Greek History and Mythology

An Enthralling Overview of Major Events, People, Myths, Gods, and Goddesses

Free limited time bonus

Stop for a moment. We have a free bonus set up for you. The problem is this: we forget 90% of everything that we read after 7 days. Crazy fact, right? Here's the solution: we've created a printable, 1-page pdf summary for this book that you're reading now. All you have to do to get your free pdf summary is to go to the following website:

https://livetolearn.lpages.co/enthrallinghistory/

Once you do, it will be intuitive. Enjoy, and thank you!

We forget 90% of everything that we've read in 7 days...

Get the free printable pdf summary of the book you've read AND much, much more... shhhh...

Enter Your Most Frequently Used Email to Get Started

DOWNLOAD FREE PDF SUMMARY

© Enthralling History

Table of Contents

Part 1: History of Greece

An Enthralling Overview of Greek History

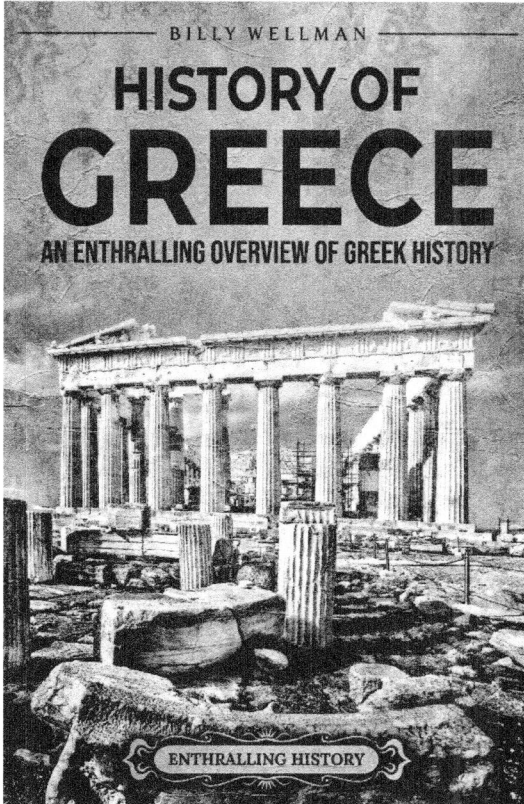

Introduction

The land of Greece and its history captures the imagination. With rugged mountains surrounded by the sea, Greece's history brings to mind epic poetry, elegant sculptures, and the inception of democracy. Greece fought unforgettable wars against the Persian, Roman, and Ottoman Empires, but its internal wars were perhaps the most memorable. For much of its history, Greece was not a single nation but a group of fractious city-states vying for supremacy. Greek settlements spread far beyond today's country of Greece to colonies around the Mediterranean and the Black Sea.

Through nine thousand years of history, several Greek civilizations rose to astounding heights before suffering cataclysmic falls. Ever resilient, new Greek powers rose from the ashes to leave their mark on the world. The Macedonian Empire under Alexander the Great and his successors stretched from the Balkan Peninsula south to Egypt and across Asia to the Indus Valley. The Byzantine Empire later claimed much of this same territory.

Greece influenced the rest of the world, especially Roman culture. But it also absorbed and further developed the scientific knowledge, technologies, and religions of its surrounding regions. This fusion of Asian, North African, and European learning formed the Hellenistic culture, a powerhouse of the arts, sciences, and philosophy. The eastern remnant of the Roman Empire continued for over a millennium as the powerful Byzantine Empire, oriented toward Greek culture and the bastion of Eastern

Orthodox Christianity. Greece's multifaceted and enduring legacy has enriched the world.

This book endeavors to guide you on an understandable, enjoyable journey through Greece's history from the Stone Age to the 20th century. This concise overview will introduce the various Greek civilizations and explain the distinctive features of each era and what made them exceptional. Of course, history isn't just dry facts and dates; it's about people. This book brings their stories to life in all their ingenuity, desperation, bravery, and artistry.

Reading history can be fascinating, but it also has immeasurable benefits. Learning Greece's history helps us understand the Greek foundation for political innovation in recent centuries and how its art and architecture influenced our sense of aesthetics. We are indebted to the Greek historians for not only recording their own history but also the histories of the Babylonians, Persians, Romans, and more. What the Greeks left behind is woven into our lives today.

Let's travel back to Greece's earliest settlements and explore the Greeks' stunning contributions to our world!

SECTION ONE:
From the Neolithic Age to the Bronze Age Collapse (7000 BCE–750 BCE)

Chapter 1: The Age of Stone, Minoans, and Cycladic Civilization

A skull! The stalagmite growing from its head looked like a horn at first glance. Christos, a Greek villager, bent over for a closer look, focusing his light on the bizarre find in the Petralona Cave. Was it human?

A year earlier, in 1959, a shepherd named Filippos had been scouring the slopes of Mount Katsika in Greece's Chalcidice, a peninsula in northern Greece. He was searching for a water source for his flocks. He discovered an opening to a massive cave. Inside, he found multiple chambers covered with stalactites and stalagmites. And now, Christos found a skull in a small cavern within the cave.

Geologists and paleontologists have investigated the skull and cave for the past six decades. The skull is missing its jawbone but still has its upper teeth. Researchers continue to debate whether the skull is male or female. Is it a *Homo sapien* (modern human) or an earlier ancestor? Just how old is it? The fiercely contested estimates range from 160,000 years old to 700,000. Anthropologists concluded that it possessed European traits, challenging the theory that the first humans emerged out of Africa.

The calcification-covered Petralona skull with a protruding stalagmite.
Nadina, CC BY-SA 3.0 <https://creativecommons.org/licenses/by-sa/3.0>, via Wikimedia Commons; https://commons.wikimedia.org/wiki/File:Petralona_skull_covered_by_stalagmiteCROP_ROTATE_ CONTRAST.jpg

Geological changes have complicated the archaeological study of Greece's prehistoric Stone Age. The Greek peninsula is located between the African and Eurasian geological plates. For millennia, as Africa slowly moved a centimeter a year toward Greece, the collision of the two plates caused constant geological folding, uplift, volcanoes, and earthquakes. Erosion produced by farmers clearing trees from Greece's mountainous landscape further disrupted the archaeological record.[1]

The Stone Age refers to the earliest period of human existence when ancient people used stone tools. Archaeologists hotly contest the beginning date for this period. Assuming that processes like radiometric decay occurred at today's rates, many scientists

---

[1] Curtis Runnels, "Review of Aegean Prehistory IV: The Stone Age of Greece from the Paleolithic to the Advent of the Neolithic," *American Journal of Archaeology* 99, no. 4 (1995): 699. https://doi.org/10.2307/506190.

estimate a date of two to three million years ago. The ending date was around 3300 BCE when humans began using bronze implements, although various civilizations progressed at different rates.

One of the earliest archaeologists studying Greece's Stone Age was Christos Tsountas, who focused on Neolithic (Late Stone Age) materials from the Thessalian plain beginning in 1901. Adalbert Markovits excavated the Zaimis Cave in Attica and the Ulbricht Cave in the Argolid Peninsula in the 1920s. He identified artifacts dating to the Paleolithic (Early Stone Age) and Mesolithic (Middle Stone Age) eras.

Meanwhile, Gordon Childe explored Neolithic finds in the Thessalian plain, noticing a resemblance between Greek artifacts and those found in western Asia. He believed Thessaly's exceptionally developed Neolithic civilization was Europe's first example of settled villages and agriculture. Radiocarbon dating places Greek sites in Thessaly and in the Peloponnese of southern Greece to be slightly younger than western Asia's Neolithic sites. Greece is located at the crossroads of early human migrations, and recent evidence points to Greece as the hub of Europe's earliest Stone Age cultures.

In the 1960s, Eric Higgs of the University of Cambridge began an archaeological exploration of Epirus in northwestern Greece. He found artifacts establishing a Paleolithic civilization with continuous occupation over extended periods. In 1967, Thomas Jacobsen of Indiana University began excavating the Franchthi Cave overlooking the Argolic Gulf in southern Greece. The cave served as a seasonal shelter for Paleolithic-era hunters. The discovery of obsidian (a black volcanic stone) from the island of Melos in the Aegean Sea proved the people had seafaring technology in the Early Stone Age.

Mesolithic-era artifacts in the Franchthi Cave showed a transition from big-game hunting to fishing for tuna and harvesting wild plants. The Neolithic-era people in the Franchthi area carved figurines of people and animals and built stone houses and terraces for crops. In 2015, divers discovered an underwater city at Lambayanna Beach just around the bend from the cave. Its earliest layers date to the transitional era between the Neolithic and Bronze

Ages. Rising sea waters buried the once-thriving city, which survived well into the Bronze Age, with fortification walls, high towers, and paved roads.[2]

Genetic studies indicate the Neolithic Greeks who practiced agriculture originated in western Turkey and spread from Greece throughout Europe.[3] The earliest Neolithic settlements in Greece did not have pottery, but they farmed, fished, and raised cattle, goats, sheep, and pigs. In the Argolid Peninsula and Thessaly, they lived in villages that consisted of up to one hundred people. They grew barley, lentils, peas, and wheat. Their tools and weaponry were made of obsidian and flint. Although they apparently sailed to Milos for its razor-sharp volcanic obsidian glass, no one lived on the island until the Late Neolithic era.

By 6000 BCE, the Neolithic Greeks had developed pottery-making, which they painted and fired in kilns. By 5000 BCE, they used stone foundations for houses, which had porches and several rooms. They lived in walled villages of up to three hundred people. They learned to carve stone and marble, producing small figurines of broad-shouldered, wide-hipped women, sometimes holding a baby. In addition to wheat, they grew rye and oats, which they used to bake bread in clay ovens. They wove garments from sheep wool. By 4000 BCE, their clay pottery featured arresting polychrome decorations.

Greece's earliest Bronze Age culture was the Minoans, who settled on Crete around 3500 BCE and later colonized other islands, including Rhodes and Thera. Crete is located in the Mediterranean Sea; it is almost halfway between mainland Greece and North Africa. The archaeologist Sir Arthur Evans named Crete's original civilization "Minoan" after Minos, who was identified by ancient historians as Crete's first king. According to Greek myth, Minos was the son of the god Zeus and a human

---

[2] Julien Beck, et al. "Searching for Neolithic Sites in the Bay of Kiladha, Greece," *Quaternary International* 584 (May 20, 2021):129-40.
https://www.sciencedirect.com/science/article/pii/S1040618220308466#!

[3] Hofmanová, Zuzana, et al. "Early Farmers from across Europe Directly Descended from Neolithic Aegeans." *PNAS.* 113 (25) (June 6, 2016): 6886–6891. doi:10.1073/pnas.1523951113. ISSN 0027-8424. PMC 4922144. PMID 27274049.

mother, Europa, a Phoenician princess living in southern Greece. Zeus abducted her from Greece, brought her to Crete, and made her his queen. They had three children, with Minos being the oldest.

The Phoenicians were seafaring people centered in Lebanon. However, they conducted trade and established colonies throughout the Mediterranean, including southern Greece. The Minos myth may reflect the blending of Crete's Phoenician and Greek colonists. DNA sampling indicates that Crete was settled by people from the central Levant (today's Syria, Lebanon, and Israel) and later by Mycenean Greeks.[4]

Greek myth said that Minos angered the god of the sea, Poseidon, when the deity sent him a magnificent snow-white bull to signify he was destined to be king. Instead of sacrificing the bull to Poseidon, Minos kept it for himself and sacrificed a different bull. Poseidon retaliated by placing a spell on Minos's wife, Pasiphaë, who became enraptured with the bull and had sex with it. She gave birth to a monster: the half-man, half-bull Minotaur who devoured humans. Minos built a labyrinth to contain the horrific creature but had to find people to feed him.

After the Athenians killed his son, an enraged Minos sailed to Athens to avenge him. Minos's father, Zeus, punished the city with disease and starvation. To escape Zeus's wrath, Minos ordered the Athenians to send seven boys and seven girls every nine years to feed the Minotaur. Athens sent fourteen children to the monster two times. The hero Theseus accompanied the children the third time. He made his way through the labyrinth and killed the Minotaur.

Minos probably was a real person (minus the Minotaur). He ruled around 2000 BCE when the Minoan culture took a great leap forward. Before then, the Minoans had gradually been cultivating a civilization on Crete for 1,500 years. They developed trade centers and a class hierarchy on the island. Around 2000

[4] King, RJ, et al. "Differential Y-chromosome Anatolian Influences on the Greek and Cretan Neolithic." *Annals of Human Genetics.* 72 (March 2008):205-14. doi: 10.1111/j.1469-1809.2007.00414.x. PMID: 18269686.

BCE, they suddenly surged forward and became a complex civilization, establishing Europe's first palaces and cities.

The Minoan civilization's transformation may well have been due to visionary leadership. The historian Thucydides said Minos built Crete's first navy (probably the first navy anywhere), enabling the Minoans to become a great sea power in the Mediterranean. Minos took possession of the Cyclades island group north of Crete with his fleet. He fought Athens and ruled the Aegean and Mediterranean Seas. The Cretans traded with Egypt and western Asia, adopting some of their technology and art techniques.

This restored section reveals the splendor of the palace at Knossos.
*cavorite https://www.flickr.com/photos/cavorite/, CC BY-SA 2.0
<https://creativecommons.org/licenses/by-sa/2.0>, via Wikimedia Commons;
https://commons.wikimedia.org/wiki/File:Palace_of_Knossos.jpg*

The Minoans began building breathtaking palaces around 2000 BCE in Crete's cities of Knossos, Malia, Phaistos, and Zakros. Earthquakes destroyed the original palaces, so the people rebuilt them around 1700 BCE. The four-story palaces towered over the landscape. They had a central court, massive colonnades, dazzling frescos decorating the walls, and archive libraries containing Europe's first two written languages.

Artisans in the palace workshops produced enchanting figurines and pottery for trading throughout the Aegean and Mediterranean.

These palaces served as regional centers of administration, religion, and trade for the surrounding farms and towns. A road network traveled outward from the palaces to nearby communities. The palaces stored grain, oil, and wine, perhaps for trade or as emergency provisions in the event of drought or other disasters.

Each palace was independent of the others during the first few centuries. After the palaces were rebuilt around 1700 BCE, Knossos rose to supremacy over the rest of the island. The palaces had no fortification walls, indicating the communities coexisted peacefully and did not fear foreign invasion. But they also had armor, bows and arrows, and swords. Perhaps this was for their naval attacks off the island. However, watchtowers on the roads between the palaces suggest bandits might have been a problem in remote areas of the island.

The Minoan civilization was remarkably advanced. The people created astounding architecture, lively artwork, aqueducts, sewage systems, and water treatment devices. The Minoans had Europe's first two writing systems (still undeciphered), which were found on seals and clay tablets. Their first writing system, used from 2100 to 1700 BCE, was Cretan hieroglyphs, which used stylized pictures to represent words or sounds. Egypt began using hieroglyphic writing around 3200 BCE, and the Minoans interacted and traded with Egypt. However, although they are superficially similar, the Cretan system was distinct. Egypt had over eight hundred symbols, while Cretan hieroglyphics only had eighty-five known symbols. Although it hasn't yet been decoded, the low number of symbols indicates that Cretan hieroglyphic was a phonetic script, with each symbol representing a sound.

The second writing system was Linear A, which came into use around 1800 BCE. It was probably a phonetic alphabet. It likely followed the same system as Cretan hieroglyphics but with simplified graphics. Linear A is unlike Egyptian hieroglyphics and Mesopotamian cuneiform, although it is possibly linked to the Proto-Sinaitic script, the ancestor of the Phoenician alphabet. Archaeologists have found hundreds of clay tablets inscribed with Linear A.

The Minoans produced high-quality ceramics, including delicately thin drinking vessels and vibrant pottery that initially featured geometric designs and later flowers and fish. Their art pictured men wearing loincloths and women in long gowns. Women seemed to be socially equal to men. The dynamic Minoan artwork showed men, women, animals, and sea creatures in bold action.

Minoan buildings and artwork suggest their religious worship included feasts, parades, and offering food and drink to their deities. The bull was an essential feature of Minoan culture. The Minoans sacrificed bulls, and their walls, jewelry, and figurines depicted bulls more than any other animal. Minoan art shows the curious practice of bull leaping, where a man grabbed a bull by the horns and flipped himself over its back.

This fresco at the Palace at Knossos shows a man vaulting over a bull.
George Groutas, CC BY 2.0 <https://creativecommons.org/licenses/by/2.0>, via Wikimedia Commons; https://commons.wikimedia.org/wiki/File:Bull_leaping,_fresco_from_the_Great_Palace_a t_Knossos,_Crete,_Heraklion_Archaeological_Museum.jpg

An important deity was a goddess holding two snakes and wearing a long, tiered skirt. Female priestesses wearing long robes are also shown sacrificing bulls and other offerings. Worship took place in palaces, mountain peaks, and caves. Archaeological excavations revealed human sacrifices; in one case, an earthquake struck while the Minoans were sacrificing a teenage boy, crushing the boy's killers.[5] The Minoans at Knossos practiced child sacrifice and cannibalism, which may have given rise to the myth of sacrificing children to the Minotaur.[6]

The Minoan society violently collapsed due to a combination of natural disasters and invasion. The 1700 BCE earthquake destroyed most of Crete's urban centers, yet the Cretans were able to recover and rebuild. But about a century later, a volcano on the island of Thera erupted catastrophically. The VEI-7 magnitude of the monstrous Minoan eruption was like multiple atomic bombs exploding. It sent ten million tons of rock, ash, and gas twenty miles up, penetrating the stratosphere.

Two hundred feet of ash and pumice buried those who hadn't escaped Thera. The volcano and accompanying earthquakes triggered a disastrous tsunami that submerged Crete's northern coast, destroying its ports and many of its cities. Some of the Minoans on Crete survived the tsunami and earthquakes, and their civilization continued until 1100 BCE, although it was significantly weakened and vulnerable.

Meanwhile, the Myceneans were thriving in the southern Greece mainland. The Minoans had lost many ports and administrative centers, so they could not maintain their sovereignty over the Mediterranean. The Myceneans stepped into the void around 1450 BCE, replacing Minoan settlements with trade outposts of their own. It appears they also invaded Crete around 1420 BCE, burning all the remaining palaces except for Knossos, which the Myceneans renovated. Archaeological finds reveal a Mycenean presence coexisting with the Minoans in Crete until the Bronze Age Collapse.

---

[5] Rodney Castleden, *The Knossos Labyrinth: A New View of the 'Palace of Minos' at Knossos* (London: Routledge, 2012), 121-22.

[6] Peter Warren, "Knossos: New Excavations and Discoveries," *Archaeology* 37, no. 4 (1984): 48–55. http://www.jstor.org/stable/41731580.

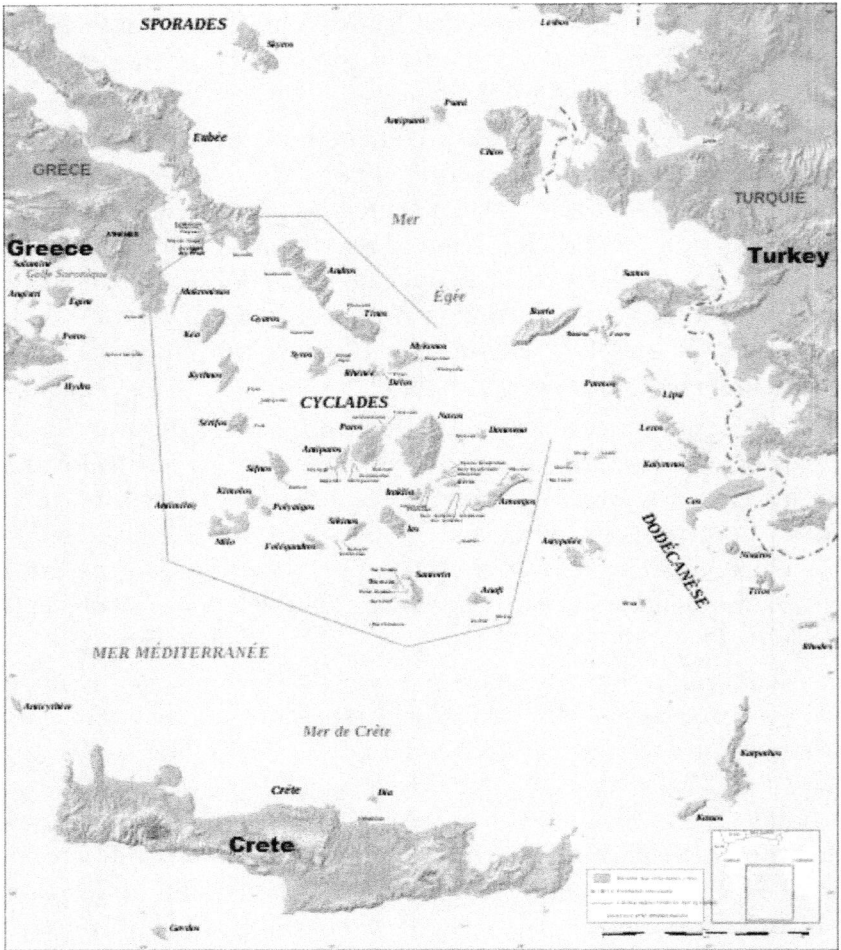

The Cyclades are between Greece and Turkey and north of Crete.

The Cycladic civilization emerged around 3200 BCE. They were seafaring people on the Cyclades in the Aegean Sea. The word "Cyclades" means "encircling islands." This island group forms a roughly circular shape around the sacred island of Delos. Delos was a worship center and later became the mythical birthplace of the Greek deities Artemis and Apollo. The Cycladic civilization and the Minoans existed in the same timeframe. They were in close proximity to each other and interacted. The Minoans colonized some of the southern Cyclades.

The Cycladic people were fishers, farmers, and herders. Their small boats were susceptible to fierce winter storms, so they spearfished for tuna mainly in the summer, which was also when the fish came closer to shore. In the Late Bronze Age, they built larger and stronger ships propelled by fifty rowers, which enabled deep-sea expeditions for fishing or trade. Today, many of the islands are sparsely populated, and fifteen of the islands are uninhabited. But before deforestation and overgrazing, the islands supported a thriving population. The people grew barley, grapevines, and olive trees on terraces going up the mountains and hills.

Some islands, like Milos, were volcanic. They provided razor-sharp black obsidian glass, which was valued for making tools and weapons. Other mineral resources that enriched the islands were copper, gold, iron, marble, and silver. With a surplus of resources, the Cycladic people sailed from one island to another, trading goods and exporting them to mainland Greece.

Archaeologists believe that Mykonos, Antiparos, and Saliagos were the first islands settled in the Late Neolithic era. Neolithic ruins on Saliagos revealed remnants of stone dwellings and a larger building about fifty by forty-six feet in diameter. Fragments of simple pottery were painted with white paint in geometric patterns. The craftsmen of Saliagos formed obsidian spear tips and arrowheads in a narrow triangular or leaf-shaped form. These characteristic obsidian pieces were found throughout Neolithic settlements in Greece, suggesting robust trade between the Cyclades and the mainland.

Marble figurines, usually female, became a hallmark of Cycladic culture. They were typically about a foot high, but a few were almost life-sized. Some were violin-shaped, with unnaturally long heads and necks and sometimes no legs. Their faces often had no features other than a nose, although the eyes and mouth might have been painted. They were usually unearthed from the graves of men and women. Scholars debate whether they had religious significance.

This marble figurine is from the island of Naxos, circa 3000 BCE.
Zoomed in. Credit: Zde, CC BY-SA 3.0 <https://creativecommons.org/licenses/by-sa/3.0>, via Wikimedia Commons;
https://commons.wikimedia.org/wiki/File:Cycladic_figurine_female,_3200%E2%80%9328
00_BC,_AshmoleanM,_AN_1946.118,_142402.jpg

Archaeologists have found forty graves on the island of Kea. The adult graves had walled crypts, each holding one to thirteen adults. Jars or tiny stone coffins held deceased children and babies. Crypt and stone coffin burials were also found on the islands of Amorgos and Syros. This burial style was far more advanced than mainland Greece in the same era, implying a distinct culture in the Cyclades.[7] A curious archaeological find in some graves in the Cyclades are hundreds of "frying pans": flat, round objects of decorated pottery or stone with a handle. Their purpose remains a mystery.

---

[7] John E. Coleman, "The Chronology and Interconnections of the Cycladic Islands in the Neolithic Period and the Early Bronze Age," *American Journal of Archaeology* 78, no. 4 (1974): 333–44. https://doi.org/10.2307/502747.

This Cycladic "frying pan" dates to about 2700 BCE.
© *Marie-Lan Nguyen / Wikimedia Commons;*
https://commons.wikimedia.org/wiki/File:Frying_pan_Syros_Louvre_CA2991.jpg

When the Minoan civilization on Crete rose to prominence around 2000 BCE, its sophisticated culture overshadowed the Cycladic civilization. The Minoans settled some of the southern Cyclades, and evidence shows a shared culture between Crete and the Cyclades. The tsunami and earthquakes accompanying the apocalyptic Minoan eruption in the southern Cyclades would have probably wiped out most life on the nearby islands. Yet, the Cycladic culture survived for several centuries until it collapsed around 1050 BCE. The Minoan culture had already disintegrated, followed by the Myceneans, as Greece fell into its centuries-long Dark Ages.

Chapter 2: The Mycenaeans and the Dark Ages

"My brother! Have you forgotten your oath?" King Menelaus of Sparta paced back and forth in agitation. Paris had abducted his wife Helen and taken her to Troy. He needed his brother, King Agamemnon of Mycenae, to help him get her back.

"Yes, Menelaus, I remember we all promised Helen's father to defend her marriage to whomever he chose. But I'm thinking of what it will take to attack Troy. It's a powerful city, and we will surely lose countless men if we go to war. We need to gather as many allies as possible if we hope to win. And if we achieve victory, it will bring us control of the Dardanelles. Greece will reap great power and wealth if we have free access to the straits and the Black Sea."

Once thought to be a myth, the prolonged and devastating Trojan War has recently found archaeological support. The "long-haired Achaeans," as Homer called the Mycenaeans, were laser-focused on controlling the trade routes of the Mediterranean, Aegean, and Black Seas. They willingly crushed their rivals, but in the end, they overextended themselves and brought down their own civilization.

Where did the Mycenaeans come from? Genetic analysis indicates they and the Minoans both descended from the ancient steppe herdsmen of today's Turkey, Armenia, and Iran. However, unlike the Minoans, the Mycenaean DNA was one-quarter linked to Siberia and northeastern Europe.[8] In the mid-Bronze Age, these Indo-European people swept into central and southern Greece, establishing the Mycenaean civilization. It thrived from 1750 to 1050 BCE, lifting the region to new heights of architecture, engineering, and military expertise.

How did the Myceneans become a great power in mainland Greece and beyond? By assimilating culture and expertise from the Minoans, the Myceneans developed a brilliantly advanced civilization. The militant Mycenaeans conquered Greece and Crete and grew wealthy through trade with the Cyclades, Cyprus, Egypt, and Phoenicia. Their ingenious engineers constructed stupendous fortresses, water and sewage systems, and bridges. The later Greek civilizations immortalized them with myths of their exploits and tales of heroes like Achilles and Odysseus.

The center of the Mycenaean civilization was the city of Mycenae in southern Greece's Peloponnese Peninsula. Mycenae was close to Athens and Corinth on a high hill just inland from the Saronic Gulf. Its limestone defensive walls are almost twenty feet thick and were constructed without mortar. Its stones are so huge that legend says the one-eyed Cyclops built the walls. Some of the walls are still standing today over three thousand years later. Mycenae's megaron (the great hall that contained the throne room) was supported by four columns with an elevated platform for the king.

[8]I. Lazaridis, et al. "Genetic Origins of the Minoans and Mycenaeans." *Nature* 548 (August 10, 2017): 214-18. doi: 10.1038/nature23310. Epub 2017 Aug 2. PMID: 28783727; PMCID: PMC5565772.

The Lion Gate still stands over three thousand years later.
William Neuheisel from DC, US, CC BY 2.0
<https://creativecommons.org/licenses/by/2.0>, via Wikimedia Commons;
https://commons.wikimedia.org/wiki/File:Lions_Gate_at_Mycenae_(5228010382).jpg

The Lion Gate has ten-foot-high rectangular boulders at each side of the entrance supporting a twenty-ton lintel. Over the lintel is a carving of two lions. It was built around 1250 BCE and is a stunning engineering feat. It resembles a gate to the Hittite city of Hattusa; however, the Mycenae gate and walls are more refined, with boulders that fit together better. How was that gargantuan lintel raised to rest on the side jambs? Some theorize that megalithic structures like this one involved building a temporary earthen ramp up to the top, lugging the huge lintel up the ramp, perhaps on rollers, getting it into place, and then removing the ramp. It must have involved massive manpower. It's no wonder the Greeks thought the Cyclops built it!

The Myceneans built their palaces within a fortified citadel called an acropolis, which was usually located at the top of a hill. The archaic and classical Greeks continued to place their palaces and temples in a hilltop acropolis. The rest of the city would be spread out below, with the majestic palace and temple area towering above, surrounded by massive walls. The high location provided dual protection: the guardsmen could survey the entire surrounding area, and it was easier to defend from attacks. In the event of an attack, the regular citizens would hurry up the hill to take refuge within the walls.

Although more humble, Tiryns was older than Mycenae, according to Greek mythology and archaeological evidence. Overlooking the Argolic Gulf, it was ten miles south of Mycenae and served as a major port. The Myceneans built its citadel around 1600 BCE and its first palace a little over two centuries later. An earthquake destroyed the palace in 1200 BCE; however, the city continued to grow to a population of fifteen thousand by 1050 BCE. It was one of the few cities in Greece that survived the Dark Ages.

The best-preserved Mycenean palatial structure is the Palace of Nestor in Pylos, which Homer mentioned in the *Iliad* and the *Odyssey*. Located on the southwest Peloponnese Peninsula coast, its earliest settlement may date back to 2000 BCE. Large-scale construction of the city began in 1600 BCE; however, the palace and other structures on Pylos's acropolis burned down in 1400 BCE. The palace was rebuilt and stood for about two more centuries before it burned again in 1180.

Colorful frescos, some still preserved, decorated the palace walls. Clay tablets contained the most extensive Mycenean Linear B script collection on the Greek mainland. Once Linear B was decoded, these tablets provided valuable information about the Mycenean culture and political system. Other major Mycenean centers with palaces included Athens, Sparta, and Thebes, although over one hundred towns and cities dotted Greece's landscape.

This vivid fresco of a dove and lyre player decorated Pylos's palace wall.
Leporello78, CC BY-SA 4.0 <https://creativecommons.org/licenses/by-sa/4.0>, via Wikimedia Commons; https://commons.wikimedia.org/wiki/File:Lyre_Player_and_Bird_Fresco_from_Pylos_Throne_Room.jpg

The major Mycenean centers served as the political head of the states, with a king (*anax*) ruling from the palace and controlling the industries in the region. Each state was divided into districts and had a central city or town, which also had a palace or fortress. Tiryns was probably one of those "district towns" under Mycenae. All the states were in a confederation subject to a "great king," who likely ruled from Mycenae.[9]

The *anax* also served as a judge and military commander. The kings came from the warrior, landowning aristocracy. A council of elders served as advisors to the king, a system that continued in the archaic and classical eras. The Myceneans had three basic social classes: the military aristocracy, the regular people (farmers, craftsmen, merchants, etc.), and enslaved people who served in the palace and temples.

---

[9]Jorrit M. Kelder, *The Kingdom of Mycenae: A Great Kingdom in the Late Bronze Age Aegean* (Bethesda: CDL Press, 2010), 45, 86, 106-7.

The Mycenean economy centered around trade. Their ships sailed as far as Spain in the west and into the Black Sea in the east. Defeating Troy meant gaining control of the Dardanelles, which connected the Aegean and Black Seas. The Myceneans established colonies around the Mediterranean and Aegean Seas to support their trade networks. They exported olives, olive oil, raisins, pottery, linen and wool textiles, and wine. They imported copper, tin, and luxury goods.

Mycenean art reflected Minoan influences, but the Myceneans put their own stamp on it. They worked with larger pieces than the Minoans, embraced new materials to work with, and used novel styles like abstract imagery. They were known for their eye-catching pottery and frescos that focused on themes of war, religion, hunting, and nature, especially sea life. The palace workshops produced glass articles, finely cut gems, and vases made from precious metals.

The Myceneans developed the Minoan's Linear A script into Linear B. They used a similar form as Linear A, although they included a few new signs. The significant difference was the two writing systems represented different languages. The Minoan language has been extinct for over two millennia, and we still don't know what sort of language it was. When archaeologists began unearthing all the clay tablets at Pylos, no one could read Linear B, but in 1952, Michael Ventris cracked the code.

Ventris was an architect but had developed a keen interest in Linear B as a teenager. As an adult, he continued trying to decipher the language. By observing patterns, he determined that Linear B had eighty-nine characters. That meant it was mostly a phonetic script, with signs representing sounds rather than whole words, although it also had over one hundred non-phonetic ideograms. Ventris eventually realized the Mycenean language was an ancient form of Greek.

When the Myceneans began building palaces, they also built shrines close to or within the citadels. The administrative centers also acted as religious centers. The palatial structures in Pyros and Mycenae contained altars in their courtyard or porch. Like the Minoans, the Myceneans sacrificed bulls in their religious observances and poured out water in libation. Mycenae's temple contained multiple figurines of what appear to be worshipers and deities, along with fifteen clay snakes.

Frescos in the temple show several women who were either goddesses or priestesses. Linear B clay tablets list sacrifices of grain, honey, scented oil, and spices. The Myceneans were polytheistic, worshiping some of the same gods as later classical Greeks, including Zeus (called Diktaios on Crete), Ares (A-re), Artemis (A-te-mi-to), Dionysus (Di-wo-nu-so), Hera (E-ra), Hermes (E-ma), and their chief deity Poseidon (Po-se-da-o). They had a powerful female deity called Potnia (mistress), possibly Athena's equivalent, and female versions of Zeus and Poseidon (Diwia and Posidaia), who were not worshiped in later Greek eras.[10]

Like the Cycladic civilization and the Minoans, the Myceneans often buried their dead in coffins, but instead of making them from stone, they usually made them from decorated clay. Shaft tombs in a circle are just outside the Lion Gate at the Palace of Nestor; the aristocrats of Pylos were buried there. The Mycenean shaft tombs were up to twelve feet deep. They were rectangular-shaped, with pebble floors and masonry walls. A wooden plank roof covered each grave. On top of that were an earthen mound and a stele or tombstone. Each shaft tomb held two to five bodies. Gold jewelry, cups, and death masks were buried with the occupants, while warriors were buried with their weapons. After scouring the writings of Homer and the 2nd-century CE Greek geographer Pausanias for clues, the amateur archaeologist Heinrich Schliemann discovered the shaft tombs in 1876.

[10] Susan Lupack, "Mycenaean Religion," in *The Oxford Handbook of the Bronze Age Aegean*, ed. Eric H. Cline, (2012). 10.1093/oxfordhb/9780199873609.013.0020.

The Myceneans put death masks over the faces of important people. This mask found by Schliemann at Mycenae dates to about 1550 BCE.

In the *Iliad*, Homer says that King Agamemnon of Mycenae led a coalition of Greek forces across the Aegean Sea to the city of Troy. The purported reason for the invasion was retrieving Menelaus's wife, Helen, from Prince Paris. However, the potential of controlling the passage from the Aegean to the Black Sea no doubt enabled Agamemnon to recruit Greek allies. After ten years of war, the Myceneans finally overpowered and burned down Troy by gaining entry via the Trojan Horse. King Menelaus got Helen back, and the Greek heroes sailed home.

Historians mostly dismissed the Trojan War as pure myth, but the ancient Greeks believed it was an actual historical event that happened around 1200 BCE. They said Troy was in today's northwestern Turkey at the entrance to the Dardanelles. In 1870, Heinrich Schliemann, the same amateur archaeologist who later discovered the graves at Pylos, traveled to Turkey. He met with Charles Maclaren and Frank Calvert, who believed that a low hill on a flat plain could be ancient Troy. Schliemann dug a deep trench from the center of the hill down to the bottom, revealing multiple layers of civilization.

Homer said an alternate name for Troy was the Hittite name Wilusa. He said that Prince Paris was also called Alaksandu. Hittite records say Wilusa was part of the Hittite Empire. It grew wealthy due to its strategic location for sea trade between the Black and Aegean Seas. Hittite documents said that Wilusa fought the "Ahhiyawa" and mentioned Alaksandu. Many scholars believe the Ahhiyawa were the Mycenaean Greeks.

Schliemann's excavation revealed nine layers of a powerful and wealthy city, with the oldest layer dating back to 3000 BCE. He found a layer dating from 1300 to 1180 BCE, with a domed citadel and other structures that matched Homer's description of Troy. This layer had evidence of a sudden catastrophic end about 1180 BCE: approximately when the ancient Greek historians said Troy fell.

Although the evidence isn't absolutely conclusive, the Myceneans may have destroyed Troy around 1180 BCE. But right about that same time, their civilization descended into chaos. Homer's *Odysseus* offers some clues for their collapse. If the Trojan War had really happened, the Greek kings and other key leaders would have been away from their realms for a decade. When they finally returned, they probably found destabilized states suffering from a lack of leadership.

With many of the warriors away, the cities were vulnerable to attack. The kings may have had to reassert their positions with whoever served as regent in their absence. King Agamemnon's wife took a lover in his absence, and when he returned home, she and her lover murdered him. Then, her son killed her and her lover to avenge Agamemnon's death. The Greeks and Trojans suffered horrific losses in the war. Many Greek cities lost their kings and countless warriors. The lives lost, the fortune expended on the war, and the destabilization it caused back in Greece may have led to an implosion of the Mycenean civilization.

But the Myceneans were not the only civilization to dissolve around 1200 BCE. From 1200 to 900 BCE, the Bronze Age Collapse saw the cataclysmic fall of numerous cultures in eastern Mediterranean regions: the Middle East, North Africa, and the Balkan Peninsula. Environmental catastrophes, including drought and earthquakes, weakened the region's societies. The mysterious marauding "Sea People" wreaked havoc on the coastal cities, from Egypt to Turkey. They shattered naval trade, cutting the Mediterranean supply chain and causing the system to collapse.

Most Mycenean cities lay in ashes, crumbling into oblivion after a destructive power crushed their majestic palaces. The Minoan and Cycladic civilizations likewise collapsed. The apocalypse was so abrupt and total that the Greek survivors lost their written languages, even in the few cities or towns that weren't demolished. Archaeologists have found no evidence of writing for three centuries in Greece.

Could the Sea People have been the Dorian Greeks? Greek legend said they had been exiled from Greece in the days of Heracles but returned from the north and took over the Peloponnese Peninsula in southern Greece. The Greek language had several dialects, and this seems to explain why. However, no definitive archaeological evidence has yet emerged to support a Dorian invasion. Cities were burned down, but new ones weren't built. Nothing innovative happened in Greece until about 1000 BCE when iron smelting slowly emerged.

The cause of the Greek Dark Ages remains a mystery. Perhaps it was a massive internal uprising or a pandemic. Large swathes of the population suddenly died, Greece's refined civilization melted away, and its economy dissipated. All the advances made by the Minoan and Mycenean civilizations were reversed. The reduced population continued farming, fishing, and herding but only to feed themselves in their small, impoverished communities. Greece's obscure Dark Ages continued for over three hundred years.

Greece slowly began emerging from the ashes of its shattered society around 800 BCE. This cultural renewal was based on the Mycenean past but was much simpler. The fluid and realistic scenes on Mycenean pottery gave way to abstract scenes and geometric patterns. The population began to increase again, building new cities or rebuilding old ones and erecting temples. Trade revived, and their economy began growing.

One technological advancement that marked the Dark Ages was the smelting of iron for tools and weapons, which transitioned Greece from the Bronze Age to the Early Iron Age. In the Bronze Age, Egypt and Mesopotamia produced small amounts of iron implements by hammering down meteorites, which are iron-nickel alloys. They didn't require smelting, but obviously, there weren't a lot of available meteorites.

Iron smelting emerged in Anatolia (Turkey) in the Bronze Age. Greece seemed to be on the brink of using this technology right before the Dark Ages, as archaeologists have found several iron tools or weapons dating from 1300 to 1200 BCE. The number of iron implements increased significantly around 1000 BCE, indicating the Greeks had mastered iron smelting in high-heat furnaces.

The Greeks began writing again around 770 BCE but not with Linear A or B. This time, they used the Semitic Phoenician alphabet as a guide but included vowels and adapted it to fit spoken Greek, which had different sounds. Over half of the letters of the ancient Greek alphabet are in today's western European alphabets, including English. Once the Greeks had a writing system again, they began using it in much broader applications than in the past. Linear B was mainly used for record-keeping, but the new Greek alphabet was used to write down the *Iliad* and the *Odyssey*. The new alphabet marked the transition to the archaic period, with its epic poetry and brilliant and prosperous civilization.

SECTION TWO:
From the Archaic Years to Roman Conquest (750–146 BCE)

Chapter 3: The Archaic Years

"Sire! I beg you! Don't sail your navy into the Bay of Eleusis. We will be at a disadvantage in the straits of Salamis. The Greeks' best naval maneuvers are in narrow waterways."

Queen Artemisia of Halicarnassus was one of King Xerxes I's naval commanders. He had led his million-man Persian force into Greece without resistance from the northern and central states. But southern Greece, led by Athens, Sparta, and Corinth, was the holdout.

"Artemisia, we've got them trapped! If we take Salamis, we can wipe out the Athenians. They're fighting each other right now. They're demoralized. This will be an easy win!"

Xerxes climbed Mount Aigaleo for the best view of his anticipated victory. Only a few Corinthian ships were floating in the bay. He couldn't see the three hundred Greek triremes hidden in the coves of Georgios Island. His self-assurance morphed into horror as he watched the debacle unfold. When his ships chased the Corinthian vessels into the straits, the Greek triremes moved in behind them, trapping the Persians in the narrow confines. Over and over, they rammed the Persian vessels until sinking ships and floating bodies clogged the water.

Greece's epic win against the massive Persian forces in 480 BCE was the defining moment in the Greco-Persian wars. From this point on, the Greeks were the aggressors, and the Persians were on the defense. It also marked the end of the archaic era, which began with the first Olympic Games in 776 BCE. Like the legendary phoenix, Greece arose from the Dark Ages more resilient and resplendent than ever. Greece's archaic era showcased enchanting poetry, novel philosophy, entrancing architecture and sculptures, and sensational advances in engineering, mathematics, and science.

Greece's Olympic sprinters on a 6ᵗʰ-century BCE amphora jar, with the newly introduced Greek letters above the runners.
RickyBennison, CC0, via Wikimedia Commons;
https://commons.wikimedia.org/wiki/File:Panathenaic_Amphora_Sprinters.jpg

The city of Olympia in the Peloponnese hosted the first Olympic Games as a festival for Zeus, which became a tradition every four years. Although the Greek city-states often battled each other, they formed a truce during the Olympics, guaranteeing safety at the games and while traveling to and from the contests. Athletes from a dozen cities came to the first Olympics for foot races. By the end of the archaic era, athletes came from one hundred cities in Greece and its colonies stretching from the Black Sea to the western Mediterranean. By this time, the competitions included chariot races, discus and javelin throws, the long jump, and military arts.

Ancient Greece was never one united country as it is today. Instead, it was a collection of independent city-states called *poleis* (singular *polis*) in mainland Greece and colonies around the

Aegean, Black, and Mediterranean Seas. A city-state consisted of a primary city with its surrounding farmland, villages, and towns. Toward the end of the archaic era, as some cities embraced democracy, the word polis meant the citizens of a city-state.

The city-states were politically independent of the others, with a variety of political structures. Some had kings, usually with an advisory council. Sparta had two kings. A small group of aristocrats called an oligarchy ruled some city-states. In Corinth, the men in their oligarchy were all from the same family. Later, tyrants ruled Corinth and some other cities. Athens went through the whole gamut during the archaic era: a monarchy, oligarchy, tyranny, and democracy.

Each polis was like its own small country, operating independently of the others, although they joined forces against a common enemy. Often, the common enemy was another Greek city-state. The most powerful and renowned cities in the archaic era were Sparta, Athens, Thebes, Corinth, Argos, Eretria, and Elis. They shared a common language, albeit with different dialects. They also shared the same polytheistic religion, with Zeus acting as the chief god. Each city-state had a patron deity. Poseidon was Corinth's patron, Dionysus was Thebe's divine patron, and Zeus's wife Hera was the head goddess of Argos.

Throughout the archaic era, Athens and Sparta were archrivals. Both were in southern Greece, only about 150 miles apart, but they were polar opposites in their philosophy, politics, lifestyle, and social structure. The Spartans were known for their rigid discipline and resistance to change. The Athenians were progressive and loved nothing better than debating the latest philosophies and ideas.

Sparta's two kings ruled with a council of elderly men who had retired from military service at the age of sixty. Sparta's lifestyle revolved around its military. Every able-bodied Spartan male citizen between the ages of twenty to sixty served in the military. Although the men married around the age of twenty, they lived in the barracks until they were thirty, making clandestine night visits to their wives. With their husbands away so much, the independent Spartan women conducted business affairs, wore short skirts, and learned martial skills.

While the rest of Greece was awakening from the Dark Ages, Sparta was in a state of anarchy. The Spartans finally pulled through with a series of reforms that set their society apart from the rest of Greece. Because all the men served in the military full-time, they needed someone to work the fields, so they conquered the neighboring Messenian and Laconian regions. They forced these people to be helots or serf laborers. The helots tended the fields. With every Spartan man freed up to serve full-time in the military, Sparta became Greece's most formidable military power by the end of the archaic era.

Athens had been a prominent Mycenean center, one of the few Greek cities to survive through the Dark Ages. Its ideal location for sea trade enabled Athens to thrive toward the end of the Dark Ages, helping to lift the rest of Greece out of inertia. Athens gained control of most of the Attica Peninsula in southern Greece, making it one immense city-state. It was the wealthiest and strongest state in the early archaic period.

While Sparta held to the same political and social structure throughout the archaic period, Athens underwent a series of changes. It had been a monarchy with a council in its Mycenean days and in the early archaic era. Then, it segued to a system of three primary magistrates called *archontes* leading the city-state. The *ecclesia* (male citizens' assembly) elected them from the elite class originally for life, then for ten-year terms, and finally for one year. One *archon* headed up the military, another led religious functions, and the third, the chief magistrate, was the administrative leader holding most of the power. Six other archons, called *thesmotetai*, served as judges.

By 621 BCE, the Athenians were increasingly unhappy with their unwritten laws, which led to confusion and exploitation. They asked Draco, Athens's first legislator, to write a law code. But Draco's laws were ridiculously harsh, mandating the death sentence for minor infractions. On the positive side, all Athenians, whether aristocrats or working class, had equal rights under Draco's legal system.

Twenty-seven years later, the Athenians asked their chief magistrate, Solon, to write a constitution. He rewrote Draco's laws and restructured the political system so males from all classes had voting rights. In his system, Athens had four classes, and each class had one hundred men appointed to the four-hundred-man council (called a *boule*). Not every citizen could vote, but one hundred voters equally represented each layer of society. It was a giant step toward democracy.

Athens's next step in its political journey was the rule of tyrants, which didn't necessarily mean a cruel despot. A tyrant came into power outside the usual channels. Instead of being the crown prince or elected by the ecclesia, he usually usurped the throne, sometimes through the assistance of oppressed citizens wanting a change. He had complete authority. He might have had an advisory council, but he had the ultimate say. As a usurper, he often ignored parts of the state's constitution, although he would generally keep most systems in place.

Although tyrants had absolute power, they sometimes used it to benefit their city-state, especially the poor and working classes. Archaic-era Greeks didn't consider tyrants bad or good; it depended on the man and his actions. Tyrants often manipulated their way into power when the current ruling powers ignored the needs of the masses. Tyrants curried the favor of the neglected and oppressed classes, promising reforms in exchange for support. But once a tyrant came into power, he had to follow through on his promises or risk losing his position. Tyranny was a stepping stone for archaic Greece between rule by a king or oligarchy to a rudimentary democracy.

Athens's first tyrant was the war hero General Pisistratus, a relative of Solon. When class conflict rocked Athens, Pisistratus portrayed himself as a champion of the lower classes, which constituted the majority of the city's population. Once in power, Pisistratus improved life for the working class and the oppressed poor. He gave farmers their lands back that had been seized due to debt and helped them develop more profitable farming with cash crops. He used his own wealth from his Macedonian gold mines to upgrade Athens's infrastructure and promoted festivals and games, which pleased all the classes. He improved Athens's navy and developed the entire Attica Peninsula into a productive and prosperous place. Athens fared so well under Pisistratus that other Greek city-states considered tyranny a viable option.

Pisistratus's son, Hippias, was Athens's next tyrant. He initially followed in his benevolent father's footsteps but then deteriorated to the point that Sparta invaded and installed Isagoras as the next chief magistrate. Isagoras exiled anyone he considered a political threat and seized their land. Finally, in 508 BCE, the Athenians revolted, expelled Isagoras, and made Cleisthenes, a democratic visionary, the next leader of Athens.

Cleisthenes's novel democratic reforms divided Athens and the rest of the Attica Peninsula into ten tribes. Each tribe had thirty units: ten from Athens, ten from the rural farmlands, and ten from the coastal region. Fifty male citizens from each of the ten tribes served on a five-hundred-man council for one year. All citizens—rich or poor, rural or urban—were equally represented, which was another significant step toward democracy. It still didn't give every citizen the right to vote, nor did it give women any representation. Still, it established a new political system that persisted into the classical age.

Perpetual warfare marked Greece's archaic age. The city-states often fought each other, but they also vied with Carthage in North Africa for control over trade and colonies around the Mediterranean. This conflict eventually erupted into the Punic Wars. The massive Persian Achaemenid Empire also warred against Greece beginning in 547 BCE, when Cyrus the Great conquered the Ionian Greek colonies on the eastern Aegean coastline. Darius the Great invaded Greece's mainland, a venture that ended in a humiliating defeat for the Persians at the Battle of Marathon in 490 BCE. Darius's son, Xerxes I, invaded Greece again in 480 BCE with his million-man army, another fiasco for Persia.

A 5ᵗʰ-century hoplite with his helmet behind him.
Jona Lendering, CC0, via Wikimedia Commons;
https://commons.wikimedia.org/wiki/File:Hoplite_5th_century.jpg

Two reasons for Greece's success in warfare were its stellar navy and almost indomitable phalanx formation in land battles. The Greek hoplite warriors wore bronze helmets covering their faces, along with bronze breastplates and shin guards. They carried bronze shields in their left hands and seven-foot spears in their right. They lined up in the phalanx position: shoulder to shoulder, with their shields slightly overlapping. Behind the first row of hoplites would be at least seven more rows. The phalanx was somewhat like a human bulldozer, approaching the enemy lines with long spears and a massive shield wall that crushed anyone not impaled by the spears.

The seafaring Greeks developed a fearsome navy in the archaic era that enabled them to fend off the Persian Empire. Their primary warship was the 120-foot-long trireme, which was propelled by rowers and sails. The ships had battering rams on their bows, and the Greeks were exceptionally skilled in ramming enemy ships in naval battles or swooping along the sides of their ships and shattering their oars. Their marine maneuvers, especially in straits or rivers, brought them a victory against Persia.

Although fierce warriors, the Greeks were also poets. Homer's epic poems, the *Iliad* and the *Odyssey*, were probably oral tales until they were finally written down with Greece's new alphabet. Hesiod wrote *Theogony* and *Works and Days* about creation and early human history. Hesiod chronicled the Golden Age when men did not sin and never knew hard labor or sadness. In the Silver Age, people had to work hard but lived long lives. The violent Bronze Age followed, which ended when Zeus wiped out the human race with the Great Flood. But Zeus told Deucalion, a man of integrity, to build an ark and fill it with food. Deucalion's family survived and formed Greece's three major tribes: the Aeolians, Dorians, and Achaeans.

Lyric poetry, sung to the lyre, became popular in the archaic age. Sappho of Lesbos wrote about love and desire between women. Mimnermus of Smyrna wrote war poetry about the Lydian Empire's invasion of his city. A choir sang and danced to choral lyric poetry, which was popular in Sparta; two favorite composers were Terpander of Lesbos and Alcman.

Corinth's Temple of Apollo, circa 540 BCE, displays Doric pillars.
Carole Raddato from FRANKFURT, Germany, CC BY-SA 2.0

A hallmark sculpture style of the archaic era was life-sized marble or limestone *korai* and *kouroi* statues of slightly smiling young women and men. The women (korai) wore long braids and modest gowns, while the men (kouroi) were naked; both represented idealized youths. The Greeks built the first stone temples in the archaic age, following similar styles of wood and brick Mycenean palaces and temples. The earliest temple architecture was Doric, with pillars bulging out in the middle and friezes decorating the top.

The pre-Socratic philosophers shaped archaic Greece's spiritual, political, and intellectual understanding. Thales of Miletus is called the Father of Science; he sought scientific answers to why and how things happened rather than the common assumption that the gods controlled everything. Thales introduced geometric concepts to Greece, such as the diameter of a circle and that an isosceles triangle has equal base angles.

One of Thales's students was Anaximander, who taught that the god Atlas wasn't holding the world up; it naturally floated free. He maintained that nature followed specific laws, which must be respected. He once correctly predicted that an earthquake would hit Sparta and got the people evacuated to safety in time. One of Anaximander's students was Anaximenes, who figured out that stars and planets differed from each other. He perceived that stars move on the same planes in the same relative positions. However, the planets that he could observe with the naked eye had more complex movements.

Pythagoras had a school in the Greek colony of Samos in southern Italy. He proposed the novel concept that the earth was a sphere rather than flat. He worked out the Pythagorean theorem: the longest side squared of a ninety-degree triangle equals the sum of the other two sides squared ($a^2 + b^2 = c^2$). However, recent evidence shows that the Babylonians used the Pythagorean theorem about one thousand years before Pythagoras.[11]

---

[11] D. F. Mansfield, "Plimpton 322: A Study of Rectangles," *Foundations of Science* 26 (2021): 977–1005. https://doi.org/10.1007/s10699-021-09806-0

Heraclitus of Ephesus taught that an unseen force called the Logos maintained and ran the universe. Humans must be in tune with the Logos to live correctly; however, most people try to live independently of the Logos and deceive themselves, failing to perceive actual reality. Xenophanes of Colophon laughed at the Greek deities who were no better than humans with their adultery, deceit, and conflict. He believed in an innately moral and benevolent supreme god who was above all gods and men.

As Greece woke up from the Dark Ages and began to prosper, its population quickly grew. But this created a problem because only 20 percent of Greece's rugged terrain could be farmed. The weather didn't help. Most of Greece's precipitation is in the winter, receiving hardly any rain during the growing season. The olive and fruit trees usually did well, but drought regularly ruined the grain crops.

Greece needed to thin out its mainland population, find a grain source to feed its people, and develop trade opportunities. The answer was colonization. During the first two centuries of the archaic era, the Greek city-states established five hundred colonies around the Mediterranean, Aegean, and Black Seas. Greek colonies extended west to today's Spain and France, south to North Africa, and as far northeast as today's Ukraine. Forty percent of the Greek population lived in its colonies, which were independent, self-governing states.

The hundreds of colonies on three continents brought unimaginable resources to Greece. The Greeks received not only grain but also lumber, textiles, and metals like copper, gold, iron, and tin. In return, Greece exported its famous red and black ceramics with scenes depicting battles, mythological scenes, and lively animals. Some of the exported pottery contained olives, olive oil, and wine from the Greece mainland. The colonies grew wealthy from trade, and some became centers for the arts or scholarly studies in mathematics, science, and philosophy.

Greece's vast trade system introduced it to coinage, which was invented in Lydia in the late 7th century BCE. Greece's first minted coins came from Aegina in the Saronic Gulf. Most ancient Greek coins were silver, but they also used gold, copper, and bronze. The city-states usually produced designs representing their city. Many used their patron deity, and the island of Thera had dolphins.

The archaic era was a high-energy age of unprecedented growth in population, colonization, technology, and scientific understanding. Archaic Greece made great strides in politics and culture. Its city-states developed formidable armies and navies that successfully allied to defeat the mammoth Persian Empire in two epic invasions. The archaic era set the stage for classical Greece's Golden Age.

Chapter 4: Classical Greece

"Are they insane? Do these Greeks think they have a chance against my million-man army?"

The year was 480 BCE, and Xerxes I of the Achaemenid Empire was swooping through Greece on his way to flatten Athens. But blocking his way in the narrow Thermopylae Pass was a small force of seven thousand Greek warriors led by King Leonidas of Sparta.

"You've got one last chance, Greeks! Throw down your weapons!"

The unfazed Spartans held their rigid discipline. "Come and get them!"

With their overlapping shields forming a wall in the phalanx position, the Greek allies held the line for two days. The pass was narrow, only sixteen feet from Mount Kallidromo's cliffs to the Malian Gulf. Behind the first line, the rest of the army stood resolute, ready to step into place if a soldier on the front line fell. But a fellow Greek eventually betrayed them, hoping for riches from Xerxes. He showed the Persians an alternate route through the mountains.

Realizing they were outflanked, King Leonidas sent most of the coalition army south, keeping only 1,400 soldiers in the pass. The joint forces heading south would guard the new wall at the Isthmus of Corinth, protecting Sparta, Corinth, and the rest of the Peloponnese Peninsula. The remaining soldiers with Leonidas fought to the death, slowing the Persians' relentless march south.

Three major military confrontations rocked Greek's classical age, which lasted from 480 to 356 BCE: the last days of the Greco-Persian Wars, the Peloponnesian War, and a fierce conflict between Sparta and Thebes. The classical age is also renowned for its temples with stunning architecture, fluid and dynamic sculptures, enlightening philosophy, and groundbreaking concepts in mathematics and science.

King Leonidas's sacrifice at the Battle of Thermopylae gave the Athenians time to flee their city and regroup on the island of Salamis. Athens fell to Xerxes, but the Persians' humiliating loss in the naval Battle of Salamis convinced Xerxes to return to Persia for good. The Greeks realized their phenomenal victory against Persia was due to the allied city-states' joint forces. To eliminate the Persian threat once and for all, the Greeks formed the Delian League in 478 BCE.

Athens was in charge of the league, and the Greeks drove the Persians out of the Aegean Sea for fifteen years and chased off the Dolopian pirates disrupting Greek trade. However, an attempt to assist Egypt's revolt against Persian domination in 460 BCE ended in disaster: Athens lost much of its fleet and twenty thousand soldiers. Unnerved, General Pericles decided to move the Delian League's treasury to Athens, fearing it was vulnerable to the Persians at Delos. However, by controlling the league and now holding its treasury, Athens became a de facto empire, and contributions to the Delian League's treasury became tribute payments.

The final face-off between Persia and Greece occurred in 451 BCE over control of the island of Cyprus. Athens's General Cimon sailed two hundred ships to Cyprus, crushing the Persian fleet and forcing Persia to agree to the thirty-year Peace of Callias in 449 BCE. The Greek colonies in Asia won independence, and Persia promised to stay out of the Aegean Sea. Greece agreed not to interfere in Cyprus, Egypt, and Anatolia (today's western Turkey).

Athens was now reveling in its golden age. The period of peace enabled it to surge ahead economically and leave a breathtaking legacy in the sciences and culture. Democracy flowered under

General Pericles's leadership, as he reformed its constitution and opened civil service positions to all social classes. He even paid the lower classes for jury service and other public administrative functions.

The remains of the Parthenon still crown Athens's Acropolis.

Athens had matured into the intellectual and artistic center of the Mediterranean. Xerxes had flattened Athens in 480 BCE, but Pericles rebuilt the citadel walls and temples on the Acropolis, which towered over the city. The Parthenon was the goddess Athena's elegant temple. A forty-foot image of the deity stood in the central room, surrounded by wall panels depicting mythological creatures and the Trojan War. The Propylaea is a colossal marble gate with Doric pillars standing in front of another image of Athena, this one made of bronze. Ictinus, the architect of Athens's Parthenon, also built the Temple of Apollo in the city of Bassae in the Peloponnese, combining Corinthian, Doric, and Ionic architecture.

Greece's Golden Age is legendary for its flowing and lively sculptures, capturing movement and emotion. The marble sculpture of *Hermes of Praxiteles* holding the baby Dionysus illustrates the relaxed contrapposto pose typical in the classical era, with the weight shifted to one leg. The classical Greeks preferred to use lustrous bronze for sculptures because of its strength, but the Romans later copied many Greek sculptures in marble.

This sculpture of Hermes and baby Dionysus was in Olympia's Temple of Hera.
Paolo Villa, CC BY-SA 4.0 <https://creativecommons.org/licenses/by-sa/4.0>, via Wikimedia Commons; https://commons.wikimedia.org/wiki/File:02_2020_Grecia_photo_Paolo_Villa_FO19002 _5_(Museo_archeologico_di_Olimpia_- _Statua_Ermes_con_Dioniso_Bambino_scolpita_da_Prassitele,_Arte_pre_Ellenistica,_d ettaglio_superiore).jpg

A favorite recreational pastime for Greeks in the Golden Age was dramatic performances, sometimes comedies but more often tragedies. The themes focused on the gods meddling in human affairs and the implications of immorality, hopeless love, and treachery. Aeschylus, Euripides, and Sophocles were the most well-known playwrights. One of Euripides's tragedies portrayed Helen's version of why she left her husband for Prince Paris of Troy. Sophocles' *Oedipus Rex* tells the story of how King Laius wanted to kill his infant son because of a prophecy that said his son would kill him. But instead of his wife, Jocasta, killing her baby, she abandoned him. A shepherd found the infant, whom the king of Corinth adopted. When the child Oedipus grew up, he killed his biological father and married his mother without knowing their true identities.

Classical Greece made incredible strides in medicine, mathematics, science, and philosophy. Hippocrates, the "Father of Medicine," introduced clinical diagnosis: checking one's pulse, temperature, urine, and bowel movements and investigating pain level and range of motion. Theaetetus of Athens advanced geometry by developing Platonic solids and irrational lengths. Leucippus and his student Democritus developed a theory of atoms as the building blocks of matter. They correctly believed atoms were constantly in motion, which Leucippus said wasn't random but controlled by Logos (the unseen force that runs the world).

Hippias of Elis was a philosopher who delved into the realms of astronomy, mathematics, and music. He discovered the geometric quadratrix, a curve trisecting an angle. He believed that a fixed and universal natural law determined morality and that it was unchanging in all situations and eras. For instance, he taught that honoring one's parents was a natural law that persisted through time.

The philosopher Socrates used a question-and-answer teaching method, encouraging his students to come to their own conclusions rather than being fed knowledge. He said an unexamined life is not worth living; we need to understand the depths of what we do not know and constantly learn new things about ourselves and life. He said people who never questioned the status quo or asked questions were "double fools." They were fools for not knowing anything and double fools for not realizing their ignorance.

Socrates's challenges to his students resulted in his trial for the corruption of Athens's youth. He was also tried for impiety because he said his god was morally good and rational. He scorned the Greek gods, who lied and cheated on their spouses. Socrates asked how humans could be moral if their gods weren't. He was found guilty on both counts and sentenced to death by drinking hemlock.

Socrates's student and close friend Plato taught the theory of forms, which stated that our concept of reality is only a reflection of actual reality. He said it is as if we live in a cave seeing shadows cast by the sun. We think the shadows are reality, but the true reality is the sun outside the cave, whose radiance is casting the shadows. Plato said most people have no clue there is more to life than the cave's shadowland, but if someone broke free and got outside, they would see the world as it is.

"He will be able to see the sun, and not mere reflections of him in the water, but he will see him in his own proper place, and not in another, and he will contemplate him as he is. He will then argue that this is he who gives the season and the years and is the guardian of all that is in the visible world, and in a certain way the cause of all things he and his fellows have been accustomed to behold."[12]

Known as the "Father of Logic," Aristotle was Plato's student and the tutor of Alexander the Great. In his *Metaphysics*, he

---

[12] Plato, *The Republic*, Book VII, trans. Benjamin Jowett. Internet Classics Archive. http://classics.mit.edu/Plato/republic.9.viii.html

argued that an unchanging, eternal, and perfect god is necessary: the "unmoved mover" who created everything. Aristotle taught the deduction principle: if a premise (belief) is accurate, its conclusion is true. Deduction enables us to understand specific truths and leads us to induction or generalized understanding.

While Athens's philosophers pondered spiritual and scientific truths, the simmering rivalry between Sparta and Athens exploded into the First Peloponnesian War in 460 BCE. At first, Sparta held back while its allies fought Athens, beginning with Corinth. Athens faltered with land wars but won brilliant victories in naval battles. Eventually, Sparta marched to Boeotia, which was sixty miles north of Athens. The Athenians met the Spartans in the Battle of Tanagra, with Sparta emerging as the victor. But Athens's navy was far superior to its land army, so it circled the Peloponnese, raiding Sparta's allies on the coast. At an impasse, Sparta agreed to the Thirty Years' Peace with Athens in 445 BCE, ending the First Peloponnesian War.

The peace only lasted fourteen years, with the Second Peloponnesian War (431–404 BCE) instigated by the Spartans invading the farmland on the Attica Peninsula around Athens. The Spartans stripped their fields, attempting to entice the Athenians into a land battle. But knowing the Spartans' superiority on land, Pericles held back, bringing the rural population into the city walls and holing up, living off of grain shipments from Egypt. Meanwhile, Athens's formidable navy formed a blockade around the Peloponnese, blocking shipments to Sparta and its allies.

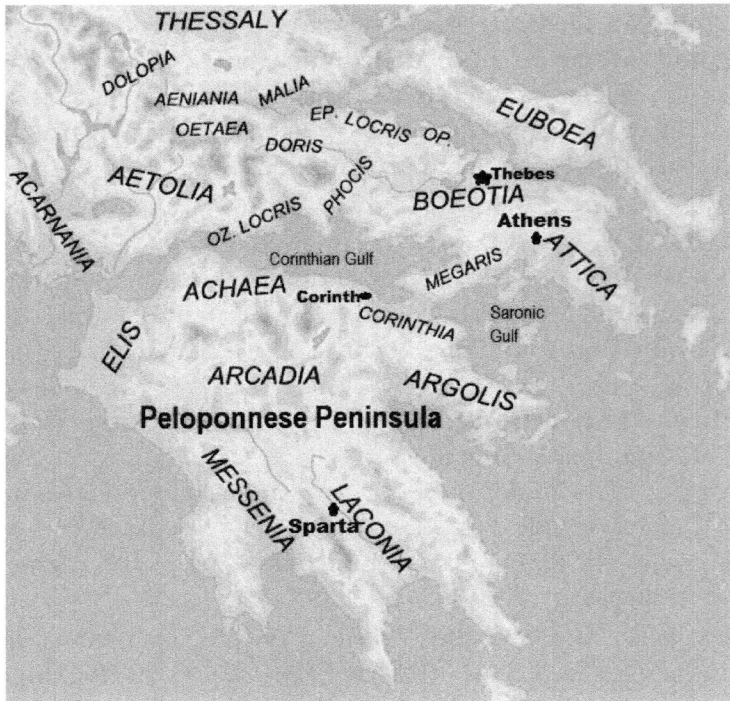

Most of southern Greece was engaged in the Peloponnesian War.
Photo modified: labels added. Credit: original:Map_greek_sanctuaries-en.svg by Marsyasderivative work: MinisterForBadTimes, CC BY-SA 2.5 <https://creativecommons.org/licenses/by-sa/2.5>, via Wikimedia Commons; https://commons.wikimedia.org/wiki/File:Ancient_Greek_southern_regions.png

Pericles never envisioned that the grain shipments from Egypt would bring rats carrying the plague, which spread like wildfire through overcrowded Athens. One-third of the population died from violent diarrhea, tissue death, and lung infection. The survivors burned the dead on pyres or threw them into huge pits by the hundreds each day. As soon as they heard about the outbreak, the Spartans fled the Attica Peninsula. In an ironic twist, the Athenian blockade protected Sparta and the rest of the Peloponnesians from the ships carrying the plague.

Pericles's death from the plague in 429 BCE left Athens without his mature and insightful leadership. But the plague eventually dissipated, and Athens resumed naval raids and fort-building on the Peloponnese. Sparta attacked Pylos, one of these forts, but the Athenians won, the first time they'd prevailed in a land battle with

Sparta. This victory empowered and energized the Athenians, as they realized the Spartan army wasn't as invincible as they thought.

Sparta responded to the loss by marching north to Thrace and taking control of Athens's silver mines in Amphipolis. Athens rushed north to regain their primary source of wealth, and in the pitched Battle of Amphipolis, both sides lost their leading generals. In a leadership crisis, the two cities negotiated the fifty-year Peace of Nicias in 421 BCE. But the peace quickly collapsed when some Peloponnese cities abandoned their alliance with Sparta and threw their lot in with Sparta's independent neighbor Argos. The deadly Battle of Mantinea, the largest land battle of the war, ended in a stunning victory for Sparta in 418 BCE, and the defiant cities were forced back into the Peloponnesian League.

Next, the war headed to the island of Sicily, across the Straits of Messina from the toe of Italy's boot. Ionian and Dorian Greeks had colonized Sicily back in the archaic era. Their mother cities were Athens for the Ionians and Sparta for the Dorians, and both cities supported their kinsmen in Sicily. When the Greeks colonized Sicily, they pushed the indigenous people inland. The town of Segesta pleaded for Athens's help against an attack by the Dorian city of Selinus. Athens agreed, and the Sicilian Expedition ensued in 415 BCE, with the Athenians launching an attack on Selinus's ally, Syracuse.

Sparta sent a fleet of eighty ships to Syracuse, and in the first two naval skirmishes, Athens's navy prevailed. But then the Spartan navy trapped the Athenian fleet in the harbor, where they could not maneuver well. Both sides lost about fifty ships in the pitched battle. Finally, the Athenians beached their ships and attempted to escape by land. But the coalition Syracusan-Spartan forces annihilated tens of thousands of the Athenians and enslaved the rest.

Back in Greece, Sparta took control of the northern Attica Peninsula, blocking trade and communications between Athens and northern Greece. Sparta then recaptured Athens's silver mines, leaving Athens financially destitute. Athens demanded more tribute from the Delian League cities, which resulted in the aggrieved Ionian colonies seceding from the league. The Persians inserted themselves into the war by building warships for Sparta.

In a downward spiral, Athens experienced internal turmoil when a four-hundred-man oligarchy usurped power, its democratic advances melting away. Then, Sparta took control of the Dardanelles, blocking Athens's grain shipments from the Black Sea. When the Athenian navy attempted to break the blockade, the Spartans sank 168 of their 180 ships. In 404 BCE, the Peloponnesian War ended with Athens's surrender. Sparta took the remaining Athenian warships and forced Athens to dismantle its protective walls. Yet, Sparta spared the Athenians from the enslavement proposed by other Greek states, remembering how Athens had rescued Greece from the Persians.

The Delian League, once led by Athens, now fell under Sparta's power. But Sparta didn't just collect tribute; it placed its own governors in the cities, which were supported by Spartan garrisons. Sparta even forced democratic states to become oligarchies. Corinth and Thebes had allied with Sparta in the Peloponnesian War, but they found Sparta's tyranny unacceptable. Persia inserted itself again, hoping to destabilize Greece further by bribing the Greek city-states to revolt against Sparta's power.

King Pausanias of Sparta marched north to meet with Spartan General Lysander, who was returning from Asia, to attack the city of Haliartus, a close ally of Thebes. Lysander arrived first and, without waiting for Pausanias, attacked Haliartus. But suddenly, a Theban army assailed him from the rear. He wasn't aware a Theban army was nearby, which was a fatal mistake since the Thebans cut him down. More Greek city-states switched to the Thebans' side.

The Spartan fleet was returning from the Dardanelles when the Persians and Athenians suddenly attacked it. General Conon of Athens commanded one Persian fleet, while Persian Governor Pharnabazus of Phrygia (in western Turkey) commanded a Phoenician fleet. The Spartans ran their ships up on the shore and fled, with the Persians and Athenians close behind. The beach ran red with Greek blood, and Sparta's naval empire folded.

General Conon and his new Persian friend Pharnabazus wreaked havoc on the Peloponnese coast and then sailed to Athens, where Pharnabazus financed the rebuilding of Athens's walls. But Sparta was still blocking Athens's grain shipments, so in

387 BCE, the Persians finally negotiated the King's Peace with Sparta, Athens, Argos, Corinth, and Thebes. The Persians got Cyprus and the Ionian Greek colonies in Asia, but all other Greek city-states were now independently ruled.

Sparta broke the treaty five years later by attacking Thebes and establishing a garrison there. But the Theban leaders had secretly trained young men in combat skills, and in 379 BCE, they killed the Spartan leaders but permitted the rest of the soldiers at the garrison to leave unharmed. Winning a land battle against the Spartans galvanized the Thebans into forming a three-hundred-man Sacred Band with highly-skilled full-time warriors. Meanwhile, Athens staged a comeback in the next decade, creating the Second Athenian League in 378 BCE. Unlike the first, all the city-states maintained their independence in a decentralized alliance.

Sparta's power over the other Greek city-states finally imploded at the 371 BCE Battle of Leuctra. The Spartans marched north to attack Thebes and caught the Thebans unaware, but the Thebans quickly rallied seven miles south of Thebes. The Thebans used their new intimidating fifty-man-deep phalanx formation and spine-chilling twelve-foot-long spears. Thebes' crushing triumph allowed it to dominate Greece for the next decade as they won one battle after another.

Thebes invaded Thessaly and Macedon to the north, taking Macedon's adolescent prince, Philip II, as a hostage, with no inkling of how that would one day change the course of history. As Thebes became stronger, a nervous Athens allied with Sparta in the consequential 362 BCE Battle of Mantinea. Thebes won the brutal battle but at a grievous cost, losing their seasoned war leader Epaminondas.

Thebes successfully invaded Sparta and freed their helots, who did Sparta's manual work. Without their helot labor freeing the Spartan men to be full-time warriors, Sparta's army floundered. But Thebes also struggled, having lost its expert generals. Neither Sparta nor Thebes could maintain control over the rest of Greece, leaving the door open for Macedon's rising star: Philip II.

Chapter 5: Philip II and Alexander the Great

"Sire, you have another letter from King Darius. He's offering peace terms again."

"I'm sure he is!" Alexander the Great chuckled. "I've conquered the entire Mediterranean coast, and I've got his women! Can you believe he abandoned them on the battlefield?"

"Yes, he asks that you return his mother, wife, and daughters. In return, you will receive half the Persian Empire, a gold fortune, and one of his daughters in marriage."

"Ha!" Alexander laughed. "I already have all that! I've got the gold of Lydia, Tyre, and Egypt. I have both his daughters, and I've conquered half the empire. Why should I stop now when I can have it all?"

Who would believe that obscure Macedon on Greece's northern frontier would rise to such heights? While Sparta, Thebes, and Athens fought for control, Macedon was nothing but a backwater at risk of being absorbed by stronger powers. And yet, under Philip II, it rose to conquer most of the Greek mainland; under Philip's son Alexander, it conquered the entire Persian Empire.

Political chaos marked Philip II's childhood and youth. After the assassination of his oldest brother, King Alexander II, he spent his teen years as a hostage in Thebes. But Theban General

Epaminondas schooled him in diplomacy and Theban military arts. Philip dreamed of reforming Macedon's military as he studied the Theban phalanx formation and weaponry. At the age of twenty-three, Philip unexpectantly became Macedon's king when his brother, King Perdiccas III, died in battle.

Philip immediately set to work transforming Macedon's military. He trained his soldiers with the sarissa: a deadly twenty-foot-long spear he invented. The men also learned Philip's innovative phalanx: sixteen rows of men eight men wide, giving them superior maneuverability. Philip quickly began expanding Macedon's borders, avenging his brother's death, and defeating the surrounding nations that had once threatened his kingdom's existence. He spread his kingdom west, encompassing today's Albania, east into today's Bulgaria, and north into today's Serbia and Kosovo. He took control of Athens's silver mines in Amphipolis.

By the end of his reign, Philip II controlled most of the Balkan Peninsula.
Photo modified: zoomed in and labels added. Credit: ArnoldPlaton, CC BY-SA 3.0 <https://creativecommons.org/licenses/by-sa/3.0>, via Wikimedia Commons https://commons.wikimedia.org/wiki/File:Balkan_Peninsula.svg

Although the Greeks only had one wife at a time, the Macedonian noblemen married multiple wives to form strategic alliances. In 337 BCE, Philip married his fourth wife, Princess Olympias of Epirus, and she gave birth to their son Alexander the following year. Philip hired the renowned philosopher Aristotle to tutor Alexander and invited the Greek rulers to send their sons to study with Alexander under Aristotle, leading to astute Greek alliances.

Philip's next military target was the Greek city-states to the south. His opportunity came when the Third Sacred War broke out in 356 BCE at Delphi in central Greece. Pythia, the Oracle of Delphi, was a priestess who would go into a trance after breathing in fumes from a fissure underneath the Temple of Apollo. People from around the Greek world traveled to Delphi to seek her advice. The city of Phocis had dared to plow farms in the sacred precinct around Delphi and then committed greater sacrilege by raiding the Temple of Apollo and stealing its treasures.

Defending Delphi not only gave Philip hero status to Apollo's worshipers but also allowed him to gain control in central Greece. Philip had been fighting Thessaly at his southern border but suddenly offered to ally with it to fight for Delphi. Together, they crushed Phocis, wiping out its military. The Thessalonians were so impressed with Philip's leadership that they made him their chief magistrate for life.

Part of Philip's peace settlement with Phocis was control of the Thermopylae Pass, which lay in Phocis' land, giving him unhindered access to southern Greece. To prevent him from invading, Athens negotiated a settlement with Philip, which he was happy to do. Philip needed Athens's navy for his long-term goal of invading and conquering the Persian Empire with a united Greek force.

Isocrates, the influential orator of Athens, encouraged Philip in his quest. "You must reconcile the four great Greek cities: Argos, Athens, Sparta, and Thebes. If they unite, everyone else will join in. We must stop this constant infighting between the Greek city-states and bring them together to fight Persia!"

Philip II's image on a gold stater coin.

But the Athenian statesman Demosthenes ranted, "Philip is the worst enemy Athens could have! He's a despot! We need to fight the Macedonians, not collude with them."

While Philip fought the Persians at Byzantium (later known as Constantinople), where Europe and Asia join, Demosthenes convinced Athens to ally with Persia against Philip. Philip desperately needed control of Byzantium because it would be his route to the Persian Empire. Exasperated with Athens, Philip marched back to Greece as Athens quickly allied with Thebes to fend him off. Thebes blocked Philip from the Thermopylae Pass, but Philip knew about the alternative route.

Philip crossed the mountains and faced off with Athens, Corinth, and Thebes in the Battle of Chaeronea. His eighteen-year-old son, Alexander, commanded the left flank with assistance from experienced officers, and Philip commanded the right side. The Greek forces lined up on the road in a two-and-a-half-mile formation, with the Thebans on the right flank against Alexander, the Athenians on an incline across from Philip, and the Corinthians in the middle.

Philip didn't want the Athenians to have the uphill advantage, so he quickly engaged and then feigned a retreat. The Athenians chased Philip's forces across the narrow valley and up the hill on the other side. Philip whirled his troops around to fight, with the

Athenians now downhill, making them an easier target for his archers. On the left flank, young Alexander proved his skills by shattering the Thebans' legendary Sacred Band.

Athens and Corinth were dumbfounded when Philip did not flatten their cities. But that wasn't his plan. He wanted the Greek states to unite under his leadership to fight Persia. He desired to fight *with* them, not destroy them. Philip was more concerned about Sparta, which had remained uninvolved. What if Sparta started wreaking havoc on Greece's cities while their forces were overseas fighting Persia? In laconic Spartan fashion, they refused negotiations.

However, the rest of Greece was ready to come to the table. They formed the League of Corinth in 337 BCE, where all the city-states (except Sparta) agreed not to fight each other but to unite against Persia. They formally declared war on the Persian Empire, making Philip their commander. Within months, Philip sent General Parmenion to Asia to free the Greek city-states in Ionia from Persian rule. But then disaster struck.

Philip was throwing a wedding for his daughter Cleopatra to her uncle, King Alexander of Epirus. As Philip entered the hall, his bodyguard and jilted lover, Pausanias, suddenly thrust a dagger into his ribs. The great warrior was dead! What would happen now? Would the Macedonian-Greek alliance still invade the Achaemenid Empire? Who would lead them?

While Philip lay bleeding out, the Macedonian military and nobles wasted no time declaring Alexander as their next king. The twenty-year-old had multiple calamities demanding his immediate attention. As soon as they heard of Philip's death, several Greek cities dropped out of the League of Corinth. Alexander had to rein them in quickly to proceed with the Persian invasion.

Alexander marched south, where the Thessalian forces waited at the Mount Olympus Pass. But he took a circuitous route and unexpectantly came up on their rear the following morning. Taken off guard, Thebes surrendered, and Alexander continued south, where Athens and Corinth apologetically acknowledged his rule. Alexander then headed north to bring Thrace and northern Greece into line.

Alexander spent the next year pummeling the northern rebels into submission, but Thebes and Athens backed out of the League of Corinth again. This time, Alexander was not so ready to forgive. He demolished the city of Thebes, sparing only the temples. He enslaved its citizens and donated its land to the surrounding towns. Athens promptly sent envoys to Alexander, pleading for mercy, which Alexander granted.

With all of Greece (except Sparta) united again, Alexander embarked on his audacious invasion of the Persian Empire. In 334 BCE, he led forty thousand Greeks and Macedonians across the Hellespont into Asia, pausing in Troy to honor the heroes of the ancient war. King Darius III of Persia wasn't especially worried. He didn't even leave Persia, assuming his governors' forces could easily repel the Greeks and Macedonians in Ionia.

General Memnon of Rhodes did not share King Darius's optimism. He had escaped to Macedon as a young man following a failed revolt against Persia's former king. He was a personal acquaintance of Philip II and his son Alexander and knew their grandiose plans. He also knew what their military machine could do. He advised the Persian satraps (governors), "We need a scorched-earth policy! Get the people off the coast! Leave nothing behind that the Greeks and their horses can eat. He needs to feed his people and their animals. Starve him, and he'll leave!"

The Persians ignored his advice. Why should they run away? They could send this upstart Macedonian packing! Instead, they lined up at the Granicus River to square off with Alexander. The Greeks would have to cross the sixty-foot-wide, swiftly flowing river, then climb up a steep bluff to meet the Persian military. As Alexander's forces drew near, the sun was about to set. Surely, he would wait until morning to cross.

But no! Instead, the Macedonian-Greek forces quickly moved into position. Alexander led the right flank with his Macedonian cavalry, elite infantry, archers, and javelin throwers. His formidable infantry formed the Macedonian phalanx in the center, and his Thessalian-Thracian cavalry took the left flank. As Alexander's right-flank cavalry plunged into the river, the Persians responded with a hail of arrows that darkened the sun.

Alexander and his horsemen galloped across the river and up the steep bank, fending off the Persians' attempts to push them down into the river. Alexander speared King Darius's son-in-law Mithridates, but then the satrap Spithridates smashed Alexander's helmet with his battle ax. The helmet fell away in two pieces but did not greatly injure Alexander. Alexander's close friend Black Cleitus impaled Spithridates before he could strike again. Meanwhile, the rest of Alexander's army was wading through the river's swift current and clambering up the embankment to form ranks with their twenty-foot sarissas. The Persians took one look at the wall of spears and panicked, running off the battlefield.

After this victory, the Ionian city-states surrendered to Alexander. Alexander next assailed Miletus and Halicarnassus, Persia's major ports, crippling Persia's naval fleet. As Alexander passed through the city of Gordium, someone pointed out the Gordian Knot, telling their leader about the prophecy. Whoever untied the massive tangle would rule Asia. Alexander smiled and slashed the knot in two with his sword. Asia was his! Most scholars conclude that this story is a myth.

This Pompey mural depicts Alexander at the Battle of Issus.
https://en.wikipedia.org/wiki/File:Alexander_the_Great_mosaic.jpg

By this point, King Darius realized he needed to lead his military in person. As Alexander marched south along the Mediterranean, King Darius unexpectedly came up on his rear, trapping Alexander's men on a narrow plain between the Nur

Mountains and the Gulf of Issus. Alexander wheeled around, and his well-trained military immediately fell into the same formation they used at the Granicus River.

On the Pinarus River's northern banks, Darius's heavy cavalry lined up next to the sea. The Persians had been hiring Greek soldiers as mercenaries for over a century, and in this battle, Darius's Greek infantry in the center faced off against their fellow Greeks. The Persian infantry extended up into the foothills, and a contingent crossed the river in an attempt to outflank the Macedonians' right wing. The Persian cavalry plunged across the river, confronting General Parmenion's Thessalian-Thracian cavalry.

The Macedonian cavalry raced over the river, breaking through the Persian infantry's left wing. But Alexander's center infantry, weighed down with their shields and heavy sarissas, were daunted by the swift current and retreated from the river. But Alexander led his elite right-flank infantry across the river unchallenged because the Macedonian cavalry had disrupted the Persian infantry facing him.

Once over the river, Alexander leaped onto a horse and charged straight at King Darius, with his Macedonian horsemen right behind him. Darius panicked and fled the field in his chariot. Once word swept through the Persian ranks that their king had abandoned them, they raced off, with the Greeks close behind, killing anyone who couldn't run fast enough.

Although injured, Alexander scored a tremendous victory in the Battle of Issus. He even captured Darius's womenfolk in the Persian camp; Persian women often accompanied their male relatives to battle. When Darius and his men ran for the hills, they left behind Darius's queen, the queen mother, and his two daughters. Alexander took them into his custody, treating them with respect. Several months later, Darius's wife died in childbirth, and Alexander gave her a royal funeral. He later married one of the daughters, Stateira II.

As Alexander's horde of warriors headed south along Lebanon's coast in 332 BCE, all the Phoenician cities except ancient Tyre surrendered. Tyre had built a new city on an island a half-mile offshore with 150-foot walls. As Alexander approached, the city evacuated their women and children to Carthage in Africa. Alexander laid siege to the city for seven months, building a causeway to the island with rubble from the old Tyre. But the sea suddenly dropped to eighteen feet deep as they got farther offshore. So, Alexander rounded up 220 ships from Cyprus, Ionia, and other Phoenician cities. Six thousand Tyrians died as the Macedonians and Greeks took the city. Alexander crucified another two thousand and enslaved thirty thousand.

Egypt had chafed under Persian rule and attempted multiple times to regain independence. Now, they welcomed Alexander as their deliverer from the Achaemenid Empire. They handed over their treasury, and the priests crowned him as Egypt's new pharaoh. At the mouth of the Nile, Alexander built the new city of Alexandria, which grew into a breathtaking center of Hellenistic culture and scientific study.

Darius met Alexander with elephants and scythed chariots.
https://commons.wikimedia.org/wiki/File:Meister_der_Alexanderschlacht_003.jpg

King Darius clashed with Alexander a final time in 331 BCE at the Battle of Gaugamela in today's northern Iraq. The Macedonians and Greeks faced war elephants from India this time, which was a new experience for them. Darius had another new weapon: four-horsed scythed chariots. Their blades extended three feet out from the wheels' hubs and could slice a man's leg in half.

Alexander led a cavalry charge around the Persian left flank, drawing them toward him and thinning out the defense in the center where King Darius was.

The Persian scythed chariots pressed toward the Greeks, but with the flexible Macedonian phalanx, the Greeks stepped aside to allow the chariots to pass through as the Bulgarian javelin throwers impaled the horses and their drivers. As the center line surrounding Darius disintegrated, Darius abandoned the field, with his men fleeing when they realized their king had left them.

Alexander headed south to Babylon, where he was hailed as the Persian Empire's new king. Darius fled east, hoping to recruit more men and retake his kingdom, but his Bactrian satrap Bessus murdered him. After arranging a proper royal funeral, Alexander appointed leadership over his new lands, keeping the governors in place who acknowledged him as their king. Next, Alexander marched east. His first objective was to find and execute Bessus. He then wanted to explore and conquer east to "the edge of the world," the Ganges River in the Indian subcontinent.

The Bactrian chieftains turned Bessus over to Alexander, who then gave him to King Darius's brother to supervise his crucifixion. While in Bactria (today's Afghanistan and Tajikistan), Alexander met Roxana, the daughter of the Bactrian chieftain Oxyartes. For Alexander, it was love at first sight. He married the young girl, despite his friends' objections, who felt he should marry a Macedonian princess or at least Darius's daughter. In their minds, Roxana's family wasn't prestigious enough for the new emperor. Alexander then marched to the Achaemenid Empire's easternmost border at the Jaxartes River.

By this time, his troops were weary and demoralized, having been away from their families for ten years. They were also wary of Alexander's abrupt mood changes, especially after he got drunk and killed his good friend Cleitus the Black. But Alexander ignored their protests and pressed on, scaling the 3,500-foot Khyber Pass over the Hindu Kush range and descending into today's Pakistan.

Alexander's hopes of traveling to the great river of India were dashed when his men rebelled. They were obstinate; it was time to go home! Alexander was livid but gave in and accompanied his men back to Babylon. When they arrived, Alexander threw a collective wedding, marrying eighty Persian princesses to his officers, uniting the Macedonian, Greek, and Persian royal families. Alexander married two princesses that day: Darius's daughter, Stateira, and Parysatis, the daughter of an earlier Persian king, Artaxerxes III.

In 323 BCE, Alexander was elated with the news that his first wife, Roxanna, was pregnant. But several months later, he became ill with a fever and died within two weeks. He had never lost a major battle. He reaped one staggering victory over another as he built a sensational three-continent empire. But he died before he could effectively rule it or name a successor. What would happen to Greece, Macedonia, Egypt, and his new Asian provinces now?

Chapter 6: The Diadochi and the Roman Conquest

Alexander's top generals met to discuss the unexpected leadership crisis of Alexander's new empire. General Perdiccas held up Alexander's ring, "Our commander and king, Alexander, gave this to me before he died. I'm to be the regent for his half-brother Arrhidaeus and for Roxana's child."

"Arrhidaeus? He's mentally deficient! How can he rule?"

"He's Alexander's closest male relative," Perdiccas explained. "Yes, he has physical and mental challenges, but we can guide him. He will marry his niece, Princess Eurydice. Roxana is due to give birth soon. If it's a girl, we'll make Arrhidaeus king, and if it's a boy, Alexander's son will be king."

"Ha! As regent, you'll be the de facto king either way," one of the generals pointed out. "So, how does Arrhidaeus feel about all this? Does he even want to be king?"

General Meleager went out to fetch Arrhidaeus. When Meleager returned with the young man, Arrhidaeus was overwhelmed at the sight of his brother's stern generals and ducked out, quivering in fear. They coaxed him back in, but tears flowed down Arrhidaeus's face. "I'm unqualified to be your king."

One of the generals asked, "Why can't we have two kings?"

The generals finally agreed on the Partition of Babylon, in which Arrhidaeus would co-reign with Roxana's baby if it were a boy. Perdiccas would be the regent for the kings and command the empire's army. As Alexander's Diadochi or successors, the other generals divided sections of the empire among themselves to rule. Two months later, Roxana gave birth to a boy, King Alexander IV.

The other generals rebelled against Perdiccas in the First War of the Diadochi (322–319 BCE) because he wanted to marry Alexander the Great's sister Cleopatra and become Macedon's king. Then Perdiccas marched against General Ptolemy, now Egypt's pharaoh, who stole Alexander's body to honor Alexander's request for burial in Egypt. But Perdiccas's men rebelled, and his three leading officers killed him, ending the first war.

With Perdiccas dead, the generals made new arrangements for the regency of the two kings. In the 321 BCE Partition of Triparadisus, Queen Eurydice became the de facto regent for her husband, Arrhidaeus. Antipater, who Alexander had appointed as regent of Macedonia while he invaded Persia, became regent over Roxana's toddler son, King Alexander IV. Antipater brought the two kings and the queen to Macedon. General Seleucus, one of Perdiccas's murderers, became Babylon's ruler. He would eventually rule as king of the Seleucid Empire, which encompassed most of the Middle East.

Two years later, Antipater died, leaving General Polyperchon as the new regent. But Antipater's son Cassander felt the regency was rightfully his and allied with Ptolemy and General Antigonus the One-Eye to evict Polyperchon from Macedon. Polyperchon escaped to Epirus with Roxana and her four-year-old boy, Alexander IV, and the three generals made Arrhidaeus the sole king of the empire.

But Alexander the Great's mother, Olympias, allied with Polyperchon in a battle against King Arrhidaeus and Queen Eurydice. The Macedonian soldiers refused to fight Queen Mother Olympias, who ordered the deaths of Arrhidaeus and Eurydice. Yet Olympias's victory was short-lived. Cassander allied with Antigonus, Ptolemy, and another of Alexander's generals, Lysimachus. They defeated Olympias, and she was stoned to death in 316 BCE. Cassander captured Roxana and the boy-king Alexander, locking them in a tower in Macedonia for years. The Second Diadochi War ended with victory for the four generals.

King Alexander IV was about to turn fourteen. He would soon be old enough to rule without a regent. Cassander poisoned him and Roxana in 309 BCE but kept their murders a secret, although it hardly mattered by this time. The five Diadochi who remained were now calling themselves king, indicating independence from the empire. Antigonus ruled from western Turkey to Egypt's border, and Cassander ruled Macedon and Thessaly. Lysimachus had Thrace, Seleucus controlled the Middle East (from Iraq to Afghanistan), and Ptolemy was pharaoh over Egypt and Libya.

The final clash in the 301 BCE Battle of Ipsus in Phrygia (western Turkey) ended the Wars of the Diadochi. Cassander, Lysimachus, and Seleucus allied against Antigonus. Seleucus was on his way back from a campaign in India and brought five hundred war elephants. As Lysimachus attacked western Turkey, Antigonus's son Demetrius rushed over from Greece to assist his father in Ipsus.

Antigonus and Demetrius had seventy-five war elephants, which they sent out in the opening charge. They were met by two hundred of Seleucus's elephants. Antigonus's stronger infantry prevailed until Seleucus released his other three hundred elephants. Seleucus's cavalry outflanked Antigonus's right wing. A javelin struck and killed Antigonus. Demetrius escaped to Greece, where he would plot a successful takeover of Macedonia.

Cassander and Ptolemy died of natural causes in 297 and 282, respectively. Only Seleucus and Lysimachus remained of the original reigning generals. Seleucus marched against Lysimachus in 281 BCE, and Lysimachus died in the battle. But a few months later, Ptolemy I's son, Ptolemy Ceraunus, assassinated Seleucus, the last of the Diadochi.

Seleucus was the last of Alexander the Great's generals.

The dynamic Hellenistic (Greek) culture permeated Asia, Africa, and eastern Europe. The Greeks assimilated the cultures of the people they led, blending Middle Eastern, Egyptian, and Indian influences with Greek art, philosophy, science, and mathematics. The Greek cities of Alexandria, Egypt, and Antioch, Syria, were the new scientific and artistic powerhouses.

Alexandria on the Nile Delta had a half million people and a thriving sea trade around the Mediterranean. Its priceless library held thousands of scrolls on history, science, religion, and literature. Its chief librarian, Eratosthenes, calculated the earth's circumference at being 28,000 to 29,000 miles, astoundingly close to today's calculations of 24,901 miles. Aristarchus of Samos taught that the earth circled the sun once a year and rotated on its axis on a twenty-four-hour day.

Archimedes of Syracuse devised a formula for determining the volume of a sphere and calculated pi (π) to 3.14 for the ratio of a circle's diameter to its circumference. He is called the founder of theoretical mechanics for developing the law of the lever. He also developed Archimedes' principle: a solid placed in a fluid is lighter by the fluid weight it displaces. He demonstrated how he could move a ship with a compound pulley.

Alexander the Great and his Hellenistic successors spread the Koine Greek dialect as the common language throughout the Mediterranean and the Middle East. A shared language enhanced trade and enabled discussions between scientific, mathematic, and religious scholars. Ptolemy II, Egypt's second Macedonian pharaoh, commissioned Jewish scholars to translate the Tanakh (Old Testament) into Koine Greek. Known as the Septuagint translation, it became the standard version used in synagogues throughout North Africa and the Middle East.

Hellenism introduced a new era of Greek sculptures. While archaic era sculptures featured stiff young women and men with slight smiles, classical Greek sculptures featured perfect bodies in sinuous and fluid motion. The Hellenistic sculptures portrayed people with imperfections, extreme emotions, flexed musculature, and exaggerated action. A dramatic example is the Laocoön Group, which features the violent deaths of the Trojan priest Laocoön and his two sons by serpents.

The Laocoön sculpture demonstrates the agony of death and despair
https://commons.wikimedia.org/wiki/File:Laocoon_Vatican_detail.jpg

The Greek world first clashed with Rome in 280 BCE. The Roman Republic had been confined to central Italy, but now it was conquering territory and extending into southern Italy. Greece had colonized southernmost Italy (the toe and heel of Italy's boot) in the archaic era. Now, several wealthy and powerful Greek city-states controlled the sea trade in the region.

"One more victory like that, and we're finished!" When King Pyrrhus of Epirus inserted himself into Italy's political scene, he discovered that a technical win could be so costly that it was a "Pyrrhic victory." It all started when Rome broke a treaty with southern Italy's powerful Greek city-state of Tarentum by sailing ten ships into the Gulf of Taranto. Tarentum angrily responded by sinking four Roman vessels, and Rome declared war.

When the Tarentines asked King Pyrrhus of Epirus in northwestern Greece for assistance, he jumped at his chance to get a foothold in Italy. A relative of Alexander the Great, he harbored ambitions of building his own empire, despite lacking soldiers, funding, and ships. He borrowed all that from Macedonia, the Seleucid Empire, and Egypt, sailing to Italy in 280 BCE. To the Tarentines' dismay, he cracked down on frivolities and drafted the men into his army.

Pyrrhus first confronted Rome in the Battle of Heraclea at the Siris River. His initial cavalry charge broke through the Roman lines. Horrified by the Roman ferocity, he demanded his lieutenant exchange armor with him. Thinking the lieutenant was King Pyrrhus, the Romans quickly killed him. Pyrrhus's war elephants turned the tide of the battle, terrifying the Roman soldiers and their horses. The Greeks won, but both sides suffered catastrophic losses: fifteen thousand Roman deaths to thirteen thousand Greeks.

Over the winter, Pyrrhus recruited troops from Ionia and Macedonia, building his military to forty thousand soldiers. He warred with Rome again in 279 BCE in a grueling two-day battle that raged in wooded terrain this time, impeding horse and elephant charges. The Romans further obstructed elephant charges by lining up three hundred anti-elephant oxcarts with spears poking out and catapults to hurl stones at the Greeks.

King Pyrrhus fought for Italy's Greek city-states against Rome.
https://commons.wikimedia.org/wiki/File:Pyrrhus.JPG

Pyrrhus guided his elephants around the end of the anti-elephant wagons on the second day. One look at the elephants and the spooked Roman horses raced off. Technically, Pyrrhus won again: the Romans lost seven thousand men, and the Greeks lost about half that. But Pyrrhus was wounded, and most of his commanders were dead.

Pyrrhus's physician, Nicias, approached the Romans, offering to kill King Pyrrhus. The Roman commanders warned Pyrrhus in a letter:

"We, being greatly disturbed in spirit because of your continued acts of injustice, desire to war with you as an enemy. But as a matter of general precedent and honor, it has seemed to us that we should desire your personal safety in order that we may have the opportunity of vanquishing you in the field."[13]

Pyrrhus thanked the Romans by freeing his Roman prisoners of war. He executed Nicias, forming the straps of a chair from his flayed skin. Then, he surprised everyone by suddenly leaving Italy and sailing to Sicily to assist the Greek city-states in their struggle against Carthage. The Sicilian Greeks said he could be their king if he rid Sicily of the Carthaginians. In his absence, Rome brought the southern Italian tribes in line and overpowered all of Italy's Greek city-states except for Rhegion and Tarentum.

Pyrrhus's Sicilian venture ended in dismal failure, and the remnants of his fleet sailed back to Italy in 276 BCE. He marched by night toward the Roman forces at Maleventum, planning a surprise attack at dawn. But his men wandered off the path into goat trails in the dark. When the weary soldiers finally came out of the woods at Maleventum, they were on a high hill in full view of the Roman troops. The Greeks suffered a brutal loss, and Pyrrhus left Italy for good. Rome now ruled all the Greek cities in southern Italy.

Rome's first offshore war was with Carthage in a successful bid to gain control of Sicily's Greek city-states. In the First Punic War (264–241 BCE), Rome forced Carthage to abandon Sicily. While

---

[13]A. Cornelius Gellius, *Noctes Atticae* (Attic Nights), Volume I, Book III (Loeb Classical Library). http://penelope.uchicago.edu/Thayer/E/Roman/Texts/Gellius/3*.html#8

battling Carthage, Rome also warred on Greece's mainland for the first time when Rome inserted itself into the convoluted politics of the Macedonian Wars.

Hannibal of Carthage had surprised Rome by crossing the Alps and swooping down on Italy from its northern border. While Hannibal was wreaking havoc in Italy, King Philip V of Macedonia allied with him to rid the eastern Adriatic Sea of Roman influence. Hannibal was too busy in Italy and Carthage to help, but Rome intercepted their communications and found out about the alliance. Rome then allied with central Greece's Aetolian League against Philip V.

The Aetolian League attacked central Greece's Acarnania, which had allied with Philip. The Acarnanians were winning until the Roman navy sailed in, captured several of their cities, and enslaved the people. Sparta jumped into the fray, allying with the Aetolian League and Rome, but Philip defeated the allied Greeks in the Peloponnese in 209 BCE. This spurred King Attalus I of Pergamon to unite with the Aetolian League, and his navy joined Rome in patrolling the Aegean Sea.

But when Bithynia invaded Pergamum, Attalus had to rush home. Rome's simultaneous war with Carthage forced it to divert its navy from the Aegean Sea, which gave Philip free rein to capture cities in the Gulf of Corinth. When Philip's allies killed Sparta's tyrant, Machanidas, Sparta pulled out of the war, empowering Philip to expel the Aetolian League from Ionia and Thessaly. The Aetolian League conceded to Philip, ending the First Macedonian War in 205 BCE.

The Second Macedonian War began in 200 BCE with a clandestine conspiracy between Philip V and the Seleucid Empire's King Antiochus to steal Egypt's throne. The Macedonian Ptolemy V had inherited Egypt's throne at the age of five, and a series of bungling regents had destabilized Egypt. The two kings agreed that if their plot succeeded, Antiochus would annex Egypt into the Seleucid Empire; Philip would get Cyrene and Egypt's holdings in the Aegean Sea.

Antiochus immediately set to work, conquering his way down the Mediterranean coast, taking the Egyptian-held cities of Damascus, Sidon, and Samaria. The Jews threw open Jerusalem's gates to Antiochus, celebrating their emancipation from Egypt, little suspecting the horrors his son would one day inflict. Meanwhile, Philip conquered Egypt's Aegean naval base of Samos and its neighboring territory in Miletus.

Rome finally crushed Carthage, ending the Third Punic War. Now it had the ships and manpower to focus on Greece and Macedonia. Rome ordered Philip to abandon all aggressions against Greek and Egyptian territories. If he complied, he could retain Macedonia and Thrace. The Roman ambassador Lepidus personally delivered the ultimatum to Philip in the final days of his siege of the city of Abydos, which would give him control of the Dardanelles.

King Philip answered Lepidus, "I pardon the offensive haughtiness of your manners for three reasons: first, because you are a young man and inexperienced in affairs; secondly, because you are the most handsome man of your time [this was true]; and thirdly, because you are a Roman."[14]

Abydos fell to Philip. Rather than face enslavement, the men killed their wives and children, throwing them from rooftops or into wells, and then stabbed or burned themselves to death. Rome responded by sending Consul Sulpicius to attack Philip in Epirus. After a few inconclusive clashes, Philip received news that the Dardanians of the central Balkans were invading Macedon, so he immediately left to defend his country.

Philip met his match in 198 BCE when Rome's new consul, Titus Quinctius Flamininus, dislodged him from Greece. As he was marching through Albania back to Macedonia, Flamininus caught Philip off guard with a rear attack, slaughtering two thousand of his men. The following year, Philip faced off again with Flamininus in the Battle of Cynoscephalae in a fog-covered valley in Thessaly. Philip's men heard the eerie sound of elephants trumpeting; this was the first time Rome used war elephants. The terrified Macedonians could hear the elephants' lumbering feet but

[14] Polybius, *Histories,* Book 16.
http://www.perseus.tufts.edu/hopper/text?doc=Perseus%3Atext%3A1999.01.0234%3Abook%3D16%3Achapter%3D34

couldn't see anything until the elephants charged at them through the dense mist. The Romans killed eight thousand Macedonians that day, and the Second Macedonian War ended with Philip's surrender and the loss of his navy and army.

Philip V faced Rome's war elephants at the Battle of Cynoscephalae.
Bernard Picart, Public domain;
https://commons.wikimedia.org/wiki/File:Eleazars_exploit.jpg

After Philip's death, his aggressive son Perseus rallied Thrace's Odrysian Kingdom and some of the Greek city-states by promising to return Greece to its former dominance and splendor. He instigated the Third Macedonian War (171–168 BCE) by conquering northern Thessaly. Rome responded by sending troops to Thessaly, but in the Battle of Callinicus, the Macedonians killed two thousand Romans while suffering only four hundred Macedonian casualties.

When the Romans scavenged the crops in the region, Perseus attacked the Roman camp, capturing the six hundred Romans left behind and Roman supplies. He didn't realize Rome's consul, Publius Licinius Crassus, was in the area until Crassus charged in with his war elephants and Numidian cavalry, killing eight thousand Macedonians.

In another nightmarish loss on Macedonia's coast in 168 BCE, Perseus fled the Battle of Pydna, leaving his men behind for the

Romans to massacre or enslave. The Romans finally found him on the island of Samothrace and hauled him to Rome. They paraded him through the streets before throwing him into prison, where he spent the rest of his life. Rome divided Macedon into four republics.

In 146 BCE, the Achaean League in Greece's Peloponnese rebelled against their former ally Rome because Rome forbade any expansion of their territory. Rome crushed the Greeks' main force at the Battle of Scarpheia. Most Greeks killed themselves or fled to Corinth, where the final battle destroyed the city, and the Romans stripped its priceless sculptures and treasures. The rest of the city-states acknowledged Rome's dominion. Yet, Greece continued to impact Rome's philosophy, art, literature, and politics for centuries, spreading its culture as the Roman Republic (and later empire) grew.

SECTION THREE:
The Roman and Byzantine Periods (146 BCE–1453 CE)

Chapter 7: The Greco-Roman World and Early Byzantine Years

What happened to Greece and the Hellenistic empires after they fell to Rome? Did they retain their culture? Why did the "Greek" side of the Roman Empire persist into the Middle Ages when the Western Roman Empire collapsed? In what ways did the new Christian religion impact the Greek world, and how did the Koine Greek language enable it to spread?

Rome ruled the Greek world for five centuries; however, Greek civilization continued to greatly impact Roman culture, just as it had since Rome's earliest history. The Greeks had colonized southern Italy in the 8th century BCE, about the same time as Rome's founding in central Italy. The Romans traded with southern Italy's Greek city-states and later with the rest of the Greek world, assimilating Greek culture.

Through the centuries, the Romans integrated Greek mythology, political ideas, philosophy, art, and architecture into their culture. The austere Romans especially admired the Greek Stoic philosophers who disdained frivolous luxuries while promoting logic and self-sacrifice. The Romans brought Greek prisoners of war back to Rome, many of whom were highly educated. These enslaved Greek intellectuals tutored the children of the Roman elite in the Greek language and literature. A status symbol for elite Romans was the ability to read and write in Greek and having knowledge of the Greek classics.

When Rome conquered Corinth and other Greek cities, it hauled priceless art and statuary back to Rome, seriously damaging the exquisite pieces in transport. However, the Romans used the Greek spoils of war as models, studying and copying the works. Free Greeks began moving to Rome to work as artists or physicians, which were in high demand. The Greco-Roman blend of Greek and Roman culture spread through the territories that Rome conquered, from Britain to central Asia.

After "freeing" Greece from Macedonian dominance, Rome initially avoided direct rule over Greece, allowing political autonomy. But in 146 BCE, Rome obliterated Corinth as a lesson against rebellion and established the Roman province of Macedonia, which initially included the previous country of Macedonia and most of today's Greece. Caesar Augustus (r. 27 BCE-14 CE) separated mainland Greece and the Cyclades from Macedonia, forming the new Roman province of Achaea.

The Hellenistic Kingdom of Pontus (today's western Turkey) revolted against Rome in the First Mithridatic War (89–85 BCE). In May 88 BCE, King Mithridates ordered an ethnic cleansing of all Romans in Pontus, killing at least eighty thousand men, women, and children on the same day. He took control of much of Greece, installing Aristion as Athens's tyrant. Rome's consul Sulla marched on Greece in 87 BCE, with most Greek cities quickly capitulating. But Athens resisted, resulting in a five-month siege of the city that ended with its fall on March 1ˢᵗ, 86 BCE. The streets of Athens flowed with blood as the Romans sacked and burned. After this horror, Greece carefully maintained compliance with Rome.

Once Greece submitted to Rome, it enjoyed an unprecedented two centuries of relative peace in the Pax Romana (Roman Peace, 27 BCE-180 CE). Rome's rule over a vast territory, stretching from the Middle East to western Europe, facilitated stability, prosperous trade, and population growth. It was an era when the arts, literature, science, and technology reached new heights, as people from three continents freely interacted and exchanged ideas.

The Romans freely copied Greek drama, sculpture, literature, philosophy, and rhetoric, putting their spin on Hellenistic culture, yet the Greeks were largely disinterested in reciprocating. Although they learned to respect Roman military power, they felt culturally superior. But one of Rome's rare contributions to Greek culture was adding gladiator and wild animal shows to the Olympics until Emperor Constantine (r. 306–337 CE) outlawed the gory shows.[15]

Most Greeks did not become Roman citizens until 212 CE when Rome extended citizenship to all free adult males in the empire under the *Constitutio Antoniniana*. Until then, Greece and some of the past Hellenistic empires, such as Egypt, continued to follow Greek law rather than Roman law. Greek architecture persisted throughout the Roman period. For instance, the outer courts of Herod's temple in Jerusalem were Corinthian in style, although the inner sanctuary followed the Torah's stipulations.[16] Buildings in Rome and throughout the empire followed the classical Greece style but with some new innovations.

Several Asian and North African religions spread throughout the Hellenistic world and later impacted the Roman Empire. In the Hellenistic age, some Greeks had begun worshiping Isis, the Egyptian goddess of fertility, motherhood, and healing, and the cult now spread throughout the Greco-Roman world. The Greeks associated the ancient Vedic god Mithra (Mithras, Mitra), worshiped by the Hindus and Persians, with Helios and Apollo. But the Romans converted this deity's worship into a clandestine cult, where initiates met secretly in caves. Judaism spread; Jewish synagogues (a Greek word meaning "gathering") were scattered in major cities throughout the Greek world.

Within the Greco-Roman milieu, a new religion launched around 30 CE. The Greeks' first contact with Christianity was at its inception. Jesus was born in Judea, which had been part of the Greek world for over three centuries since Alexander the Great conquered the land and was greeted by the Jewish priests at the

---

[15] A. H. M. Jones, "The Greeks under the Roman Empire," *Dumbarton Oaks Papers* 17 (1963): 1–9. https://doi.org/10.2307/1291187.

[16] Jones, "The Greeks under the Roman Empire," 10.

---

gates of Jerusalem. The Talmud records that Jewish High Priest Shimon HaTzaddik petitioned Alexander the Great to preserve the temple, and Alexander granted their request.[17]

The Judaeans spoke both Koine Greek and Aramaic. When Jesus read from the scroll of Isaiah in the synagogue (Luke 4:17-21), it was the LXX (Koine Greek Septuagint translation), not the Hebrew Tanakh.[18] Jesus and his apostles quoted from this Greek translation more often than the Hebrew version, and the apostles wrote the New Testament in Koine Greek. Apostle John began his Gospel with "Εν ἀρχῇ ἦν ὁ Λόγος" ("In the beginning was the *Logos*"),[19] which had special meaning to the Greeks. The Greek philosopher Heraclitus said the Logos was the invisible fire that drives the systems of the universe. Leucippus said the Logos controlled the movement of atoms. Stoic philosophy taught that the Logos was the universal, divine reason from which life and order proceed.

Apostle John mentioned Greek converts to Judaism who traveled to Jerusalem for the Passover celebration, requesting an audience with Jesus.[20] The Greek-speaking Apostles Paul, Barnabas, Silas, Luke, and Timothy took Christianity to the Greek city-states in Asia, mainland Greece, and Macedonia.[21] When Paul arrived in Athens, he debated with the Epicurean and Stoic philosophers, quoting from the Greek poem *Phaenomena* by Aratus. "In him, we live and move and have our being ... we are his offspring."[22]

---

[17] Yoma 69a, *The William Davidson Talmud (Koren - Steinsaltz)*. https://www.sefaria.org/Yoma.69a.14?lang=bi&with=all&lang2=en

[18] Luke 4:18, "Commentaries," *Bible Hub*. https://biblehub.com/commentaries/luke/4-18.htm

[19] John 1:1, "Interlinear Bible," *Bible Hub*. https://biblehub.com/interlinear/john/1-1.htm

[20] John 12:20-21

[21] Acts 13-17

[22] Acts 17:18-33

Paul in Athens in the Catholic Basilica of St. Dionysius the Areopagite. Paul was not one of the original Twelve Apostles, but he is called an apostle for this importance in early Christianity.

Paul and his cohorts received a mixed reaction from the Greeks. Some were interested and wanted to hear more. Others laughed in contempt. Dionysius, a magistrate in the Areopagus

Court, converted and became the first bishop of Athens.[23] In Ephesus, so many people converted from Greek polytheism to Christianity that the silversmiths lost business selling cult images, so they stirred up a mob against Paul.[24] In Cyprus, the Roman proconsul Quintus Sergius Paulus converted.[25] In Macedonia, a wealthy female merchant named Lydia converted.[26]

Within Paul's lifetime, Christian churches sprang up throughout the major cities of the Greek world. Ten books of the New Testament are letters written by Paul to Greek churches or Greek bishops, in which he quoted the Greek philosophers Epimenides and Menander.[27] Some Christians died as martyrs since they were considered an affront to traditional Greek beliefs. In 60 BCE, Apostle Andrew, brother of Simon Peter, was crucified in Patras. Barnabas was stoned to death in Salamis.

The Apostolic Age, the first generation of Christianity, was followed by the ante-Nicene period, which began in 100 CE and continued until 325 CE when the First Council of Nicaea met. Christians experienced several periods of intense persecution by local leaders and various emperors, especially Nero (r. 54–68 CE), Valerian (r. 253–260 CE), and Diocletian (r. 284–305). The Romans considered Christianity a socially divisive cult because the monotheistic Christians refused to bow to the Greco-Roman pantheon of gods or acknowledge the Roman emperor as a deity. The Jews were likewise monotheistic, but their religion was so ancient they were generally tolerated.

Quadratus, the bishop of Athens, was a disciple of the original apostles. When Emperor Hadrian visited Athens in 124 CE, Quadratus presented an explanation of Christianity. Hadrian responded with a favorable proclamation, stating that Christians could not be persecuted merely for being Christian but only if they did something illegal. However, after Hadrian's death, persecution

---

[23] Acts 17:32-34

[24] Acts 19

[25] Acts 13:6-12

[26] Acts 16:11-15

[27] Titus 1:12, 1 Corinthians 15:33

emerged again in some regions of the Roman Empire. Polycarp of Smyrna, who had been schooled by John the Apostle, refused to burn incense in worship of the emperor and was burned at the stake around 156 CE. Despite persecution, about 10 percent of the empire's population was Christian by 300 CE.

Roman Emperor Diocletian divided the empire's leadership into a tetrarchy (four co-rulers) under his authority. He moved his capital from Rome to Nicomedia (in today's Turkey) and ruled western Turkey, Syria, Palestine, and Egypt. Constantius administered Britain and Gaul, Maximum governed Spain, Italy, and Africa's northwestern coast, and Galerius controlled Greece and the rest of the Balkan Peninsula.

When Diocletian fell seriously ill, Galerius pushed him out of the tetrarchy, making himself the lead ruler. He passed the Edict of Toleration in 311 CE, ending Diocletian's great persecution of Christians. Torture and death had done nothing to deter Christianity, which continued growing in vitality and numbers. By 313 CE, the tetrarchy had crumbled, with two emperors left: Constantine (the son of Constantius) and Licinius (a close friend of Galerius). They jointly passed the Edict of Milan, granting Christians and everyone else the freedom to follow the religion of their choice.

The uneasy truce between the two remaining emperors crumbled in 321 CE, and a series of battles ensued. In 324 CE, Constantine defeated Licinius's navy and land army but spared his life, allowing him to live as a private citizen in Thessalonica. After Licinius reportedly tried to stir up support from the Goths in a ploy to regain power, Constantine had Licinius hanged, making himself the sole emperor of the East and West. Constantine rebuilt the ancient Greek colony of Byzantium, where Asia and Europe meet at the Bosphorus Strait, renaming it Constantinople. His new capital represented the union of the East and West.

Constantine called the Eastern and Western church leaders together in Nicaea to iron out the doctrine of the Holy Trinity. Arius, a priest in Alexandria, Egypt, had been teaching that Jesus' existence began at his birth, making him unequal to God the Father, who was infinite. However, most priests held to the Gospel of John, which made it clear that the Logos was with God in the beginning and the creator of all things.[28] The First Council of Nicaea formed the Nicene Creed, which is still used in different forms in many Christian churches:

"I believe ... in one Lord Jesus Christ, the only-begotten Son of God, begotten of the Father before all ages; Light of Light, true God of true God, begotten, not created, of one essence with the Father through Whom all things were made."

After Emperor Constantine died, the Roman Empire went through a period of instability. In 364 CE, Valentinian became emperor, ruling the Western Roman Empire from Milan, Italy, and appointing his brother Valens to rule over the Eastern Roman Empire. He ruled from Constantinople. Valentinian died suddenly of a stroke amid an angry tirade, and his two sons inherited the Western Roman Empire while Valens continued to rule the East. Soon, Valens would confront his greatest nemesis: the Goths, a nomadic Germanic tribe.

The Greek world's history of fending off Indo-European tribes crossing the Alps and moving into southern Europe stretched back for centuries. Celtic-speaking tribes had taken advantage of the destabilization caused by Alexander the Great's untimely death, penetrating Thrace, Illyria, Macedon, and the region around the Black Sea. Ptolemy Ceraunus, the son of Egypt's first Macedonian pharaoh, had seized Macedon's throne, but the Celts killed him, mounting his head on a spear in 279 BCE.

Led by King Brennus, eighty thousand Celtic-speaking Gauls invaded Greece in 279 BCE, targeting the treasures at Delphi's Temple of Apollo. A Greek coalition force led by Athenian General Calippus rushed to defend the sacred land, a holy sanctuary for all Greeks. In a savage battle at Delphi, Brennus committed suicide after being wounded, and the Greeks chased the Gauls out of Greece. The Gallic survivors settled in today's western Turkey, establishing the Kingdom of Galatia.

---

[28] John 1:1-5

The Dying Gaul is a Roman copy of a Greek original.
BeBo86, CC BY-SA 3.0 <https://creativecommons.org/licenses/by-sa/3.0>, via Wikimedia Commons; https://commons.wikimedia.org/wiki/File:Dying_Gaul.jpg

Germanic-speaking tribes also began migrating east and south, reaching the Balkans before 200 BCE. But the Antigonid dynasty of Macedonia (descendants of Antiochus the Great's son Demetrius) barred them from crossing the southern Danube. Centuries later, one tribe called the Heruli migrated to the Black Sea, sailing along its northern shoreline and attacking and conquering its Greek city-states.

In 267 CE, the Heruli ships sailed to southern Greece's Peloponnese Peninsula, raiding Sparta, Corinth, Argos, and Olympia. Heading to the Attica Peninsula, they sacked Athens, destroying the temples, library, and courthouse in the Agora. However, the Heruli left the residential areas in the north and southwest of Athens intact and seemed only interested in looting, not settling in Greece.[29]

---

[29] Lamprini Chioti, "The Herulian Invasion in Athens (267 CE): The Archaeological Evidence," *Destructions, Survival, and Recovery in Ancient Greece* (American School of Classical Studies at Athens: May 16, 2019). https://www.academia.edu/39196609/The_Herulian_invasion_in_Athens_267_CE_The_Archaeological_Evidence

A century later, the Eastern Emperor Valens marched his army to Thrace, facing off against ten thousand Germanic Goths. The Goths killed Valens in the 378 CE Battle of Adrianople, and the catastrophic war obliterated two-thirds of the Eastern Roman Empire's military, including most of its commanders. The Western emperor appointed Theodosius I, the son of a war hero, as the Eastern Roman Empire's new emperor. Rather than fighting the Goths, Theodosius permitted them to settle in the empire and hired them as mercenaries.

Greece's Olympic Games had always been a religious festival to Zeus, with the ritual slaughter of one hundred oxen at the Temple of Zeus followed by a riotous barbeque. The Roman emperors supported the Olympics; Nero even added musical and acting contests to the repertoire and joined the contests. Of course, he won every competition he entered, even a chariot race where he fell out of his chariot and failed to finish. But to discourage traditional Greek polytheism, Theodosius banned animal sacrifices, which put a damper on the Olympic festivities. Nevertheless, the games continued for a few more years until the reign of Theodosius II (402–450 CE), who ordered the Temple of Zeus to be burned.

The Western Roman Empire fell apart within decades, unable to fend off the relentless onslaught of Germanic tribes and Central Asia's Huns. While Rome suffered a horrific famine in 410 CE, Alaric, king of the western Goths, sacked the city. In 455, the Vandals, another Germanic tribe, sacked Rome again. In 475, the eastern Goths forced the Western emperor to abdicate, and the Western Roman Empire collapsed.

Greece and the rest of the Eastern Roman Empire continued until the Ottoman Empire completed the conquest of the Byzantine Empire in 1453 CE. Modern historians refer to the Eastern Roman Empire as the Byzantine Empire after its capital Byzantium (renamed Constantinople). The Byzantine Empire reigned for over a millennium and was a cultural, economic, and military powerhouse. With borders that receded and advanced, it also ruled Egypt, Turkey, and the western Mediterranean coastal areas for some of the time it was in power.

The Byzantine Empire in 476 CE.
Photo modified: labels added. Credit: Darylprasad, CC BY-SA 4.0
<https://creativecommons.org/licenses/by-sa/4.0>, via Wikimedia Commons;
https://commons.wikimedia.org/wiki/File:Byzantium476.png

In 529 CE, Emperor Justinian I revised Roman law into the Justinian Code, which shaped the Byzantine legal system for nine centuries and even influenced modern Greece's laws. It made Christianity the state religion and a requirement for citizenship. Hellenistic culture was still strong in the Byzantine Empire, with Greek philosophy shaping Christian theology. However, the emperors suppressed polytheism. In 529, Justinian I cut state funding for the Neoplatonic Academy, a revival of Plato's original school, which the Roman dictator Sulla destroyed in 86 BCE. The academy's scholars carried their scrolls of philosophy, literature, and science to Ctesiphon in today's Iraq, continuing for another century through its Sassanian dynasty.

The Greeks and the people of the former Hellenistic empires spoke and wrote in Koine Greek during the Roman era. Latin was the official administrative language for the entire Roman Empire, but in the East, it was mainly used in the military and for some administrative functions. When the Western Roman Empire collapsed, the Byzantine Empire continued using the Greek language as the "lingua franca," or common language. Emperor Heraclius (r. 610–641 CE) made Greek the official language of the Byzantine Empire and the only language for governmental affairs.

By this point, Koine Greek had segued into Byzantine Greek or Medieval Greek, a stepping-stone from Koine Greek to Modern Greek. Koine Greek continues to be used today as the liturgical language of the Greek Orthodox Church.

Chapter 8: Byzantium under Greek Influence

The wind rippled through Heraclius's hair as he stood near his ship's bow, to which he had attached an image of the Virgin Mary. Observing Constantinople's skyline from the sea, he could see the Hagia Sofia's dome and the palace, now occupied by the incompetent tyrant Phocas. As his fleet approached, the people of Constantinople immediately overthrew their oppressive ruler, who had tortured and executed anyone he considered a threat. The patriarch of Constantinople crowned Heraclius the new emperor, hoping he could rescue the empire from its multiple crises.

As the people handed Phocas over, Heraclius asked, "Is this how you run our empire?"

"Can you do any better?" Phocas bitterly retorted before being hewn into pieces.

Turning the beleaguered Byzantine Empire around was a daunting challenge for Heraclius. Eight years earlier, in 602 CE, Phocas had assassinated Emperor Maurice, killed his wife and three little girls, and usurped the throne. Taking advantage of the chaos in Constantinople, the Persian Sassanid Empire invaded the Byzantine provinces of Armenia and Mesopotamia. By 608, Constantinople's horrified citizens watched the Persians burn villages across the Bosphorus Strait. Meanwhile, the Avar confederation swept into the Balkan Peninsula from today's

Ukraine, Russia, and Kazakhstan. Wreaking havoc in Thrace and northern Greece, they demanded tribute payments from the Byzantine Empire.

Emperor Heraclius's first decade in the war against Persia did not go well. The Persians took Antioch and Damascus, and in 614, they conquered Jerusalem, murdering over fifty thousand citizens, including thousands of nuns and priests. They burned down the city's churches and captured the True Cross, believed to be the one upon which Jesus died. In 618, they invaded Egypt and conquered Alexandria. Egypt was Constantinople's primary grain source, so the city now faced famine.

Heraclius finally launched a successful counteroffensive in 622, marching directly toward Iran and impelling the Persian forces to hurry back to defend their homeland. He overwhelmingly defeated the Persian troops before rushing home to fend off the Avars laying siege to Constantinople. The patriarch rallied the citizens by marching around the wall of Constantinople, carrying an icon of the Virgin Mary. Meanwhile, Heraclius arranged to meet the khan (king) of the Avars in Thrace to discuss a settlement. On his way, Heraclius narrowly escaped an Avar ambush. He threw off his purple robe, tucked his crown under his arm to avoid recognition, and scurried back to the city unharmed.

After successfully defending his capital, Heraclius led his army back to Asia in 627, scoring a crushing victory in the eleven-hour Battle of Nineveh. The disgruntled Persians overthrew their king and crowned his son, who immediately reached out with peace terms. The Byzantine Empire got their Asian and African territories back, and the Persians returned the True Cross.

The Byzantine Empire reigned as one of the world's longest multi-continent empires in a millennium of palace intrigues, wars on multiple fronts, and religious controversies. The people of the empire never called it the Byzantine Empire; in their minds, it was still the Roman Empire. However, the Western Roman Empire had collapsed, and Rome wasn't within the Eastern Roman Empire's borders, nor did Rome exercise power over the East. Thus, the Renaissance scholars renamed it the Byzantine Empire, although it was a predominantly Greek state culturally. The Byzantine Empire left a rich and lasting legacy of architecture, art, literature, and mystical Eastern Orthodox Christianity. Its imaginative abstract art with spiritual themes reflected the diverse cultures that graced the three-continent empire.

This 6th-century mosaic of Jesus Christ Pantocrator ("all-powerful") in Hagia Sofia reflects the distinctive religious art of the Byzantine Empire.

In 610 CE, the same year Heraclius ascended the Byzantine throne, a man in a cave in Arabia was experiencing visions. Muhammad gathered a following and eventually conquered Mecca. While Heraclius was successfully fighting the Persians, Muhammad conquered all of Arabia. After Muhammad died in 632, his impassioned Islamic followers led a holy war to spread their new religion, and the Byzantine Empire was in their crosshairs.

The Muslims began with raids on the Palestine border, which was nothing new. Yet, Heraclius took the threat seriously and remained in Asia. But his age and failing health prevented him from personally commanding his troops. The zealous Muslim troops took Palestine, Transjordan, Syria, and Egypt. Heraclius pulled back and fortified Anatolia (Turkey) against the Islamic tide while the Arabs turned east and crushed the Persian Sassanid Empire.

By Heraclius's death in 641, the Byzantine Empire had lost all of Asia except Anatolia but still held North Africa west of Egypt. Spain was lost, but the Byzantine Empire held the ancient Greek colonies in southern Italy and the islands throughout the Mediterranean. The empire ruled the coastal regions of Greece and the other Balkan territories, but the Avars and Slavs controlled a vast swathe of the central Balkan Peninsula.

Surprisingly, although massively outnumbered by the Arab caliphate forces, the Byzantine Empire kept it from taking more territory. Heraclius's grandson, Constans II, restructured the army, spreading them into units throughout the empire. Instead of receiving a salary, the soldiers received farmland parceled out from former imperial estates. During the next three centuries, the Byzantine Empire recovered its Balkan territories, doubled in population, and became fantastically rich and powerful. In awe, the Russians, Serbs, and Armenians converted to Eastern Orthodox Christianity.[30]

Despite calling itself "Roman" and ruling from a city at the intersection of Europe and Asia, the Byzantine Empire transformed into a culturally Hellenistic power through the spread of the Greek language and culture. Hellenistic art, architecture, literature, theater, and language surged forward in the Byzantine Renaissance, which lasted from the 9th to 11th centuries. Scholars studied Plato and other ancient Greek philosophers, incorporating

---

[30] Warren Treadgold, "The Persistence of Byzantium," *The Wilson Quarterly* 22, no. 4 (1998): 76-7. http://www.jstor.org/stable/40260386.

their ideas into Christian theology.

Anna Komnene, a medical doctor, hospital administrator, and daughter of the 12th-century Emperor Alexios I Komnenos, wrote the *Alexiad*, chronicling the First Crusade. Thoroughly educated in Greek classics, sciences, and rhetoric, she wrote her history in Athens's Attic Greek dialect with an epic poetry style reflecting Homer and Xenophon. The work conveyed the alarm in Constantinople generated by the western European Crusaders marching through the Byzantine Empire on their way to emancipate Jerusalem.[31]

By embracing Hellenistic culture, the Byzantine Empire played an integral role in preserving classical Greek philosophy, literature, and art. Greek culture shaped the Byzantine Empire, which, in turn, transmitted Greek culture to western Europe and the Islamic world.[32] Greek colonists in the archaic and classical eras strongly influenced the region over which the Roman Empire ruled. Later, Alexander the Great and his successors' Hellenistic empires left their stamp on eastern Europe, western Asia, and North Africa. As Rome's importance faded, the Hellenistic cities of Antioch, Alexandria, and Pergamum rose to ascendency as cultural centers.

Despite the inherent incompatibility of Greek polytheism with monotheistic Christianity, the Byzantine Empire fused Hellenistic culture with the Eastern Orthodox Church. They did so cautiously. For instance, the 4th-century Bishop Basil of Caesarea encouraged his students to explore Greek literature and philosophy but to reject anything contradictory to Christianity. Christian theologians found parallels between Plato's ethics and philosophy and the teachings of Christ.[33]

---

[31] Romilly J. H. Jenkins, "The Hellenistic Origins of Byzantine Literature," *Dumbarton Oaks Papers* 17 (1963): 37–52. https://doi.org/10.2307/1291189.

[32] Anthony Kaldellis, *Hellenism in Byzantium: The Transformations of Greek Identity and the Reception of the Classical Tradition*, (Cambridge: Cambridge University Press, 2007), 11.

[33] Rakesh Mittal, *Hellenism and the Shaping of the Byzantine Empire*, Marquette University, 2010.
https://epublications.marquette.edu/cgi/viewcontent.cgi?article=1001&context=jablonowski_award

Byzantine monks, like the 15th-century Bessarion who studied Neoplatonism in Greece, copied and preserved the texts of ancient Greek philosophers. Bessarion translated Aristotle's *Metaphysics* and Xenophon's *Memorabilia* and attempted to reconcile Plato and Aristotle with Christianity. Students in the Byzantine Empire studied Homer as the founder of literature and received tutoring in Greek rhetoric and philosophy, which were considered essential to a well-rounded education.

Byzantine literature represented a continuation of ancient Greek tradition, replicating the literary styles of Lucian, Homer, and Herodotus. The Byzantine monks who collected, translated, copied, and studied the Greek language and literature safeguarded these extraordinary works well into the Renaissance era. These preserved works impacted Renaissance thinkers and revolutionary politics centuries later.

In *Dialectica*, the 8th-century monk John of Damascus commented on Aristotle's *Prior Analytics*, which deals with deductive reasoning. John's work employed Greek logic to deal with controversies rocking the church regarding the nature of Christ. Aristotle taught that if certain principles are known to be factual, we can make deductions from that. John of Damascus used this deductive process to tackle theological arguments.

Classical Greek scholar and Arab-Christian monk John of Damascus.
https://commons.wikimedia.org/wiki/File:John-of-Damascus_01.jpg

The 9th-century Photius, Patriarch of Constantinople, wrote *Amphilochia*, which included a commentary on Aristotle's *Categories* and his concept of substance and theory of predication. The 11th-century monk and savant Michael Psellos reintroduced the study of Plato and wrote *De Omnifaria Doctrina*, which deals with Aristotle's *Categories* and *Prior Analytics*. Psellos was so engrossed in Greek philosophy that his friends began to doubt his Christian faith.

In the early Byzantine Empire, the only cities with a population of over 100,000 were Alexandria, Antioch, and Constantinople. Constantinople was the largest, with around 400,000 at its height. Despite the urban prosperity, about 90 percent of the Byzantine Empire's population were illiterate rural farmers scratching out a living, which was typical of medieval society. Even so, throughout most of its history, the Byzantine Empire outshone western Europe with its efficient government and diversified economy.[34]

How did the Byzantine Empire survive almost a thousand years after the Western Roman Empire fell? One reason was economics. The Western Roman Empire enriched itself through conquests, but once it stopped gaining additional territory, the flow of wealth slowed to a trickle. Although the Byzantine Empire gained some wealth from conquering the Persian Empire, the costs involved in the decades-long war blunted its impact. The Byzantine Empire's economy centered around sea trade. The Greeks had traded and colonized around the Mediterranean, Aegean, and Black Seas since the archaic era, and their vast sea trade continued with the Byzantine Empire.

Ancient Troy had once grown unimaginably wealthy by reigning over the straits linking the Aegean and Black Seas. Constantinople's strategic location likewise gave it control of ship traffic between the two seas. The other two major cities— Alexandria and Antioch—were situated for profitable sea trade in the Mediterranean. Alexandria lay on a branch of the Nile that emptied into the sea. Antioch, Syria, was on an island in the Orontes River close to the Mediterranean. After Antioch fell to the

---

[34]Treadgold, "The Persistence of Byzantium," 69-70.

Arabs in 637 CE and Alexandria in 641, Thessaloniki in northern Greece on the Aegean Sea rose in prominence, becoming the empire's second-largest city.

The city of Constantine lay on a triangular-shaped peninsula surrounded on three sides by water. The Sea of Marmara was to the south, the Golden Horn waterway to the north, the Bosphorus Strait to the east, and Greece and Thrace (Bulgaria) to the west. The Bosphorus connected the Black Sea to the Aegean Sea and was the boundary line between Europe and Asia. Constantinople's location positioned it for wealthy sea trade and lucrative intercontinental land trade.

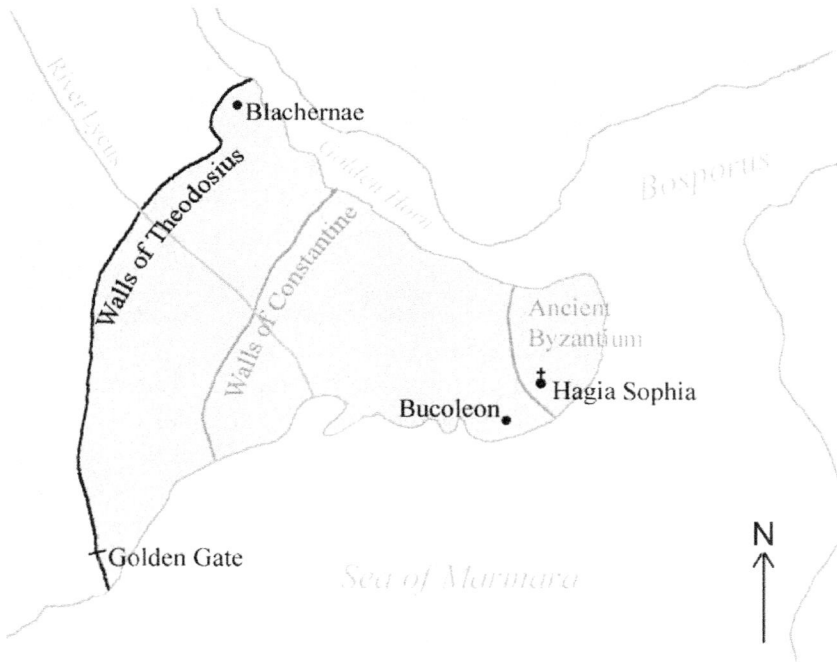

Constantinople (today's Istanbul) was the capital of the Byzantine Empire.
Jniemenmaa, CC BY-SA 3.0 <http://creativecommons.org/licenses/by-sa/3.0/>, via Wikimedia Commons; https://commons.wikimedia.org/wiki/File:Constantinople.png

When Constantine enlarged and transformed the ancient Greek city of Byzantium into Constantinople, he built a new wall. It stretched from the Sea of Marmara to the Golden Horn estuary, protecting the city from invasion by land. He brought priceless art pieces and sculptures from Rome. Constantine needed people to fill his lavish new city, so he enticed noblemen with land grants and free food for the working class.

The Byzantine emperor technically had almost unlimited power. Still, he needed the acknowledgment and favor of his citizens and the patriarch of Constantinople. If he became a tyrannical despot, he risked being overthrown, which happened to Andronicus I Komnenos in 1185 CE after a two-year rule. The church expected the emperors to comply with its moral standards. Although none came close, the patriarch of Constantinople wasn't as likely to excuse them as the Roman pope. Some Byzantine religious artwork showed emperors burning in hell.[35]

Like in Rome, the Byzantine emperors worked with a senate. Unlike Rome, the senators were not from the elite class but military men who had worked their way through the ranks. The Byzantine government followed the rule of law, but the emperor could change the laws. Despite being hierarchal, a fascinating aspect of Byzantine society was that it allowed for upward mobility. A prostitute could become an empress, like Justinian I's wife Theodora, and an uneducated peasant could become an emperor, like Basil I.

Basil's skills in winning wrestling matches and taming unruly horses caught the attention of Emperor Michael III. The emperor made Basil his bodyguard and confidant, then had him marry his mistress Eudokia, who was pregnant with Michael's son Leo. When Leo was born in 866 CE, Michael made Basil his junior co-emperor so that his son with Eudokia would be of "legitimate" royal birth. The whole affair backfired on Michael when Basil assassinated him the following year. As junior emperor, Basil automatically ascended the throne. Amazingly, he was a competent emperor. He reconquered the ancient Greek city-states of southern Italy, trounced the Arab caliphate, and rewrote the legal code of the Byzantine Empire.

The Greek Orthodox Church, as it was known after its 11th-century schism from Rome, profoundly influenced the Byzantine Empire's government and culture. It was called the "Greek" Orthodox Church then, not because it was only in Greece or for

---

[35] Treadgold, "The Persistence of Byzantium," 70-71.

Greek people but because Koine Greek was the liturgical language. Today, the name "Greek Orthodox Church" refers to the Orthodox churches in Greece or among Greek people worldwide and is part of the larger Eastern Orthodox Church (or Orthodox Catholic Church).

The Byzantine emperor appointed the patriarch (a major archbishop) of Constantinople and had the authority to remove him. Beginning in the 4th century, the patriarch of Constantinople held the second place of honor among archbishops after the pope in Rome. The Byzantine church was known for its monasticism, where men and women, often from the nobility, abandoned their luxurious lives to live as ascetics in monasteries and convents.

This mosaic of Empress Theodora, wife of Justinian I, is in the Basilica of San Vitale (built 547 CE) in Ravenna, Italy.
https://commons.wikimedia.org/wiki/File:Mosaic_of_empress_Theodora,_Ravenna,_San_Vitale,_547.jpg

The monastics devoted themselves to communal worship and scholarly pursuits in the monasteries' libraries of ancient texts. The monks and nuns also cared for orphans, the elderly, the needy, and the sick. Empress Theodora, the wife of Emperor Justinian I (r. 527–565), had been a prostitute before her marriage. After becoming empress, she bought and emancipated girls sold into prostitution, sending them to a convent she established so they could learn a trade to support themselves.

A fierce controversy that rocked the Orthodox Church, especially in the 8th century CE, was the question of icons: images of Jesus, the Virgin Mary, and the saints. These statues and paintings had been an integral part of worship in Rome and the Eastern Orthodox Church. But Emperor Leo III and others felt that icons were essentially idols and banned them in 730. Fifty-seven years later, Empress Irene became the de facto ruler as regent for her ten-year-old son. She organized the Seventh Ecumenical Council at Nicaea, which made icons legal again. The decision was overturned in 815, but Empress Theodora, the widow of Emperor Theophilus, restored the veneration of images in 843.

Hagia Sophia was completed in 537 CE. The Ottomans added the minarets.
Photo zoomed in. Credit: Dennis Jarvis from Halifax, Canada, CC BY-SA 2.0
<https://creativecommons.org/licenses/by-sa/2.0>, via Wikimedia Commons
https://commons.wikimedia.org/wiki/File:Turkey-3019_-_Hagia_Sophia_(2216460729).jpg

Isadore of Miletus, a brilliant Greek architect and scientist, and Anthemius, another Greek architect and master of Euclidean geometry, designed the Hagia Sofia Cathedral. Commissioned by Emperor Justinian I and completed in 537 CE, Hagia Sofia (the Church of Holy Wisdom) was the world's largest cathedral for almost a thousand years. An earthquake damaged the dome in 558, and Isadore's nephew rebuilt it, making it higher and more resilient to earthquakes. When the Ottomans conquered Constantinople in 1453, they converted it into a mosque. The 6th-century Hagia Sofia still graces Istanbul today.

Chapter 9: Last Years of Byzantium

"Theodora! I haven't much longer to live, and we need to get the succession sorted out." Constantine VIII rose on one elbow on his bed. "I haven't any sons, so you must marry Romanos Argyros. That's the only way he'll be accepted as the new emperor."

"I cannot marry Romanos!" Theodora paced back and forth in agitation.

"Why not? You'll be the new empress!"

"Father! He's married! At least he was until you forced him to divorce his wife and send her to a nunnery! I will not bring God's judgment down on myself by marrying him. Besides, Romanos is my cousin! We're too closely related to marry."

"Oh, Theodora!" Constantine sighed and fell back on his pillow. "Go back to your religious devotion, and send your sister to me. I'll see if Zoe will marry Romanos."

Theodora's sister Zoe did marry Romanos, and Constantine died the next day, making the couple the new emperor and empress in 1028. Theodora escaped the palace drama by sequestering herself in a monastery. After six years, unhappy in her marriage, Zoe and her young lover Michael drowned Romanos in his bath and married each other the same day. They bribed the patriarch of Constantinople to crown Michael as the new emperor and adopted Michael's nephew, Michael Kalaphates, since they had no child to inherit the throne.

When Emperor Michael died six years later, Michael Kalaphates became emperor and banished Zoe to a monastery. But the people of Constantinople revolted, sending Michael off into exile. They retrieved both Theodora and Zoe from their respective monasteries. And that was how the Byzantine Empire came to be ruled by two empresses, not as regents or wives but in their own right.

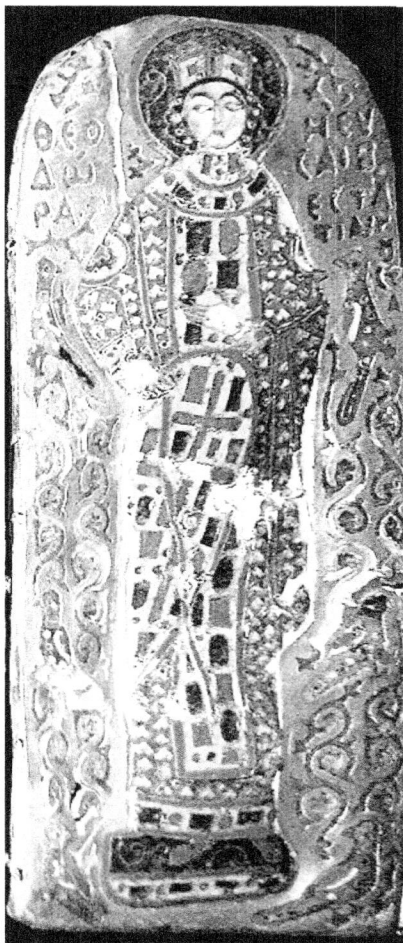

Theodora Porphyrogenita was co-empress with her sister Zoe and then ruled as sole emperor.
https://commons.wikimedia.org/wiki/File:Theodora_Porphyrogenita_in_the_Monomach us_Crown_(2).jpg

Although outraged at being forcibly removed from her beloved monastery, Theodora was a diligent empress. Zoe quickly married an old lover, Constantine Monomachos. All three ruled the empire; however, their neglect of the military left the empire vulnerable to the Turco-Persian Seljuk Empire. After Zoe died in 1050 and Constantine in 1055, the imperial guard proclaimed Theodora "emperor." Theodora reigned as the Byzantine Empire's sole emperor for twenty months until her death.

Church history took a dramatic turn during the co-reign of Theodora and her brother-in-law Constantine. Roman Pope Leo III excommunicated the patriarch of Constantinople, Michael Cerularius, in the Great Schism (1054 CE). The Eastern and Western Churches had disputed complicated religious issues for centuries, including how to observe Holy Communion and the precise wording of the Nicene Creed. The Eastern Church thought priests could marry, and the Roman Church believed they should be celibate.

Then, there was the question of who had ultimate power. Pope Nicholas I (in. off. 858–867 CE) claimed his dominion extended over all the earth. Now that Rome was a backwater and Constantinople was the largest and most powerful European city, Constantinople claimed its patriarch was equal to the pope. For one thing, Constantinople was a theocracy, with its emperor acting as the "Viceroy of God" and the "interpreter of the Word of God."[36]

The simmering tensions between Rome and Constantinople reached a boiling point in 1054 when Rome excommunicated Constantinople's Patriarch Michael Cerularius. Constantinople fired back by excommunicating the Roman pope and his representatives in July 1054, although Leo had died three months prior, and a new pope had not yet been selected. Despite attempts to heal the breach, the Christian Church existed as two self-governing factions from this point forward.

---

[36] Steven Runciman, *The Byzantine Theocracy: The Weil Lectures, Cincinnati* (Cambridge: Cambridge University Press, 2004). ISBN 978-0-521-54591-4.

Hard on the heels of this crisis followed the 1071 invasion of the Seljuk Turks. The Battle of Manzikert in Anatolia (Turkey) ended in catastrophe: the Turks decimated most of the Byzantine Empire's professional troops and captured Emperor Romanos IV Diogenes. Sultan Alp Arslan of the Seljuk Empire pushed the emperor's neck to the ground with his foot.

"What would you do if I were in your place?" the sultan asked.

"Maybe kill you. Or parade you through the streets of Constantinople."

The sultan smiled. "I'm giving you a heavier punishment. I'm forgiving you and setting you free."[87]

For the next week, Romanos dined with Alp Arslan while they hashed out terms of surrender. Romanos agreed to pay 1.5 million gold pieces in ransom and an annual tribute of 360,000 gold pieces. The emperor offered his daughter in marriage to the sultan's son, and the sultan provided safe passage back to Constantinople. Things weren't so rosy back home. The Doukas family had staged a coup; they captured Romanos when he returned and gouged out his eyes. Romanos died from the infected wounds shortly after.

Two decades later, the First Crusade set out from western Europe to retake Jerusalem and other holy sites from Islamic control. Although it still lagged behind the Byzantine Empire, western Europe was recovering from its Dark Ages, which saw an economic and cultural decline following the fall of the Western Roman Empire. The Byzantine Empire had lost many territories in Anatolia, Syria, and Palestine to the Seljuk Turks, so Emperor Alexios Komnenos reached out to Pope Urban II for help.

Forty years had passed since the Great Schism, and the strained relationship between the Greek Orthodox Church and the Roman Catholic Church continued. Yet both the Eastern and Western Churches were disturbed that the Seljuk Turks, who had converted to Sunni Islam a century earlier, now controlled the Holy Land. And not just the Holy Land; the Seljuk Empire stretched from the

---

[87] R. Scott Peoples, *Crusade of Kings* (Rockville, MD: Wildside Press LLC, 2013), 13. ISBN 978-0-8095-7221-2

Hindu Kush mountain range of Afghanistan to the Mediterranean and from the Black Sea in the north to the Persian Gulf. Emperor Alexios wanted the empire's lost lands back and to protect the European side of the empire from the Turks.

Pope Urban II thought that assisting the Byzantine Empire and retaking the Holy Land might reunite the two churches with him at the helm. In 1095, he rallied Christians in Europe to march east to defend the Byzantines from the Turks and retake Jerusalem. Ordinary citizens and professional armies, stirred with religious zeal, marched through the Byzantine Empire toward Constantinople in 1096, their launching point for Asia. While appreciative of their help in retaking the Byzantine Empire's former territory, Byzantine Emperor Alexios and his people were unnerved by the tens of thousands of armed western Europeans gathering in their capital city. Moreover, the soldiers had freely scavenged from farms as they passed through Byzantine lands.

A 13th-century depiction of Godfrey of Bouillon leading the First Crusade.
https://commons.wikimedia.org/wiki/File:Krizaci.jpg

Alexios required all Crusaders to swear loyalty to him, confirming that the Crusaders would return any former Byzantine territory they recouped to his empire. Alexios did not command the western forces, nor did many Byzantines join in, but the empire provided logistical support. The soldiers of the First Crusade (1095–1099) recaptured the ancient Greek cities of Nicaea, Edessa, and Antioch. Finally, in 1099, they retook Jerusalem, slaughtering thousands of Muslims in the process.

Almost fifty years later, the Second Crusade set out after the Seljuks recaptured Edessa, killing and enslaving its Christian citizens. King Louis VII of France and King Conrad III of Germany led their forces in 1147, but their efforts to retake Edessa and Damascus ended in abject failure. In 1187, Jerusalem fell to Saladin, a Sunni Muslim of Kurdish descent and sultan of Syria and Egypt, sparking Pope Leo III to call for the Third Crusade.

The Crusaders headed east, led by England's King Richard the Lionheart, King Philip II of France, and Holy Roman Emperor Frederick I Barbarossa. King Frederick led his forces out first in 1190 but drowned in a river in Turkey. The French and English arrived by sea in 1191 in time to help a French knight, Guy of Jerusalem, in a successful counterattack against Saladin at Acre in northern Israel. When terms of surrender fell apart, King Richard decapitated 2,700 Muslim prisoners, and Saladin killed all his Christian prisoners. Finally, Richard and Saladin agreed to a treaty that permitted safe passage for Christian pilgrims traveling to the Holy Land.

The Crusades enabled the Byzantine Empire to reclaim most of its holdings along the eastern Aegean coastline, wealthy city-states that had been established by the Greeks two millennia earlier. However, the Byzantine Empire continued to neglect its military, happy to let the western European Crusaders fight on their behalf. The western Europeans passing through Constantinople took note of the city's staggering wealth, weak military, and unstable monarchy.

And then, it happened. Instead of fighting the Turks, the Crusaders turned on the Byzantine Empire and attacked Constantinople. It all started with a series of coup d'états beginning in 1183. Andronikos I Komnenos, who had been seducing princesses throughout Europe and Asia, suddenly turned on his thirteen-year-old cousin, Emperor Alexios II, usurping his throne. Andronikos mercilessly killed the boy, his mother, and thousands of western Europeans living in Constantinople.

Andronikos's chaotic reign ended two years later when Constantinople's citizens revolted. The emperor tried to flee with his wife and mistress (yes, both) by boat, but he was captured, tortured for three days, killed, and left unburied. A distant relative, Isaac II Angelos, became emperor in 1185 and successfully fended off Norman King William II of Sicily, who had invaded the Balkans. When the Third Crusade launched, some of the Crusaders looted Byzantine settlements, an ominous foretaste of what was to come. Nevertheless, Isaac failed to shore up his land forces or naval fleet, which had shrunk to only thirty ships.

In 1195, Isaac's brother, Alexios Angelos, staged a coup. He blinded Isaac, threw him into a dungeon, and usurped the throne. Alexios III emptied the state treasury, passing out bribes to secure his position. He looted the former emperors' tombs and crushed his citizens with heavy taxes. The empire was in dire straits, with the Hungarians, Bulgarians, Romanian Vlachs, and Seljuk Turks launching raids from the north and east.

Isaac II was still in the dungeon, but his son, Alexios IV Angelos, approached the soldiers gathering in Venice for the Fourth Crusade. He struck a deal: if they could make him the empire's new king and get rid of his uncle, Alexios III, he would end the Great Schism with Rome and fund their Crusade. In 1203, the Crusaders besieged Constantinople, burning part of the city. Although Alexios III's men outnumbered the Crusaders, he was afraid to fight and escaped to Thrace.

Constantinople's citizens retrieved Isaac II from the dungeon. They clothed him in purple, but because he was blind, the Crusaders insisted Alexios IV should be the new emperor. Alexios needed to pay off the Crusaders but was horrified to discover that his uncle had emptied the state coffers. He melted down gold and silver icons from the churches but could only meet half the amount he had promised the Crusaders. Enraged at the desecration of their sacred statues, the citizens of Constantinople took to the streets in violent protests. The usurper Doukas Mourtzouphlos took advantage of the chaos and imprisoned and strangled Alexios IV. Isaac II died about the same time, and Mourtzouphlos was crowned Alexios V.

The Crusaders were furious at not receiving the total promised amount of money and at the murder of the king they had installed. Pope Innocent III commanded them *not* to attack Constantinople again, but the priests accompanying the Crusaders ignored his order. In April 1204, the Crusaders sailed across the Bosphorus and sacked Constantinople for three days, looting priceless artwork, raping nuns, and murdering Orthodox priests. They desecrated the Hagia Sofia Cathedral, destroying ancient sacred texts and drinking wine from the Holy Communion vessels.

Following Constantinople's fall, the western Europeans quickly conquered northern Greece, Thessaly, and Thrace. Most of the Greeks in the conquered territories fled to the three states still held by the Byzantines. The "Empire of Nicaea" stretched from the Aegean to the Black Sea. Alexios III's son-in-law, Theodore Lascaris, was crowned in 1205. Nicaea became the new patriarchal seat of the Orthodox Church. The second remaining Byzantine state was the Despotate of Epirus on the Adriatic coast, ruling over northwestern Greece and a section of Thessaly. On the southwestern shore of the Black Sea lay the third state, the Empire of Trebizond, which had been captured by former Emperor Andronicus's grandsons.

In Nicaea, Theodore I immediately faced an attack from Baldwin, the first emperor of what was now Latin Constantinople. Theodore suffered a bitter loss of territory along the Black Sea coastline. However, the Greeks who remained in Thrace struck an alliance with Tsar Kalojan of Bulgaria. In 1205, he attacked Emperor Baldwin's army, capturing the emperor, who died in prison. By 1241, Latin-held territories in the previous Byzantine Empire had shrunk to little more than the city of Constantinople. Emperor John Vatatzes of Nicaea was setting the stage to retake Constantinople. With the Bulgarians distracted by the Mongols sweeping in from Asia, he brought Thessalonica and Epirus under his control.

After Vatatzes's death, his son, Theodore II Lascaris, incompetently continued his quest until he died four years later from epilepsy. A palace coup brought the crown to Michael VIII Palaiologos, who descended from all three of Constantinople's imperial families. He ruled as co-emperor with Theodore's seven-year-old son John IV. In 1261, his general, Alexius Strategopoulos, was heading to Thrace when he learned that the Latin military was away from Constantinople attacking Daphnusia Island (Kefken Island) in the Black Sea. He also learned of a narrow, unguarded gate in Constantinople's walls and sent a small detachment of men through.

They overcame the unsuspecting guards and opened the main gate to Strategopoulos's army, who poured into the unguarded city. Emperor Baldwin and most of the Latins escaped to Euboea. Michael was crowned emperor of Constantinople, but he blinded his co-emperor of Nicaea, John IV, on his eleventh birthday. The patriarch of Constantinople excommunicated Michael for his crime, but blindness eliminated John's ability to rule either Nicaea or Constantinople.

For the next two centuries, Michael's descendants—the Palaiologan dynasty—ruled the restored Byzantine Empire. Initially, they recouped much of the empire's former glory and power, but they repeated some fatal flaws: neglecting their military and engaging in a brutal civil war. This left the empire vulnerable to the Ottoman Turks, who took most of Anatolia by 1305.

In 1348, the Black Death reached the Byzantine Empire: a pandemic of bubonic plague that caused huge lymphatic boils to break out all over the body and ooze bloody pus. People would vomit blood, and their fingers, toes, noses, and lips would turn black with gangrene. The Black Death was the deadliest pandemic in world history and killed up to 90 percent of those infected, sometimes within one day of symptom onset. At least one-third of Europe's population died from the Black Death, even more in the coastal regions. Located between two seas, Constantinople suffered dreadfully, as did the Greek islands and coastal cities.

Finally, the plague burned out, and Constantinople limped along for another century before the Ottoman conquest. In the empire's latter years, ancient Greek philosophy began to reemerge, specifically, Neoplatonic thought. The Byzantine Empire was the world's only postclassical culture that continued to speak and write

Greek, which gave them immediate access to Hellenistic literature. The Byzantine Empire was "a fascinating laboratory for cultural and intellectual fusion, reception, combination, and reinvention."[38]

The Byzantines applied Plato's philosophy to the new political world that was no longer pagan but Christian. They realized that Aristotle, Plato, and other Greek philosophers had rejected the concept of multiple gods who sinned as flagrantly as humans. Texts by Byzantine's Komnenian dynasty used Aristotelian terms to interpret historical conflicts. Byzantine intellectual history contextualized classical Greek thought to fit their milieu, and it continued to shape their worldview. They didn't just use Neoplatonic theory and other Greek philosophies to push their agenda; they were committed to its truth. Hellenism and Christianity weren't necessarily worldviews in tension but parallel discourses.[39]

Constantinople had withstood multiple sieges through the centuries thanks to being surrounded by water on three sides. Three defensive walls and a moat guarded the western side facing land. Yet, the Islamic Ottoman Empire of western Turkey was encroaching on Europe, having already taken Thrace, Serbia, and Thessaloniki. The Byzantines foiled two Ottoman attacks on Constantinople in 1394 and 1422. But in 1453, Sultan Mehmed II blockaded the city, preventing whatever help the western Europeans could lend.

---

[38] Anthony Kaldellis, *Hellenism in Byzantium: The Transformations of Greek Identity and the Reception of the Classical Tradition* (Cambridge: Cambridge University Press, 2007). https://www.cambridge.org/core/books/cambridge-intellectual-history-of-byzantium/introduction/6301571643465C8A8D0D73A01EA92AD1

[39] Kaldellis, *Hellenism in Byzantium*.

A restored section of Constantinople's walls.

Constantinople only had five thousand fighting men and twenty-six ships under the command of Emperor Constantine XI to fend off the massive Ottoman army. They had catapults, but the Turks had even newer technology: the Turkish Bombard, a twenty-seven-foot-long cannon that could launch six-hundred-pound stones. For six weeks, the Ottoman Turks pulverized Constantinople's walls, and on May 29th, 1453, the Ottomans flooded the city, killing Emperor Constantine. They pillaged the city, slaying thousands. They enslaved fifty thousand inhabitants. The Muslims converted the Hagia Sofia Cathedral into a mosque and renamed Constantinople Istanbul, which became the capital of the Ottoman Empire.

But the ancient Greek culture persisted. Some Greek scholars had prudently left when the Ottomans were attacking surrounding regions. Others were able to escape during or immediately after Constantinople's fall. They made their way to Italy with priceless Greek manuscripts from classical philosophers like Plato and Aristotle, which were then translated into Latin. These scholars' knowledge of astronomy, architecture, poetry, music, and political theory helped create the early Renaissance: the rebirth of culture, art, and philosophy in western Europe.

SECTION FOUR:
New and Modern Greek History (1453 CE–20th Century)

Chapter 10: Ottoman Rule and the War of Independence

"Domenikos! What will we do about the *paidomazoma*? They'll be coming soon!"

"Don't worry so much, Philippa. They might not choose our children."

"They take one in five, Domenikos! The strongest and most handsome boys. They'll take Nicholas! I know they will!"

Domenikos tried to soothe his wife. "It might not be so bad. They'll train him to fight in the elite corps or serve as a civil servant. He would have a chance at a better life."

"Domenikos! They'll force him to become Muslim. What if they castrate him and make him a eunuch? And Agatha! She's growing into a beauty. They'll take her for the harems, and she'll never see the light of day again!"

Domenikos cleared his throat. "If we convert to Islam, they won't take our children. We needn't really convert; we'll become crypto-Christians. In our hearts, we'll follow Christ."

But tears rolled down Philippa's cheeks. "We're forced to choose between our children and our God? I fear for all our souls!"

Greece crumbled, bit by bit, to the Turkish Ottoman Empire within fifty years after Constantinople fell in 1453. For over three centuries, the Greeks suffered brutal atrocities and humiliations under the Ottoman occupation. The Ottomans forced Christian communities to hand over one-fifth of their children as "tribute." They forbade them to carry weapons or travel by horse. If a Christian family converted to Islam and was found secretly practicing Christianity, they were executed. Greece's economy suffered, literacy declined, and its population dwindled.

Sultan Mehmed II and Patriarch Gennadios II.
https://commons.wikimedia.org/wiki/File:Gennadios_II_and_Mehmed_II.jpg

However, the Muslims allowed the Orthodox Church to continue; they even appointed the patriarchs. Sultan Mehmed II, the twenty-one-year-old who had conquered Constantinople, handed the patriarchal staff to Gennadios Scholarios, his choice for the new ecumenical patriarch. Mehmed declared the patriarch the supreme representative of all Greek Orthodox Christians in the Ottoman Empire. The patriarch was responsible for the Christians' law-abiding behavior and was their highest judicial authority, especially regarding family and inheritance law.[40]

Part of Mehmed's rationale for restoring power to the patriarch was maintaining the schism between the Greek Orthodox Church and the Roman Catholic Church. He didn't want the pope in Rome telling Christians in his empire what to do. And yet, the patriarchate played a pivotal role in shaping modern Hellenism into a cohesive, unified body and carrying on the Greek intellectual tradition. Orthodox priests were now essentially the leaders of Greek communities, controlling the schools and courts.

The Ottoman Empire's ongoing conflict with the Republic of Venice for control of the Aegean, Ionian, and Adriatic Seas began before Constantinople fell. The Turks scored a decisive victory in the 1499 Battle of Zonchio, the first time they used cannons on their ships. In the Ottoman-Venetian War (1537–1540), Sultan Suleyman I allied with France against Holy Roman Emperor Charles V. They planned a simultaneous attack on Italy: France from the north and the Ottomans from the south. But the French got distracted with the Netherlands and didn't make it to Italy. So, the Ottoman forces left Italy, sailed to the Adriatic Sea, and trounced the Holy League alliance of European states in the 1538 Battle of Preveza. The wars with Venice raged for almost two more centuries; the Ottoman Empire won all but one, chipping away at Venetian territory.

Through the years of Ottoman occupation, Greek uprisings and revolts sprang up, often taking advantage of the times the Turks were distracted by their wars with Venice. The Kladas brothers, Epifani and Krokodeilos, fought to take Greece's Peloponnese Peninsula back from the Ottoman Empire in the late 1400s. They allied with the Venetians and won some territory, over which Epifani governed. Krokodeilos continued to lead guerilla attacks on the Turks in the Peloponnese for another eleven years until he was captured and flayed alive.

---

[40] Constantinos Svolopoulos, "The Ecumenical Patriarchate in the Ottoman Empire (1453-1923): Adaptation and Change," *Journal of Modern Hellenism.* 17-18 (2000-2001): 107-110.

Makarios Melissourgos, a bishop in the Peloponnese, conspired with the Spaniards to instigate an insurgency. Spain had joined a coalition promoted by the pope against the Ottoman Empire, which threatened sea trade in the Mediterranean. The 1571 Battle of Lepanto, fought in the Gulf of Patras in western Greece, was an overwhelming (and rare) victory for the coalition forces against the Ottoman Empire. Melissourgos and his family continued to lead rebel raids on the Ottomans in the Peloponnese, but once the western Europeans left the area, they fled to Italy.

The Society of Friends (*Filiki Eteria*) sprang up in Odesa, Ukraine, in 1814 as a secret organization to rid Greece of Ottoman rule and set up an autonomous Greek government. Odesa was an ancient Greek city colonized in the archaic era. Many members were "Phanariotes" from wealthy Greek merchant families in Constantinople and Russia. Other members were political leaders from Greece or Orthodox priests from the extended Greek world. A key leader was Alexander Ypsilantis, born to a noble Greek family in Constantinople that fled to Russia when it was fighting the Turks. Ypsilantis lost his right arm fighting for Russia against Napoleon Bonaparte but devoted himself to recruiting and training fighters and raising funds. He sent fiery letters to Hellenistic centers, drumming up support for Greek independence.

When the Ottoman Turks conquered Greece, the last holdouts fled to the rugged mountains rather than submit to Islamic rule. The Ottomans were never able to root them out, so these *klephts* (independence fighters) were like the Greek version of Robin Hood and his merry men, stealing from Ottoman tax collectors. They survived as bandits, plundering the Turkish settlements for livestock and goods.

Their ranks grew, with those fleeing oppressive poverty or criminal charges joining them, but they had a violent, dark side. They were prone to vendettas. They robbed Greeks as well as Turks and extorted money from Greek communities in return for protection. Sometimes, the Ottomans even hired them as an area's "peacekeepers" or *armatoles*. Eventually, the klephtic bands became the local rulers of Greece's mountainous regions.

Since the Ottoman Empire forbade Greek Christians from bearing arms, the klephts were among the few Greeks who had weapons. More importantly, they had centuries of fighting experience and knew how to use Greece's rugged mountainous terrain to their advantage against the Turks. As nationalistic fervor grew, they launched guerilla raids on the Ottomans, boosting morale among the Greeks. One of their most powerful chieftains was Dimitrios Makris, who had been initiated into the Filiki Eteria and was a leading fighter in the Greek Revolution.

Dimitrios Makris, klepht and Greek freedom fighter.
https://commons.wikimedia.org/wiki/File:Makris_Dimitrios_Greek_Fighter.JPG

But to give the Greek Revolution justice, we should start at the beginning. Through the centuries of Ottoman occupation, the Greeks were mainly in survival mode, giving scant attention to their cultural heritage. However, Greek literature, philosophy, and art sparked the Renaissance in western Europe. This generated the Age of Reason, with new political discourse leading to sweeping changes in Europe and the British colonies in America. In the 18th century, the universal admiration of the ancient Greek culture led to the Enlightenment among the Greek intelligentsia, encouraging nationalistic fervor. Even non-Greek Europeans began questioning the miserable existence to which the Greeks had been reduced in their homeland.

Inspired by their classical past, the Greek Enlightenment leaders initially disdained their "priest-ridden" Byzantine history. But then, Konstantinos Paparrigopoulos, a history professor at the University of Athens, promoted a continuum of Greek history with links from the archaic era to modern history. Thus, Enlightenment thinkers began to focus on the glories of the Byzantine era and how it preserved and developed classical thought and art.[41]

Turkish occupation and ultra-conservative Greek Orthodox clerics had isolated Greece from western Europe and America's political, scientific, and industrial revolutions. Yet, as early as 800 BCE, the Greeks had colonized the Mediterranean, Aegean, Ionian, and Black Seas. They had always been seafaring traders. In the late 1700s CE, Greek merchants redeveloped a trade empire stretching from the Mediterranean to India, eventually expanding into the world's largest commercial sea empire.[42] Emigrants escaping Greece's political and economic systems began following these trade routes and went farther afield, reaching America by 1800. The Greek Enlightenment movement spread due to this Greek diaspora.

As the Ottoman Empire slid into economic and military decline, the Greek trading class grew increasingly prosperous. Their interactions with the outside world exposed them to new, revolutionary ideas. With the support of the diaspora and wealthy merchants, Greece now had the economic power to fund a war. Russian Empress Catherine the Great (r. 1762–1796) encouraged Greece's nationalistic flames. She hoped to annex the eastern section of the Ottoman Empire, including Constantinople, with a simultaneous attack on the Ottomans from the Russians and Greeks. But when Russia did go to war against the Ottomans in 1768, the Greeks weren't yet ready to launch their own revolution.

---

[41] Richard Clogg, *A Concise History of Greece* (Cambridge: Cambridge University Press, 2021), 1-3.

[42] Clogg, *Concise History of Greece*, 4-6.

Yet, Russia's war and the French Revolution of 1789 stoked the fires of Greek revolutionary zeal.

Rigas Feraios was an author and publisher who rallied support from both klephts and Greek Orthodox bishops for the cause of an independent Greece. He wrote and published the patriotic hymn "Thourios," which became an anthem of the revolution, part of which read:

> "Shall we dwell in caves, just looking out at the branches,
>
> Leaving from the world into bitter slavery?
>
> Better live one hour in freedom
>
> Than forty years in slavery and prison."

The Greek diaspora that clustered in Odesa (in today's Ukraine) lived in Greek neighborhoods with their own churches, schools, and theaters. Their merchants traded among Greek settlements in the Black Sea and the Mediterranean while recruiting soldiers and supporters for the cause. They used a code. When they greeted someone as "friend," it wasn't just a warm greeting but an indication of belonging to the Filiki Eteria (Society of Friends). The "Great Fair" referred to the revolution, and "market readiness" meant how many soldiers were ready to fight in a given area.[43]

In 1818, the Filiki Eteria moved to Constantinople under the leadership of Panagiotis Sekeris, a wealthy merchant. He helped fund the organization and introduced the small society to the Greek elite in the Ottoman capital. The Eteria recruited "apostles": Greek veterans who had fought on the Russian side against Napoleon. They sent the apostles throughout the Greek lands to recruit and train a military force.

The aristocratic Alexander Ypsilantis took the helm of the Filiki Eteria in 1820, bringing his brothers and friends from the wealthy upper class into the fold. The leaders met in October 1820 to hash out the "Great Plan": how and where to start the war of independence. They first considered beginning the war in the

---

[43]Mark Mazower, *The Greek Revolution: 1821 and the Making of Modern Europe* (New York: Penguin Press, 2021), 10-11.

Peloponnese on November 15th. Ypsilantis reconsidered and decided to launch the war from across Russia's border in Moldovia and Wallachia in the spring. Although within the Ottoman borders, these lands were semi-autonomous, mostly Christian, and led by Christian governors with no Turkish garrisons. Moldavia's Prince Michael Soutzos was a secret member of the Filiki Eteria.

On February 21st, 1821, Ypsilantis launched the revolution in Galati with the rallying cry, "Fight for faith and the fatherland!" Ypsilantis crossed a tributary of the Danube with 4,500 Greek and eastern European soldiers. They marched to Bucharest in Romania, where Ypsilantis discovered he had overestimated Russian and Romanian support, despite sharing the Orthodox faith. The Ottoman army soon crossed the Danube with thirty thousand troops and fought several battles against Ypsilantis's outnumbered Greek forces.

In Istanbul (formerly Constantinople), the Ottomans responded to the uprisings by forcing Patriarch Gregory V to excommunicate the revolutionaries on Easter Sunday. One week later, Turkish soldiers burst into St. George's Cathedral during Divine Liturgy, dragged the patriarch out, and hanged him at the gate, leaving his body suspended for three days. That same day, the Ottomans began the mass execution of bishops, priests, Greek officials, and Greek merchants in Constantinople and Greece, demolishing churches throughout the empire.

The June 19th Battle of Drăgăşani ended the conflict in Moldovia when the drunken Greek commander Karavias ordered an attack before most Greek forces had arrived on the field. Only 500 cavalry units charged out and quickly retreated just as the Sacred Band of about 350 student volunteers marched out. Only about one-third survived, but their sacrifice spurred the resistance movement in the Peloponnese and central Greece, where the revolt erupted on March 25th.

After the debacle at Drăgăşani, Ypsilantis fled to Austria, where Emperor Francis II placed him under house arrest for seven years. But southern Greece's Peloponnese had already scored a major victory in the May 12th, 1821, Battle of Valtetsi. A Turkish force of five thousand attacked the village of Valtetsi, where several companies of Greek revolutionaries had assembled. The Greeks fought from four tower houses, with 80 to 350 men in each tower.

While the Turks besieged the towers, a Greek force of seven hundred arrived and attacked their flank, holding an advantage over the Ottomans on a steep slope. Another Greek battalion entered near the end of the twenty-four-hour battle, completely turning the tide, and the Greeks routed the Turkish forces. By the end of the year, the Greeks were in firm control of central Greece and the Peloponnese in the south. They declared independence in January 1822.

The Battle of Valtetsi in the Peloponnese was the first decisive Greek victory.

Europe's conservative heads of state were disturbed by Greece's rebellion, as they preferred to maintain the status quo. However, many Europeans applauded the Greeks' audacity. Pastors and professors reminded everyone of their rich heritage of Greek philosophy, literature, and art. Men from all over Europe, especially France and Italy, sailed to Greece to fight with the revolutionaries. Greek organizations in the United States sent supplies and funding. Appalled by Patriarch Gregory V's execution, Russia severed diplomatic relations with the Ottoman Empire.

The island of Crete had always resisted Ottoman rule, and once Greece declared independence, Crete also revolted. Muhammad Ali Pasha was the Albanian governor of Egypt (part of the Ottoman Empire), and Sultan Mahmud II offered him Crete if he could bring the Cretans in line and help fight the Greeks. Muhammad Ali sent his son-in-law and thirty warships to subdue Crete. Meanwhile, Cyprus (under Ottoman control) sent shiploads of supplies and one thousand Cypriots to Greece to fight. In July 1821, the Ottomans retaliated by executing Archbishop Kyprianos of Cyprus, three other Cypriot bishops, and all the abbots and monks in Cyprus.

Albanian-speaking islanders from the Aegean Sea manned the Greek revolutionaries' naval fleet, but they usually had merchant ships rather than warships. Since the Ottoman Empire overshadowed them with bigger and better-armed warships, the Greeks resorted to an ancient tactic: fireships. They filled small ships with highly flammable materials. A skeleton crew then steered the vessel toward the Ottoman fleet. At the last moment, they set the ship on fire and escaped on a small boat that was pulled behind them. When the wind or tide was just right, the burning ship would drift into the enemy ships, setting them afire and sometimes exploding. A fireship successfully blew up the Ottoman Empire's flagship, killing Commander Kara Ali and over two thousand people. Sadly, some who died were Greeks captured at Chios being transported to the Turkish slave market.

An internal conflict threatened to derail the Greek Revolution, with a civil war erupting between the guerilla fighters from the mountains and General Theodoros Kolokotronis, the Greek commander-in-chief in the Peloponnese. After two civil wars, Kolokotronis was eventually confirmed as the revolution's commander. Still, the infighting left them vulnerable to the Egyptians, who attacked on behalf of the Ottomans. The Egyptians wreaked havoc in the Peloponnese and captured ancient Athens in 1827.

In April 1827, the Greeks elected Ioannis Kapodistrias as their *kyvernetes* or governor. Meanwhile, the Turkish atrocities, Egypt's interference, and hopes of promoting their own interests in the region finally swayed the British, French, and Russian powers to intervene. After the Turks rejected mediation, the allied forces sailed a naval fleet to Navarino Bay in the Peloponnese on October 20th, 1827. A Turkish and Egyptian naval fleet of seventy-eight ships was moored there, and the Ottomans fired first, which was a suicidal act since the allies had longer-range cannons. They sank all but eight of the Turkish and Egyptian ships. Bonfires and the ringing of church bells spread through Greece as news of the overwhelming victory circulated.

Kapodistrias, Greece's first governor, arrived in January 1828 after touring Europe to drum up support. Four months later, Russia declared war on the Ottoman Empire, forcing it to fight on two fronts. Egypt pulled out of Greece in 1828, and the Greeks swiftly expelled the remaining Ottoman garrisons in the Peloponnese. In December 1828, the British, French, and Russian ambassadors hashed out a protocol for an autonomous Greek state ruled by a king but under the authority of the Ottoman sultan. But the Greeks were unhappy with the proposed borders, and Sultan Mahmud declared he would never grant Greece its independence.

The final clash was the September 1829 Battle of Petra in central Greece. A unified Greek army (rather than guerilla bands) led by Demetrios Ypsilantis (Alexander's younger brother) scored a glorious victory, losing only three men but killing one hundred Turks and eliminating the Turkish military presence in Greece. The Ottomans finally agreed to an autonomous Greek state, but by this time, the British and French insisted on a completely independent Greek state with a king.

In May 1832, Britain, France, and Russia offered the Greek throne to the seventeen-year-old Bavarian prince Otto von Wittelsbach, who descended from two Byzantine royal lines. For the first time in its history, Greece was a united, independent country, with a king ruling the entire land.

Chapter 11: Greece in the 19ᵗʰ Century

As he stood at the HMS *Madagascar*'s forecastle, a bead of sweat dripped from Otto's temple, despite the sea breeze. He gazed at the villages dotting the shoreline at the base of rugged mountains as the frigate sailed up the Argolic Gulf toward Nafplio. Forty-two ships accompanying him transported the Bavarian Auxiliary Corps: a three-thousand-man force sent to replace the French allied troops struggling to maintain the peace in Greece.

When Otto was born, his grandfather, Maximilian I, was king of Bavaria. When he was ten, his father, Ludwig I, ascended the throne, and his older brother became crown prince. And now, the Great Powers (Russia, Britain, and France) had offered Otto the newly created throne of Greece. He wasn't their first choice; they had chosen Prince Leopold of Saxe-Coburg and Gotha, but he turned them down because of Greece's instability and poverty. Leopold's reluctance was well-founded; Governor Kapodistrias's assassination in 1831 plunged the country into near-anarchy.

The Great Powers' second choice was Otto, who had distant ancestors from the Byzantine-Greek Komnenos dynasty. No one bothered to check with Greece. Otto wasn't old enough to be king, so a regency council of Bavarian advisors was to rule for the next few years until he turned twenty. He'd never been to Greece, didn't speak the language, and was Roman Catholic, not Greek

Orthodox. He'd heard Greece didn't have beer, so he brought his Bavarian brewmaster.

As the HMS *Madagascar* approached Nafplio, Otto wondered if the Greeks would accept him. Could he do this? Could he lead Greece out of chaos and into greatness? He saw thousands of people crowding the docks, and then a great cheer arose. Otto breathed a sigh of relief. As he disembarked, an excited murmur passed through the crowd at the sight of their handsome, young king. They nodded in approval when he changed his name to the Hellenistic "Othon" and wore Greek clothing, including the fustanella skirt.

Greece's first king: Otto Friedrich Ludwig.
https://commons.wikimedia.org/wiki/File:Otto_of_Greece_litograph.jpg

Otto moved Greece's capital from Nafplio to Athens, but by this point, the ancient city had disintegrated into a village of several hundred houses. He immediately set to work restoring Athens, building universities, gardens, a national library, a palace, and a parliament building. Although Otto constructed hospitals and schools throughout Greece, the people's adoration quickly wore off. His regency council disregarded Greek culture, as it was intent on imposing Bavarian ways and an authoritarian government with no Greeks in key positions. They attempted to suppress the Greek monasteries. And then there were the taxes, which were higher than what the Ottoman Empire had levied.

When Otto turned twenty in 1835, his regency council disbanded, but Bavarians continued to serve in the highest administrative positions. King Otto replaced them with Greek ministers in 1837. When he was twenty-one, Otto traveled back to Bavaria and married the beautiful seventeen-year-old Amalia of Oldenburg. She was Lutheran, but any child born to the couple would be baptized in the Greek Orthodox Church.

Amalie of Oldenburg, Queen of Greece. Painting by Karl Joseph Stieler.
https://commons.wikimedia.org/wiki/File:Joseph_Karl_Stieler_-
Duchess_Marie_Frederike_Amalie_of_Oldenburg,_Queen_of_Greece.jpg

At first, the petite, vibrant, and youthful queen charmed the Greeks with her enthusiastic patriotism regarding her adopted country. She labored tirelessly to improve social conditions. But she and Otto never had any children. Who would rule Greece if their king had no sons? The Greek women whispered, "It must be all that dancing and riding horses that are making her infertile."

Otto faced massive challenges as king. Ottoman rule had impoverished Greece, and the years of revolution plunged it into desperate straits. Its rocky, mountainous terrain with inconsistent rainfall had never provided enough farmland to feed a large population. In the distant past, Greece traded for grain with its former colonies around the Mediterranean and Black Seas. But now, it had little funding or goods to exchange.

Most of the arable land was in the hands of powerful clans like the Mavromichalis family, which had assassinated Greece's governor, Kapodistrias. The Great Powers loaned money for Greece to survive, but in exchange, their three legates in Athens interfered in political affairs. Rather than gradually fading out of the picture, the Great Powers inserted themselves more and more into Greek politics.

The Greeks demanded a constitution and legislature to balance Otto's absolute monarchy. Issues reached a boiling point in 1843, and the heroes from the Greek War of Independence revolted. They insisted on a constitution, the right for all males to vote, and the elimination of Bavarians in the government. After a bloodless coup, Otto granted the Greeks their constitution in 1844, and most Bavarians left. Universal voting rights would have to wait until the next king, though.

The Greeks' next dilemma regarded the Greeks outside their borders. These Greeks lived in lands like Macedonia, Thrace, Epirus, the Aegean Islands, Cyprus, and Crete, which had all been part of the Greek world since ancient times. However, in the mid-1800s, they were still under Ottoman domination. The Greeks' "Great Idea" was to bring all these territories into the Greek state, reviving the Byzantine Empire with Constantinople as its capital.[44]

The Crimean War (1853-1856) erupted when Russia made a power grab for Ottoman territories in the Middle East and the

---

[44] Roumen Daskalov and Tchavdar Marinov, *Entangled Histories of the Balkans - Volume One: National Ideologies and Language Policies.* (Leiden, Brill, 2013), 200.

eastern Mediterranean. Britain, France, Sardinia, and Turkey jumped in against Russia, and the Greeks thought it was an opportune time to retrieve Thessaly and Epirus. But Britain and France stymied their attempts. Russia lost the war, and Greece failed to regain any territory.

The Greeks were dissatisfied with King Otto's authoritarian rule, his dismissal of Prime Minister Konstantinos Kanaris, and his lack of support in invading Thrace and Epirus. When he and the queen visited the Peloponnese in 1862, a rebellion arose, and the Greeks deposed King Otto after a thirty-year reign. In Otto's mind, as he and Amalia boarded a British warship for their voyage to Germany, his exile was not permanent.

Yet, the Greeks were ready for a fresh start and liked Prince Alfred of Britain. However, Queen Victoria had other plans for her second son. Following the Great Powers' recommendation, the Greeks elected a seventeen-year-old prince of Denmark to become their new king: George I. He was the son of Denmark's heir presumptive, Christian IX, who would become the Danish king a few months later. George I was a distant descendant of Emperor Isaac II Angelos of the Byzantine Empire through his mother.

Although George spoke Danish, English, French, and German, he didn't know Greek but quickly mastered the language. His siblings' marriages into European royal families brought him a stellar network of alliances that served Greece well. His sister, Alexandra, married the future King Edward VII of Britain, and his older brother, Frederick, became Denmark's king. Another sister, Dagmar, married the Russian tsar's son, Alexander III, and became Empress Marie in 1881.

In 1863, shortly after George was crowned king of Greece in Copenhagen, Dagmar introduced him to the twelve-year-old Grand Duchess Olga Constantinovna of Russia, whom he married four years later. George was Lutheran, but Olga was an Orthodox Christian, which pleased their Greek subjects. They had eight children together, and their descendants ruled Greece until 1967. Their grandson, Prince Philip, married Princess Elizabeth, later Queen Elizabeth II of England.

George I and Olga with Olga's sister, Grand Duchess Vera Constantinovna of Russia.
https://commons.wikimedia.org/wiki/File:Vera_with_her_sister_Olga_and_brother-in-law_George.jpg

Since he was still a minor, King George traveled to Greece with two Danish advisors: his uncle, Prince Julius, and Count Wilhelm Sponneck. In his first year, he asked the Greek Assembly to write a new constitution, which provided voting rights for all male citizens (the women would have to wait another ninety years). He sent his uncle Julius back to Denmark in his second year when he caught him attempting to remove Sponneck. Sponneck continued to serve as George's advisor for another twelve years, although the Greeks disliked him because of his boorish, ethnocentric attitude. He even questioned whether the modern-day Greeks were descendants of the ancient classical Greeks.

The seven Ionian islands just off Greece's western shore in the Ionian Sea had been settled by the Greeks at least as early as the 9th century BCE. The Republic of Venice gained control of the islands in the 13th century CE, followed by Venice in 1797, then France, and lastly, Britain. But Greek nationalist groups on the islands began pushing for *enosis* (incorporation into Greece). Finally, in 1864, the Great Powers transferred sovereignty of the islands to Greece, honoring King George I's request when he ascended Greece's throne.

The island of Crete was settled by the Minoans around 3500 BCE and was the earliest Bronze Age culture in the Greek world. Cretan revolutionaries could accurately say that Crete was and always had been an intrinsic part of the Greek world. The Cretans had opposed the Ottoman occupation, and now that King George I was titled "King of the Hellenes" (not just Greece), they declared Crete was part of the Kingdom of the Hellenes.

From 1866 to 1869, the Great Cretan Revolution raged against the Turks. The November 1866 Holocaust of Arkadi was an Ottoman attack on the Arkadi Monastery, the rebel headquarters. Hundreds of women and children had fled to the monastery for safety when the Ottomans began raiding their villages. But as the Greek rebels ran out of ammunition, the Turks' gigantic cannons blew down the monastery's gates on the second day of fighting.

The situation was hopeless. If the Cretans surrendered, the women would be raped, the children sold into slavery, and the men executed. The abbot called on the men to retreat to the monastery's vault where the gunpowder was stored and blow it up once the Turkish forces got inside. The explosion killed about 850 Greeks, including most of the women and children, and over 1,500 Turks.

The incident incited a passionate uproar throughout Europe and America, as the newspapers printed letters from French poet Victor Hugo describing the tragedy. People sent supplies to Crete and traveled there to help fight. Ottoman Grand Vizier Ali Pasha arrived in Crete in 1867 and reconquered Crete section by section but gave the Cretan Christians some local autonomy. By 1869, the rebels had either fled to Greece or submitted to Ottoman rule.

At the beginning of George I's reign, the new constitution instituted a single-chamber parliament and did away with the senate. King George could choose his prime minister, call for parliamentary sessions, and dissolve parliament if his cabinet endorsed his decree. For the first decade of George I's reign, his parliament was a disaster. George ignored public opinion when it came to his choices for prime minister and continually dissolved parliament.

Charilaos Trikoupis, a liberal leader of parliament, published an anonymous manifesto in the Athens newspaper in 1874 titled "Who's to Blame?" He criticized King George for frequently dissolving parliament and allowing multiple minority parties. He recommended the *dedilomeni* principle of parliamentary confidence: before a politician could be appointed prime minister, he must have majority support in parliament. He believed this system would force various factions to collaborate. Once Trikoupis admitted to authoring the article, King George invited him to form a government, declaring he would only appoint the leader of the parliament's majority party as prime minister.[45]

Greece continued to pursue annexing Thessaly and Epirus. When Russia and Turkey went to war in 1877, it provided a golden opportunity. George's sister Dagmar interceded with her father-in-law, Emperor Alexander II of Russia, asking him to ally with Greece in the war. But the other two Great Powers, Britain and France, would not permit Greece's involvement. Yet, when Russia won in 1878, and the Congress of Berlin met to hash out the new borders, Greece claimed Thessaly, Epirus, and Crete.[46] The British and French were favorable toward the idea, but the Ottoman Turks kept Crete and granted Thessaly and a section of Epirus to Greece in 1881.

The thirty-two-day Greco-Turkish War broke out in 1897 in Crete, which had always been a hotbed of dissent in the Ottoman

---

[45] Richard Clogg, *A Short History of Modern Greece* (Cambridge: Cambridge University Press, 1979), 86.

[46] Clogg, *Modern Greece*, 89.

Empire. As fighting erupted between the Ottoman Empire and Greece, the Great Powers surrounded the island with their ships, attempting to disrupt the conflict. Germany supported Turkey, which was awkward for King George since his son, Constantine, was married to Sophie, the German Kaiser's sister. Crown Prince Constantine was the general of the Greek forces when the fighting spread to Thessaly and Macedonia.

This was Greece's first war since its revolution. It was outmanned and outgunned and lost most of the battles. Nicholas II of Russia (Alexander III's son) mediated a peace treaty, which forced Greece to pay war reparations to Turkey. But the following year, the Great Powers removed the Ottomans and made Crete an autonomous state. King George's son, Prince George, served as high commissioner of the Cretan State for fifteen years until Crete formally became part of Greece in 1913.

In 1913, King George was looking forward to his Golden Jubilee in October, celebrating fifty years as king. He intended to abdicate after the ceremonies, with his son Constantine then taking the throne. But on March 18th, as he was enjoying an afternoon stroll in Athens, a mentally ill man shot him in the back at close range. The king died instantly. Constantine I succeeded him as the first Greek king born in Greece. He was also the first Greek king who was already a member of the Greek Orthodox Church.

Although King George I contended with multiple challenges, Greece became stabilized, gained territory, and improved its infrastructure during his long reign. In 1881, construction began on the Corinth Canal across the Isthmus of Corinth, linking the Saronic Gulf and the Gulf of Corinth: a shortcut between the Ionian and Aegean Seas. The ancient Greeks had dreamed of building the canal, and Roman Emperor Nero began construction in 67 CE, digging the first basketful of dirt. But he died several months later, and construction stopped. The Greeks finally completed the channel in 1893. It is still used by smaller vessels today, although it temporarily closed in October 2022 following catastrophic landslides.

King George also revived the Olympic Games, opening the first modern Olympics in 1896 in the Panathenaic Stadium of Athens. Crown Prince Constantine served as president of its organizing committee and raised the necessary funds to host the games. The Panathenaic Stadium was built of marble in 144 CE, and businessman George Averoff paid 920,000 drachmas (about one million USD) for its restoration.[47] The stadium is still used today and served as an Olympic venue in 2004.

Greece had been isolated from the Renaissance during Ottoman rule, except for the Ionian islands and Crete, which had been under European control for part of the time. The Cretan School and Ionia's Heptanese School assimilated the European artistic revolution and combined Eastern and Western traditions. El Greco (Doménikos Theotokópoulos) trained at the Cretan School.

During the 19th-century reigns of Greece's first two monarchs, the country experienced a flourishing of the arts. Greek artists often studied in Munich and put their spin on Romanticism, incorporating Greece's landscapes, history, and revolutionary ideals. The works of this era display raw emotion and theatrics. Historical paintings feature the heroism and sacrifices of the Greek Revolution. In the latter half of the 19th century, historical themes gave way to depictions of everyday life and nature.

---

[47] David C. Young, *The Modern Olympics: A Struggle for Revival* (Baltimore: Johns Hopkins University Press, 1996), 128.

Chapter 12: Greece in the 20th Century

The Balkan Wars, which lit the fuse to World War I, erupted after years of simmering tensions among the Slavs and other ethnic groups within the Ottoman Empire. Worried about the Balkan powder keg and how a revolution might throw the rest of Europe out of balance, Europe's Great Powers used their diplomatic power to quell aspirations of a revolt.

But Greece had similarly suffered under the Ottoman Empire, and its people felt a sense of camaraderie with those still struggling for independence in the Balkans. In 1912, Greece and the Slavic states secretly formed the Balkan League, which consisted of Bulgaria, Serbia, Greece, and Montenegro. The alliance represented distinct ethnic groups that usually fought each other but joined forces against Turkey while it was distracted with Italy's invasion of Libya.

On October 5th, 1912, the first day of the war, Greek Lieutenant Dimitrios Kamberos flew a reconnaissance flight over Thessaly: history's first military aviation mission. Within one month, the Balkan alliance shocked the world by driving the Ottoman forces out of southeastern Europe. The Great Powers scrambled to regain control, calling everyone to London to sort out the Balkan's new boundaries. Finally, after sixty-three meetings, they hashed out a treaty ending the First Balkan War on May 30th, 1913.

The Bulgarians were displeased. Serbia and Greece had crushed Bulgaria's hopes of getting most of Macedonia by deciding to keep the territories their own forces had conquered. Exactly one month later, Bulgaria incited the Second Balkan War by launching a surprise attack on Greece and Serbia. Bulgaria ended up getting attacked on all sides when the Ottoman Empire jumped back into the fray, and Romania invaded Bulgaria's northern borders.

The war ended within six weeks, and this time, the players, rather than the Great Powers, negotiated the Treaty of Bucharest. Turkey regained Thrace in Bulgaria, and Serbia got northern Macedonia. Greece got southern Epirus and Macedonia, the Aegean Islands, and formal control of Crete, expanding to over twice its size. The Balkan Wars were notable for Greece's submarine *Delfin* launching the world's first torpedo attack (albeit unsuccessfully) against a warship: the Ottoman light cruiser *Mecidiye*.[48]

World War I detonated in 1914 after a Serbian nationalist, Gavrilo Princip, shot and killed Austria-Hungary's Crown Prince Franz Ferdinand and his wife, Sophie. Austria-Hungary declared war on Serbia, and multiple other nations jumped in. The war saw the Central Powers (Germany, Austria-Hungary, Bulgaria, and the Ottoman Empire) facing off against the Allied Powers (Great Britain, France, Russia, Italy, Romania, Canada, Japan, the United States, and eventually Greece).

Greece's treaty with Serbia at the end of the Balkan Wars promised mutual military assistance in the event of a third-party attack. But since the third party referred to Bulgaria, Prime Minister Eleftherios Venizelos advocated remaining neutral unless Bulgaria got involved. If that happened, which Venizelos thought likely, he promoted joining the Allied Powers.

But King Constantine I and his foreign ministers thought that Germany and the Central Powers would win the war and didn't want to be on the losing side. Moreover, the king had attended university in Germany, trained in the German Imperial Army, and

---

[48] E. R. Hooten, *Prelude to the First World War: The Balkan Wars 1912-1913* (Gloucestershire: Fonthill Media, 2014).

married Sophie, the German Kaiser's sister. Yet, his mother, Olga, was living in her native Russia, which was fighting against Germany. Constantine was in an awkward position and wanted to stay out of the war entirely.

Prime Minister Venizelos and King Constantine I.
https://commons.wikimedia.org/wiki/File:158_14_Constantin_Venizelos.jpg

In September 1915, Bulgaria invaded Serbia, so Prime Minister Venizelos mobilized the Greek troops to honor their treaty. Needing more men, Venizelos asked the French to send additional troops, which they did. But Venizelos failed to clear the matter with the king and parliament; consequently, King Constantine dismissed him. Alexandros Zaimis became the new prime minister, and he informed Serbia that Greece could not help.

King Constantine and the parliament desperately tried to remain neutral in the war but still suffered. The Allies blocked coal and wheat coming into Greece and seized the Greek islands of Lesbos and Corfu. The French took Greece's Fort Dova Tepe on the Macedonian-Greek border. Two weeks later, the German-

Bulgarian columns attacked and seized Greece's Rupel Fortress in central Macedonia. French General Maurice Sarrail imposed martial law in Thessaloniki, controlling all communications, railways, and the harbor. In June, the Allies commanded Greece to demobilize its military. Bulgaria invaded, occupying eastern Macedonia by late August 1916. In October, the Italians attacked and occupied Greek-held northern Epirus.

Enough was enough! Former Prime Minister Venizelos and many other exasperated Greeks formed a separate Greek government on October 9th: the Provisional Government of National Defense. They joined the Allies and declared war on Germany and Bulgaria. The Allied Powers insisted King Constantine abdicate, and when he left for Switzerland in June 1917, Greece's Provisional Government took control of the whole country. Greece routed Bulgaria from Macedonia and retook all of Serbia in tandem with the Allied Forces. World War I ended in November 1918, and Greece received Thrace through the ensuing treaties.

When the Allied Powers forced Constantine's abdication, they ruled out Crown Prince George as the next king, believing he shared his father's pro-German leanings. They permitted Constantine's second son, Alexander, to become Greece's king, though.[49] King Alexander ruled until his sudden death in October 1920 from a monkey bite. He was walking in the summer palace gardens when the gardener's Barbary macaque attacked the king's German shepherd. As the king tried to separate the animals, another monkey attacked him, leaving him with several bites that went septic. Three weeks later, the king died. At that point, Greece invited Constantine I to return, and he resumed his rule in December 1920.

By this time, Greece had already entered the Greco-Turkish War (1919–1922). After WWI ended, Greece staked its claim to Anatolia (Asia Minor or western Turkey), which had once been part of the Byzantine Empire. The crumbling Ottoman Empire

---

[49] "Downfall of King Constantine," *Current History* (1916-1940) 6, no. 1 (1917): 83–85. http://www.jstor.org/stable/45328408.

still had 2.5 million Greeks, even though the Muslims systematically killed hundreds of thousands of Greek Christians in Turkey during WWI.[50] Venizelos's goal of claiming Asia Minor was to expel the Ottoman rule "from those territories where the majority of the population consists of Greeks."[51]

Greece's military landed at Smyrna on Turkey's western coast in May 1919, which it had received in the 1918 Armistice of Mudros. The Greeks and Armenians in the region joined forces with the Greek military and quickly gained control of western Asia Minor. The Turks fought back with guerrilla warfare, and both sides committed ethnic atrocities against the local citizens caught in the warzone. The Greeks slaughtered Muslims, and the Muslims murdered Greek Orthodox citizens, forcing the survivors out of their villages and east to the Smyrna region.

In the two months between King Alexander's death and King Constantine's reinstatement, the Greeks voted out Venizelos, forcing him to leave the country. When they brought King Constantine back to the throne, the Allied Powers cut financial and military aid to Greece. Russia was in the midst of a civil war, but the Soviet faction provided munitions to the revolutionaries of the Turkish Nationalist Movement. In 1921, the Greeks suffered a bitter defeat at the Battle of the Sakarya, losing 80 percent of its officers. In August 1922, the Turkish Great Offensive pushed forward with more than 100,000 soldiers. The Greeks had twice as many men but were disorganized and demoralized. The Turks crushed the Greek army, capturing fifteen thousand soldiers and forcing a retreat to the Aegean Sea.

The Turks burned down the Greek and Armenian sections of Smyrna. Trapped between the Turkish forces, the fire, and the sea, the frantic citizens had nowhere to flee. Nearly 100,000 people died as the city burned for nine days. The Allies decided a population exchange was the only way to end further atrocities.

---

[50] Adam Jones, *Genocide: A Comprehensive Introduction* (London: Routledge, 2006), 154-55.

[51] "Not War Against Islam – Statement by Greek Prime Minister," *The Scotsman*, June 29, 1920, 5, 29.

The 1923 Treaty of Lausanne forced 1.2 million Orthodox Christians to leave Turkey for Greece and moved 400,000 Greek Muslims from Greece to Turkey.

The September 1922 burning of Smyrna.
https://commons.wikimedia.org/wiki/File:Smyrna-burn-1922.jpg

Following the catastrophe at Smyrna, Venizelos's supporters compelled King Constantine I to abdicate again in September 1922, installing his oldest son, George II, as monarch. But when the Liberal Party came into power two years later, they exiled George, declaring Greece to be a republic. The new government threatened a minimum six-month jail sentence for anyone advocating a return to a monarchy or questioning the election results. The fragile new government limped along, interrupted by a one-year dictatorship when General Theodoros Pangalos staged a coup in 1925. He was ejected the following year, and the republic was restored. Venizelos regained control in 1928, bringing a measure of stability. Yet, the Great Depression (1929–1939) crushed Greece economically, and political chaos resumed.

The Greeks voted Venizelos out in 1932, and three military coups rocked the country between 1933 and 1935. Finally, in October 1935, General Georgios Kondylis forced himself into the position of prime minister, dissolved the republic, and staged a rigged election that restored the monarchy with 98 percent of the vote. George II, who had been living in two rooms at Brown's

Hotel of London, returned to Greece in November 1935. Refusing to be a puppet king, he immediately butted heads with Kondylis, dismissed him, and appointed Konstantinos Demertzis as prime minister.

Demertzis dropped dead of a heart attack four months later, so George appointed Minister of Defense Ioannis Metaxas as the new prime minister. This appointment was highly unpopular among the rising Communist Party, and workers went on strike throughout Greece. Metaxas declared a state of emergency in August 1936, citing industrial unrest and the "communist danger." He disbanded parliament and formed the totalitarian August Regime, imitating Benito Mussolini's fascist Italy. He banned political parties and strikes and censored the media. His dictatorship remained in power for five years until his death in 1941.

As World War II loomed, Metaxas strengthened fortifications at the Bulgaria-Greece border with tunnels, machine-gun nests, and "dragon's teeth" structures to impede tanks. Mussolini's Italian forces invaded northwest Greece in October 1940, officially bringing Greece into World War II. The Greeks resisted with fierce tenacity and chased the Italians out of the country. In April 1941, three months after Metaxas died, Adolf Hitler invaded Greece. The king and parliament fled to Crete as Germans, Bulgarians, and Italians swamped Greece.

The occupying forces plundered the farms and requisitioned food to feed their troops. Greece had always required grain shipments from outside the country for its population; the Allies' blockade now cut that off. As the Great Famine set in, dead bodies littered the streets of Athens, with as many as one thousand dying of starvation each day. The situation in other towns and cities was just as bleak, with an estimated 5 percent of Greece's population starving to death.

But Greece had relied on resistance forces in its rugged mountains during the Greek War of Independence, and similar mountain guerilla troops launched a successful defense against the invaders. Italy surrendered to the Allies in 1943, the Germans and Bulgarians withdrew from Greece in 1944, and the Greek king and government returned to Greece. World War II ended in September 1945.

A cavalry brigade of the Greek People's Liberation Army.
https://commons.wikimedia.org/wiki/File:IPPIKO-ELAS-1.jpg

Greece's two largest resistance movements—the National Liberation Front and the Greek People's Liberation Army—were communist and backed by the Soviet Union and Yugoslavia. Their clash with Greece's government exploded into the Greek Civil War, which lasted from 1944 to 1949 and wreaked even more devastation on the war-torn country. The civil war killed 100,000 people and mangled the economy, which was already on the brink of ruin. Finally, Soviet Union's Joseph Stalin told the Greek communists to fold up their operations; it would be too hard to fight Britain and the United States. One positive aspect of the liberal influence in Greece was women finally getting the right to vote on May 28th, 1952.

After World War II, the Dodecanese Islands in the Aegean and Mediterranean Seas went to Greece with the stipulation that they remain demilitarized. The Minoans and Myceneans had settled the islands beginning in the 2nd millennium BCE, and they had always had close ties to Greece. During the 20th century, the islands passed through the hands of Italy, Germany, and Britain before uniting with Greece on March 7th, 1948.

In the 2nd millennium BCE, the Myceneans also settled the island of Cyprus in the eastern Mediterranean Sea, south of Turkey and west of Syria. In the 20th century, about 80 percent of the population was Cypriot-Greek-speaking people of Greek lineage who belonged to the Greek Orthodox Church. The Ottoman Empire occupied Cyprus until the Russo-Turkish War (1877–1878), when Britain took over its administration.

In the 20th century, the Greek population of Cyprus pressed for a union with Greece, which the ethnic Turks resisted. When Cyprus gained independence in 1960, the Cypriot Turks, who consisted of 20 percent of the population, got 30 percent representation in parliament. Many Greeks considered this overrepresentation. In 1963, violence broke out, with 174 Greeks and 364 Turks dying. The Greeks destroyed 109 Turkish villages, displacing 30,000 ethnic Turks. In 1974, the Cypriot Greeks staged a coup, still desiring to unite with Greece, which triggered a Turkish invasion. The end result was a line dividing the island into a northern section under Turkish rule and a southern section under Cypriot-Greek control.

In mainland Greece, the struggle between the communist-leaning liberals and right-wing conservatives reached the boiling point in 1967. The United States had inserted itself in 1947 with the Truman Doctrine, which supported an authoritarian government in Greece to guard against Soviet influence. In the 1964 election, the more progressive Centre Union Party won a landslide victory, with its founder, Georgios Papandreou, becoming Greece's new prime minister.

Papandreou wanted to weed out military officers involved in the CIA-funded, anti-communist IDEA society (*Ieros Desmos Ellinon Axiomatikon* or Holy Bond of Greek Officers), which advocated a dictatorship. When twenty-four-year-old Constantine II ascended the throne in 1964, he clashed with Papandreou, forcing his resignation in 1965. The king replaced Papandreou with a series of prime ministers from the Centre Union Party, which still held the majority, but none served more than a few weeks. Papandreou's supporters considered these men to be defectors or "apostates" from the party, labeling Constantine's actions the *Apostasia* or Royal Coup.

Greece stumbled through this political crisis. On April 21st, 1967, the people of Athens awakened to the sound of gunfire and tanks rolling into the city. Military songs blared on the radio, followed by the announcement, "The Hellenic Armed Forces have taken the country's governance." Right-wing military officers had staged a coup called the Greek Junta, which established a seven-year dictatorship. They censored the media and arrested left-wing politicians and ten thousand blacklisted citizens, sending them to prison or a concentration camp on Yaros Island. Thousands endured torture by the Security Police and Greek Military Police.

King Constantine attempted a counter-coup in December 1967 with the navy and air force members that were still loyal to him. When the coup failed, he fled Greece with his family, and the junta appointed Major Georgios Zoitakis as regent in the king's absence. Zoitakis appointed Colonel George Papadopoulos, one of the coup's three ringleaders, as prime minister. In 1972, Papadopoulos became the joint regent and prime minister and abolished the monarchy in June 1973.

In November 1973, several hundred students launched a protest at Athens's National Technical University, demanding the military junta abandon power. The next day, thousands of citizens poured onto the campus to support the student protestors. The students constructed a radio system that broadcasted throughout Athens. Three days later, a tank crashed through the university's gates, and the military brutally cleared out the protestors.

The following week, Dimitrios Ioannidis, Papadopoulos's protégé, initiated a counter-coup that ejected Papadopoulos, accusing him of straying from the 1967 revolutionary ideals. But the Greek military pulled support from Ioannidis when he sponsored the disastrous 1974 coup in Cyprus, which resulted in Turkey invading the island. The second-generation junta leadership decided to put Greece back on track for elections. They invited Konstantinos Karamanlis, who had served as prime minister in the early 1960s, to return from exile and serve as Greece's interim leader until elections resumed.

With elections restored and a new administration in place, Constantine II confidently expected to return as Greece's monarch. However, the electorate voted against restoring the monarchy. Constantine remained in London, as he was a close friend of his cousin Prince Charles (now King Charles III) and godfather of William, Prince of Wales. In 2013, Greece finally permitted Constantine to return to live in Greece as a private citizen.

On January 1ˢᵗ, 1981, Greece joined the European Economic Community (EEC), to which it had first applied in 1959. In 1961, Greece and the EEC signed an Association Agreement, but the ensuing political chaos froze the process. With democracy restored in 1974, Prime Minister Karamanlis reactivated the procedures to integrate Greece as a full member of the European Union. His goal was to restore economic and political stability and modernize Greek society. Greece adopted the single currency euro in 2002.

In August 2004, Athens again hosted the Olympic Games in its twenty-fifth competition since King George I revived the modern games in 1896. Athens built a new airport, ring road, and subway system to welcome over eleven thousand competitors and an estimated one million visitors. Despite the media's dire predictions, all the venues were completed on schedule, and the transportation systems and venues awed everyone. "Unforgettable dream games!" exclaimed President Jacques Rogge of the International Olympic Committee.

Conclusion

Greece immensely impacted our world as the cradle of Western civilization. The Minoans were the first advanced European culture, a people who built breathtaking palaces, created dazzling art, and devised Europe's first two written languages. The Myceneans followed soon after, elevating Greece and its surrounding islands to new levels of urban organization, engineering, architecture, and warfare proficiency. Their ships sailed around the Mediterranean and Black Seas, exchanging goods, establishing colonies, and spreading an advanced culture.

After Greece's Dark Ages, the archaic era emerged to introduce Europe to written literature, such as Homer's *Iliad* and *Odyssey*. We are indebted to the ancient Greeks' stunning breakthroughs in mathematics, science, and medicine. Greek philosophers developed a logical observation of the physical world, and early Greek physicians devised the systematic diagnosis of common diseases. Greece left an indelible stamp on Roman culture, the Christian Church, the Byzantine Empire, the Renaissance, and modern-day politics. Greece's experimentation and development of political systems contributed enormously to democratic republics worldwide.

Cretan hieroglyphs and Linear A used in Crete and southern Greece were the first European writing systems. Tablets with Linear B dating to at least 1350 BCE document an ancient form of the Greek language still spoken today. Spoken and written Koine

Greek dates to the 4ᵗʰ century BCE and became the lingua franca of the vast territories covering three continents conquered by Alexander the Great. Scholars translated the Hebrew Tanakh (Old Testament) into Koine Greek (the Septuagint version) in Hellenistic Egypt, and the apostles wrote the New Testament in Koine Greek.

The Byzantine Empire left an enduring legacy, especially its contribution to developing the Eastern Orthodox Church. Byzantine architecture spread to Russia and south to Egypt. Byzantine monks, philosophers, and artists cultivated a unique cultural blend of Christianity with Greek philosophy, science, art, and literature. They preserved Greek and Roman art, literature, philosophy, science, technology, and law through the centuries until the Renaissance.

Modern Greece has trailblazed through multiple challenges, employing innovations and silencing doubters. After freeing itself from Ottoman rule, Greece established the oldest parliamentary democracy in the eastern Mediterranean and southeast Europe. It has endured since 1864, with three brief non-democratic regimes lasting a combined total of twenty-three years. With a few bumps along the way, Greece has emerged from abject poverty to economic prosperity in the past seven decades. While its ancient classical past is an intrinsic element of Greece's national identity, the nation is a world player today, developing an impressive geopolitical identity in the eastern Mediterranean.

Part 2: Greek Mythology

An Enthralling Overview of Greek Myths, Gods, and Goddesses

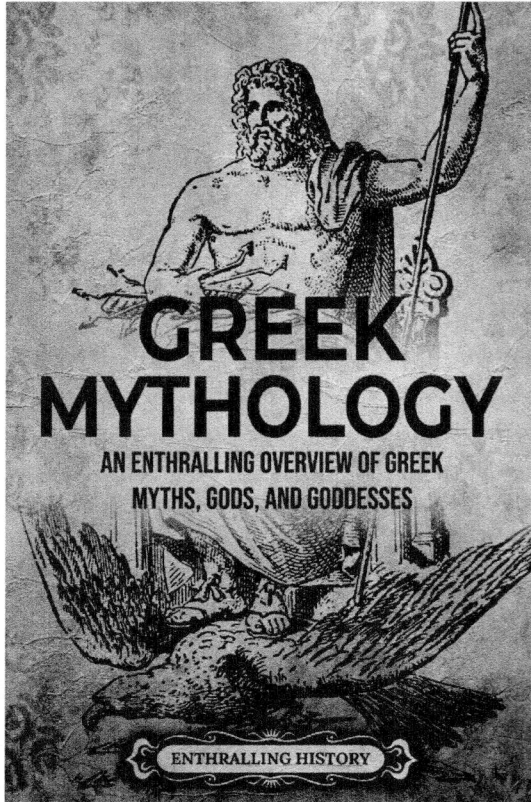

Introduction

Similar to other kinds of mythologies within a pagan-based society, Greek mythology has adjusted itself throughout the centuries. It has been at the whims of redactors, philosophers, and storytellers who shifted narratives for the purposes of revealing some deeper meaning about the actions of gods, goddesses, and heroes.

For instance, the birth of the god of wine, Dionysus, is hotly debated and has been rewritten multiple times. In the version composed by Hesiod, Dionysus was born of Zeus and Semele, a princess. In another version composed by Hesychius, he is the son of Dione, a female Titan. The switch in mothers is by no means a coincidence; the two men could have heard the story differently, or they could have made the adjustments themselves.

This diversity reflects the variation of realities in the Greek world. Greece was not considered to be a united kingdom in the sense that there was one monarch who ruled over all of Greece. The mainland and islands were governed under distinct *poleis* (singular *polis*, meaning "city"), which led to great variations in Greek culture, art, literature, and oral histories. The diversity of that world is reflected in this book, which seeks to marry the different versions of myths together in an attempt to represent the whole of the Greek world and the surrounding nations.

Our main goal is to bestow a comprehensive and compelling worldview of Greek mythology in all the multifaceted aspects that go into good storytelling. The versions of these myths below are very much in the spirit of mythology. They might be a bit different than the myths you remember at times, as we have sometimes taken the more dramatic version of a myth and married it into its traditional telling, but the core of the story will remain the same.

Chapter 1: From Chaos to Uranus

Which came first, the chicken or the egg? The creation of the world for many ancient cultures, including the Greeks, began with a place where there was no beginning and no end. It began in Chaos, a deep but not entirely empty void. Chaos would give birth to the first gods. The primordial ones' hot-headed and ballsy (pay attention because there is a great joke there) behavior gave birth to a world that would soon be engulfed in the drama of their children.

It is unclear whether Chaos's children gave birth to themselves, springing forth from the emptiness of their sire, or if Chaos squatted low and painfully birthed these beings. Also highly debated amongst scholars is the gender of Chaos, who, for the sake of argument, we shall consider to be female. This makes sense since she delivered a couple of kids, but the gender and biology of the Greek gods, Titans, and other miscellaneous non-human characters are not dictated by the black and white laws of biology. In Greek mythology, babies could be born from a head, a thigh, a volcano under the earth, or a dark swirling black hole at the beginning of time.

And so, Chaos gave birth to Gaia, whose body would lay the foundations for the earth, which would spring all forms of life. The second born was Tartarus, who is also referred to as Erebus. His body comprised the underworld, the realm of the dead, where all souls went for judgment at the end of their life. Both gods and men feared what lay in the darkness of the underworld. After Tartarus came Pontus, who was the first god of the sea. But he was more than this—he was the sea itself, a raw form of power that would be inherited by the godly generations that came later. This was the case with all the primordial beings. They were the stadium in which the Olympians played their games, and they were also the source of the Olympians' weapons and power.

Chaos also gave birth to other children considered to be among the original primordial beings. Eros, the fabled and cherub-like god of love, who some consider to be the child of the Olympians Aphrodite and Ares, is actually believed to have been born at the beginning of time. Nyx, the literal night who took the form of a woman, also emerged from Chaos. Her name and characterization as a shadowy figure can give you the impression that she is evil. However, she is an ambivalent goddess, holding both light and dark qualities, which would be embodied by her numerous children.

Nyx and her brother Erebus brought Aether and Hemera into the world. Aether filled up the space between the heavens and the earth with a fine mist that gave the sky its blue hue. His sister-wife Hemera, the literal day, was an entirely independent entity from Helios (the sun), and she brought forth her brother's mists each morning. Oftentimes, the sibling-partner combinations in Greek mythology represent the duality of the natural world, such as the water and the rain cycle.

Nyx also gave birth to several other divine beings, pushing them out from her own dark mass. These children shaped a vast range of human experiences, both positive and negative. This list is lengthy, but there was Moros (fate), Hypnos (sleep), Oneiroi (dreams), Geras (old age), Oizys (pain), Nemesis (revenge), Eris (strife), Apate (deceit), Philotes (sexual pleasure), Momos (blame), Thanatos (peaceful death), Ker (violent death), and finally the Hesperides (the daughters of the evening who were typically depicted as nymphs). During this same time, Nyx's sister Gaia birthed her son Uranus, who would become the lord of the entire cosmos. Their union would produce the old gods of Greece, the famed and ferocious Titans.

Chapter 2: The Titans

It is safe to say that out of all the divine beings of Greek mythology, Gaia and Uranus were overachievers when it came to the number of children. Not only did they produce hundreds of children, but they also gave birth to several different types of monsters and Titans. Uranus was determined to have not only as many children as possible but also perfect children with considerable gifts and beauty. Their firstborn children were not a success, at least according to Uranus. These were the three Hecatonchires. These accursed monsters, with their hundred hands and fifty heads to one body, were the least favored amongst Uranus and Gaia's children.

Their second attempt at children resulted in three one-eyed Cyclopes. These children were closer to what their father had hoped for, as they were born with unmatched physical strength and had a prowess for metalworking. Later, the Cyclopes would form the gods' first weapons.

Still, Uranus hated his monstrous children. In fact, he hated them so much that he threw them into the deepest and darkest pits of Tartarus. Those children never saw the light of day; instead, they were cast into the darkness as soon as they were pulled from Gaia. This broke her heart. Naturally, she was hesitant to produce any more children for Uranus, but the lord of the heavens gave her little choice in the matter. He would keep going until he had his perfect children. Thankfully, Gaia's next several pregnancies resulted in twelve ideal children, who are known as the Titans.

These twelve beings are referred to in sources as the Uranides. There were six males and six females. Four of the brothers—Coeus, Crius, Hyperion, and Iapetus—held up the heavens and suspended their father Uranus just above the earth. However, the official firstborn was Oceanus, the patron god of fresh water. He was responsible for overseeing the rivers, lakes, aquifers, springs, and even the clouds in the sky. The second-born, Coeus, was the Titan of intellect and questioning. Coeus was also responsible for keeping the northern axis around which the heavens spun, which he held along with three of his brothers.

The next brother, Crius, the Titan and lord of the constellations and the yearly calendar, kept sway over the north axis of the heavens. The next brother, Hyperion, the lord of light, sired the lights that come from the cosmos, including the dawn (Eos), the sun (Helios), and the moon (Selene). The final brother, Iapetus, the Titan of mortality, would give birth to the gods that created humanity.

After the five brothers came their sisters. The female Titans would lay with their brothers and create generations of Titans and gods. Theia was the Titan of foresight and mother to Hyperion's three godly children. Rhea was the goddess of feminine fertility and would soon become the queen of the Titans. Themis, the Titan of the law of fate by which all men must abide, would later become pregnant by her nephew and give birth to the seasons and the Fates, the old crones of time. Next came Mnemosyne, the goddess of memory. She would also give birth to a couple of Muses by the very same nephew that impregnated her sister Themis. The second youngest daughter, Phoebe, the Titan of prophecy, was the wife of "intellect" (her brother Coeus) and the patron goddess of the legendary Oracle of Delphi. The youngest daughter Tethys was the wife of her brother Oceanus and sired for him the source of every freshwater source that would fall under his dominion.

These Titans became the world around which humanity would grow. They were the foundations of knowledge, culture, and tradition. However, there was still one more Titan to be born. Cronos, the youngest, was the Titan of time. And he had all of time's most destructive qualities, such as aging, erosion, and decay. He was by far the most ruthless and hateful of the Titans. He despised his accursed father for the mistreatment of his brothers, the Cyclopes and the Hecatonchires.

Obviously, Gaia was not so thrilled with her husband. She also despised his cruel and greedy nature, as he had forced her to bear him children he either rejected or abused. Over time, her hatred grew deep. It molded itself, forming the first metals of the earth that would be used to fashion a god-killing weapon—the sickle that would destroy Uranus for all time. Gaia approached her children and asked them all to search their hearts and to take up the blade that grew from her hatred and kill Uranus. Her children stood silent, as they were afraid to rise up against the wrath of their father. Cronos, the youngest, was the only one to heed his mother's call. He, along with his brothers who held up the heavens, would concoct a plan to exact terrible vengeance and murder their father.

That night, Uranus returned and brought the darkness of night with him. He laid over his wife, meaning to take her yet again in his lustful greed. Uranus was aroused and prepared to enter Gaia, but before he could, the four pillars of the earth—Coeus, Crius, Hyperion, and Iapetus—seized their father, pinning him down. Cronos leaped forth from the shadows and cut his father from root to stem and tossed his genitals into the sea. The combination of sea and sperm birthed one of the most famous Olympians in history: the goddess of love herself, Aphrodite.

With his dying breath, Uranus spoke his last cruel words to his son Cronos, a terrible prophecy that would lead to the loss of the remainder of Cronos's compassion. He told his son that one day, one of his own children would seek to overthrow him and that they would do to him what he had done to his father.

The Mutilation of Uranus by Saturn (Cronos) *by Giorgio Vasari (1556)*.
https://commons.wikimedia.org/wiki/File:The_Mutilation_of_Uranus_by_Saturn.jpg

Chapter 3: The War of the Titans

After the fall of Uranus, Cronos usurped his crown as "King of the Cosmos" and took Rhea, his sister, as queen. Despite having succeeded in dispatching their wicked father, the Titans could do nothing to remove the foreboding prophecy from their brother's mind. Uranus had won. Cronos's fear that he would one day be dispatched by his own children turned him into ten times the monster his father was. Upon the birth of each of his children, Cronos swallowed them whole. These were the gods who would take up residence on Mt. Olympus and seize control of the earth and heavens: Hestia, Hera, Demeter, Poseidon, Hades, and Zeus.

The last child, Zeus, was not swallowed but hidden away by his mother Rhea, who gave her husband a rock swaddled in a blanket to consume in Zeus's place. The rest of her children remained alive, continuously growing in their father's stomach. Zeus was raised in secret far away near Mount Ida, which was on the island of Crete. He lived in a cave guarded day and night by the Curetes, and he was nurtured by the milk of Amalthea, a she-goat. When Zeus came to power, he honored Amalthea by placing her likeness in the stars. He fashioned his shield from her hide and created the cornucopia of plenty from her horn. The Curetes were also the children of Gaia, but they were not Titans. They were thought to be the first inhabitants of Crete. They performed the first war dances, banging together their spears and shields so as to drown out the cries of the infant Zeus so that his location would not be discovered.

When Zeus reached manhood, he sought to rise against Cronos, but he needed the help of his siblings. Their father and the Titans were too strong to take on alone. So, Rhea approached her mother Gaia and beseeched her to reveal the secrets of the earth and make her a concoction that would cause Cronos to vomit up his now fully grown children. Metis, the sister of Rhea, presented it to Cronos so that he would not suspect their plan, and he drank the mixture with no hesitation. Up came all of his swallowed children. They, along with their brother Zeus, retreated to the safety of Mt. Olympus and began a terrible ten-year war against Cronos and the Titans. It was the old gods versus the new. Some Titans would be forced to choose sides, and Zeus used all of his wits and strength to recruit the most valuable. Out of the numerous Titans, though, only two would stand against Cronos: Themis, the goddess of divine law and wisdom (daughter of Gaia and Uranus), and her son Prometheus, who would later bestow the gift of knowledge to humanity.

After ten years of war, there seemed to be no victor in sight, and both sides were beginning to lose heart. However, the turning point eventually came, and it was due to the most unlikely allies in the war: the monsters that Uranus had imprisoned in the depths of Tartarus. Cronos, who had vowed to release his brothers from the underworld, had broken his promise and left them to rot away in the dark. Zeus freed his uncles, the Cyclopes and Hecatonchires, from captivity. As a reward, the Cyclopes made Zeus and his brothers weapons of monumental power. They were cast from the forces of nature that stirred inside Gaia and the heavens. These weapons were none other than Zeus's thunderbolt, Poseidon's trident, and Hades's pitchfork.

With the tides now having turned in favor of the Olympians, the last day of the ten-year war, known as the Titanomachy, would occur. This final day of battle, as recorded in Hesiod's *Theogony* (Hesiod was a Greek poet), speaks of the might of the Hecatonchires. With their hundred hands, they hurled down a rain of gargantuan boulders upon the Titans, forcing them to take cover behind the mountains. Zeus delivered the final blow to his father

Cronos, and with no more allies or strength to resist his son, the king of the universe and this terrible father of time had been defeated, and he was cast down into the underworld along with his brothers and sisters. Their dark prison would be guarded by its former inhabitants, the hundred-handed Hecatonchires. However, Themis and Prometheus would live since they had aided the gods. Prometheus's brother Atlas, who sided with Cronos, was tasked with holding up the sky as punishment for his crimes.

With their enemies defeated and imprisoned, the Olympians set to the task of deciding who would rule which domains of the earth. The three brothers—Zeus, Poseidon, and Hades—drew lots for the largest kingdoms. Zeus would become the king of the gods, lord of the skies, and the god of thunder and lightning. Poseidon came to rule the vast depths of the sea; he was the shaker of mountains and the creator of new lands. Hades drew the shortest straw, so he was made the lord of the underworld, and he rarely emerged from his dark domain.

Chapter 4: The Gods

Zeus

Zeus was the king of the Gods, the ruler of the heavens and the earth, the manipulator of weather, and the wielder of lightning and thunder. In addition to these many titles, Zeus was also the god of reason and justice. He is shown in representations of Greek wall art and pottery as a man in his later years on account of his well-developed beard and large build. No doubt, the god himself was an attractive and incredibly powerful god, but his greatest strength was his skillful mind. It was through his cunning and prowess that he was able to defeat his numerous enemies and claim the throne of Olympus.

Despite his keen sense of justice and wisdom, Zeus was quite rash in his actions as a god. He was prone to quick decision-making, which probably contributed to the fact that he had more children than most of the other Olympians. Although Zeus technically had several wives, he also had coitus with a number of nymphs and mortal women, producing hundreds of children in the process. Most of these children became notable heroes and figures in Greek mythology, such as Helen of Troy and Perseus, the slayer of the Gorgon Medusa, as well as several major gods and goddesses.

When Zeus first came to power, he took Metis as his wife, the very same Metis who had freed Zeus's siblings from the belly of their father. Metis was the daughter of Oceanus and Tethys, and she was the goddess of good counsel. It is easy to understand Zeus's initial attraction to Metis, and she became his most trusted confidant and mentor. Well, up until the time he swallowed her whole but more on this later.

Zeus had many other wives, both mortal and immortal, but his main queen, at least in keeping with Greek mythological tradition, was his sister Hera. Zeus, like many other gods, could shapeshift, and most of the time, he approached his sexual partners and conquests in the guise of an animal. This was how he won the affections of Hera.

The ancient Greeks connected with the gods through their interactions and usage of the natural world. Zeus was identified with the natural world through symbols like the bull and the eagle or through various species of plant life, mainly the oak tree.

Out of all the qualities a king is meant to possess, perhaps the most important is wisdom. Without a doubt, the kings who last the longest and are the most loved tend to be wise. These are the kings who seek the advice and counsel of others. Zeus took his role as a king very seriously, and he was constantly attended by a multitude of lesser gods, goddesses, and spirits who acted as his advisors and bodyguards. At each foot of his throne sat a guardian spirit: Kratos (Strength), Zelos (Rivalry), Nike (Victory), and Bia (Force). Hermes, one of Zeus's sons, acted as his herald, and the official summons and messages of the king could only be delivered by Iris, the iridescent goddess of the rainbow. After Zeus consumed Metis, the position of the hand of the king was vacant. Themis, the Titan who had stood beside Zeus during the decade-long war with Cronos and the other Titans, was charged with the order and peace of the cosmos and attended the king in all of his endeavors. She even kept her loyalty to Zeus after he banished her son Prometheus to the underworld to undergo the torture of having a vulture (or eagle in some versions) continuously eat his magically regenerating liver until the end of time.

Poseidon

Poseidon, the god of the seas, master of earthquakes, and the creator of new lands and islands, had a temper that was as reckless and destructive as the sea itself. With his great trident, he moved the waters, carrying ships safely across the sea or bringing waves on land and washing away whole villages and cities.

Poseidon was not only destructive. He also possessed a more creative side and manifested the first horses and hippocampi, fish-tailed horses that he used to draw his golden chariot from the sea to Mt. Olympus. His physical appearance is not that different from his brothers. He is often depicted as an older man with a beard, and there is usually a wreath of celery around his head instead of olives like Zeus. One of his natural symbols is the celery stalk; another one is the pine tree.

Just like his brother, Poseidon was tempted by the beauty of mortals, goddesses, and nymphs. However, he was far less of a gentleman than his brother. Calling a spade a spade, Poseidon was a habitual rapist. There are several notable tales of him raping young women, with the two most notable victims being his wife and queen of the seas, the "ebony-eyed" nymph Amphitrite, and his own sister Demeter, whom he took against her will while they were both horses. Rape in the ancient world was not thought of as a crime in the same way it is perceived today. In other ancient sources, including legal corpora, rape was not an act of violence but rather uncontrollable passion. That being said, Poseidon still seemed to have a bit of an issue with the topic more than other gods and goddesses. It was perhaps a way to characterize his wildly violent and rash behavior, as the people could compare his behavior to the sea, an entity that has very little regard for its victims since it cannot control its raging waters.

Poseidon had many affairs with magical beings, including his own grandmother, the primordial being Gaia. Thus, he produced some of the most famous children in Greek mythology. The winged horse Pegasus sprung from the severed head of Poseidon's sexual conquest Medusa. Triton, his son by Amphitrite, controlled and quelled the waves of the Aegean Sea. The depictions of Triton look like something from an Old Spice commercial. Picture a merman with a set of washboard abs and sometimes an unruly beard. Other times, his face was meant to resemble that of a Greek youth, one perhaps around the age of twenty or twenty-five, given the fact that beards signaled a mature age in Greek culture. His symbol is a conch shell. Poseidon's daughter, Rhode, a sea nymph and the goddess protector of the Greek island of Rhodes, would become the wife of Helios, the sun.

Hades

The lord of the underworld was as gloomy as his domain. Hades had a burning resentment toward his siblings for his lot in being looked down upon and rejected as the god of the dead. (He was not the god of death, though; that role belonged to Thanatos.) Although Hades was not prone to common decencies, like manners or smiling, he was the richest of the gods, for all the treasures that lay inside the earth were his property. This is one of the reasons that his most recognizable symbol is the cornucopia, the horn of plenty. At the end of their lives, the dead would be led to the underworld by the wing-footed god Hermes. At the edge of the River Styx, they would wait with two gold coins for the boatman Charon to ferry them across to Hades's dark dominion. The underworld had various sections, and people would be assigned to these sections according to the life they had lived. While the underworld was meant to be a realm for punishment and pain, it was also a place of final rest for those souls deserving of peace.

However, Hades was also the guardian of proper funeral rites, and any soul that did not receive a proper sanctified burial according to the laws of Hades was not allowed to enter the gates of the underworld. This is why Hades kept the gates guarded day and night by his most loyal disciple, the three-headed dog Cerberus. Any sort of dark magic or ritual was the niche of the god of the dead, particularly the cult activity of attempting to raise the dead. If an ancient Greek really wanted their curse on someone to stick, they invoked curses that called upon the powers and prowess of Hades.

Like his brothers, Hades is considered to have the physical appearance of an older man with a dark beard and more of a medium build. Unlike his brothers, however, who seemed to be attracted to just about anyone and everyone, Hades was far more selective with his lovers and often formed deep attachments to them. His main queen was Persephone, the goddess of spring vegetation and the daughter of his own sister Demeter. Although their union deeply upset Persephone's mother, over time, her daughter learned to come to terms with her predicament, and she must have developed at least some sort of feelings for her uncle.

When he went off with his lovers and left her to tend to the underworld alone, she exacted terrible revenge on these women, often throwing her husband into deep grief. One of these women, Minthe, was trampled under the goddess's foot (some versions say Demeter did this). Hades was so distraught that the goddess transformed Minthe's body into a mint plant and named the mountain where she died in her honor. To this day, the site is said to be a very holy domain that the god of the underworld visits often. The other concubine of Hades was Leuce, the daughter of the Titan Oceanus. She was carried off by Hades and also murdered by his wife. However, in later versions, she lived out her days in the underworld. Regardless of the myth you look at, Hades transformed her into a white poplar tree and wears a laurel of poplar leaves around his head as a crown.

The god of the dead was indeed a hopeless romantic, and he showed favor toward heroes that embarked on their quests in the name of love. The singer Orpheus traveled to the underworld to retrieve his recently departed and dearly beloved wife, Eurydice. Hades and Persephone were so moved by his plea that they agreed to release his wife. However, she would trail behind him, and he must not look back, or else she would return to the land of the dead. Orpheus did as he was instructed and did not look back to check for his wife, even though the temptation was great. Right as he stepped foot into the world above, he decided he didn't trust Hades (some say he wanted to make sure she was there, while others say he was so eager that he could wait no longer). He looked back to see if the soul of his wife had indeed followed him out. He turned and saw that it was his wife, and he was filled with unspeakable joy. As a smile crossed his lips, the earth closed its gates, swallowing up Eurydice and taking her back into the darkness.

Hermes

As far as gods go, Hermes is by far the most approachable and likable. This silver-tongued prince was the god of trade, athletics, healthy competition, medicinal knowledge, and thievery. Although this last quality is classically unsavory, Hermes could be considered the original gentleman thief, as he used his finely tuned skills to steal from his marks. Think more along the lines of pickpocketing instead of mugging. Hermes is also rarely ever seen in Greek art without his caduceus, more commonly known as a herald's scepter or that thing you see on the side of ambulances in the United States. At times, he favors his father's looks, sporting a long thick beard, and other times, he is depicted as a young, effeminate, and beautiful man. He is often thought to have the youngest physical appearance of all the Olympians.

Although Hermes was by far the most mischievous and diabolically cunning of all the gods, he was, without a doubt, one of his father's personal favorites. That's saying a lot, considering Zeus had hundreds of children. Hermes started displaying signs of cunning intelligence when he was only an infant. Only a few hours after his birth, he managed to sneak away from his mother Maia as she was resting and stole his brother Apollo's cattle, wiping away their footprints in the dust. Apollo searched high and low for his herd. Little Hermes revealed his cruel actions but would not return the cattle until he was forced to do so.

As a child, Hermes was also a gifted craftsman, and he created the lyre from the shell of a turtle. He gifted this to Apollo in order to appease the sun god over the theft of his cattle. Apollo was so delighted that he relinquished the herd to Hermes willingly and showered him with additional gifts. Zeus was so impressed by this young savant that he gave him a permanent throne on Olympus and made Hermes his personal messenger and attendant of the dead, as he would accompany them to the underworld. With his winged sandals, he traveled fast on the wind, not unlike the comic book hero Flash. Hermes is often equated with any kind of herding activity; whether it's a flock of animals or a flock of souls, Hermes is the god you would call when you want to move a crowd.

The romantic life of the god of messengers was not unlike the other gods on Mt. Olympus. Hermes consorted with mortals and immortals alike. However, unlike his father, who used his shapeshifting to deceive and/or seduce women or his rapist of an uncle Poseidon, Hermes used plenty of sweet words to seduce his lovers. His skills as a smooth talker afforded him the company of some of the most beautiful goddesses and humans of the age, including the goddess of love herself, Aphrodite. The two, in fact, share a son, the love god of intersexuality and androgyny, Hermaphroditus.

Hermes is often considered to be the god of male sexuality, both homosexuality and heterosexuality, making his coupling with the living embodiment of female sexuality logical. Some even say that Hermes took the hero Perseus as a lover. A few of his other notable male lovers were the king of Thebes and a young boy named Crocus, who Hermes mortally wounded in a game of discus. He felt such grief for his actions that he transformed the youth into a beautiful crocus flower.

Apollo

Apollo was the master of the sun. With his great golden chariot, he would bring forth the warmth of Helios each and every morning. He was also the god of medicine, prophecy, healing, and archery. He and his twin sister Artemis were both skilled archers. They could hunt with the skill of most grown mortal men when they were only infants. Apollo was also the patron god of youth, and as such, he is never depicted with a full raging beard like his forefathers.

Apollo's father was Zeus, and his mother was the immortal second-generation Titan Leto, patron goddess of motherhood, modesty, and womanly demure. The story of Apollo's birth, as well as that of his sister Artemis, is similar to other tales that surround the many lovers of Zeus and their offspring. Leto was hunted to the ends of the earth by Hera, Zeus's lawful wife, who was a woman of unparalleled jealousy and callousness. She once even dared to steal Zeus's thunderbolt because she was so upset. The thunder god showed his wife no mercy and hung her from the sky with anvils attached to her ankles until she repented and returned the lightning bolt. After being chased around the globe by Hera, Leto finally found a place to birth her twins on the floating islands of Delos. After the birth of the twins, Hera gave up her pursuit, and Zeus gave both his children thrones on Mt. Olympus.

Like the rest of the gods and goddesses of Mt Olympus, the sun god had no shortage of lovers in his immortal life, and just like Hermes, he had an affinity for both men and women. However, most of the love myths surrounding Apollo are about women and, in particular, nymphs. One of the most famous of all myths involving Apollo was his pursuit of the Naiad nymph Daphne. One trademark of the nymphs was their ability to outrun the various gods, monsters, and creatures that sought to have or harm them. Daphne gave the sun god a good sprint, running all over Greece. Finally, in frustration, Daphne called out to Gaia to save her from Apollo's grasp. Gaia then transformed the nymph into a laurel tree. Even in her tree state, the sun god longed for her. He made the laurel wreath one of his main totems and placed laurel branches around the temple of the Oracle of Delphi.

Apollo probably had the highest number of relations with nymphs out of all the gods, and he produced some very ethereal and earthly divine children. One of the most notable is the god of olive oil, beekeeping, and the Etesian winds, Aristaeus.

Apollo was also the slayer of the mighty Python of Delphi. Sources offer contested opinions as to the origins of the great beast and its form, but what is certain is that Python was older than all the Olympians. He was a relic from the days of Chaos and the great flood. Some say that Python was one of the beasts sent by Hera to destroy Apollo's mother, Leto. Seeking revenge, Apollo shot the serpent right in the eye with one of his golden arrows. Others say that the serpent was set by Gaia to guard the Oracle of Delphi, a being of immense prophetic power. In fact, the Oracle was so powerful that she caught the attention and patronage of the sun god. The great serpent was bested with one shot from Apollo's bow, and the god usurped the patronage of Delphi.

Ares

Ares was a son that even a mother would find hard to love. He had an undeniable bloodlust, but his brutal antics suited him nicely since he was the god of war. He was not the most well-liked god of all the Olympians. Mortals feared Ares far more than they respected him. There were several deities that personified war activities, but there was nothing philosophical or redeemable about Ares's take on battles. He loved to kill for sport, desecrating and defiling the bodies of the men he fought. Despite his warlike ways, Ares has always been characterized in mythology as an irrefutable coward. And since he was the son of Zeus and Hera, he had a guaranteed throne on Olympus, unlike many other gods and goddesses.

He is usually depicted in ancient renderings as a mature man or a slender youth in full body armor. The god's seemingly one likable quality was that the god of war has never been recorded in Greek mythology as a rapist, despite the fact that rape and war always seem to pair together. He preferred a style similar to that of his father Zeus, as he had an arsenal of tricks in order to seduce mortals and immortals alike. One of Ares's most notable lovers was the goddess of love herself and the lawful wife of Hephaestus, Aphrodite. In fact, the god of blacksmiths and metallurgy, Hephaestus, caught the lovers entangled within a golden net he had made special for the occasion. He then invited the rest of the Olympians to laugh at the adulterous lovers.

From their union, the goddess of love and the god of war had four divine children: Anteros, Deimos, Phobos, and Harmonia. All of their children represented different possible outcomes or human tendencies when it comes to relationships. Anteros was the god of both unrequited and requited love. Deimos was the god of fear, while Phobos was the god of panic. Harmonia was the goddess of harmony and the mother of Semele, who would become the mother of Dionysus, the god of wine and merriment.

In addition to his warlike attributes, Ares was also the god of civil order and had a very strong sense of right and wrong. He was very protective of his loved ones, especially his children. When his daughter with Aglauros (the daughter of the king of Athens) was raped by Halirrhothius, the son of Poseidon, Ares caught the rapist in the act and slit his throat on the spot. Poseidon was outraged and brought Ares to the court of the gods to be tried as a murderer, but the gods declared by unanimous vote that Ares should be acquitted of all crimes.

By all accounts, Ares seems to be the god most invested in his children. He could be defined in modern terms as a very "hands-on father." Almost all of his children were given attention, especially if they showed promise and prowess on the battlefield. It didn't matter whether they were a boy or a girl; Ares treated all his children the same. Some of his most famous fearless sires are the Amazonian race of warrior women. Yes, the very same Amazons who would later inspire the iconic female warrior culture of Wonder Woman herself. Ares had his selected favorite daughters but doted on all the Amazons, showering them with weapons and artillery and constantly backing their war efforts. His two favorite daughters were Amazonian Queens Hippolyta and Penthesilea, to whom he gifted war belts, shields, and spears in their honor. He could definitely be considered the "dad of the year."

Eros

Eros is more commonly depicted and personified as a baby in modern representations, but his characterization in ancient Greek works of art is far more adult. He still has his signature wings, as well as his bow and arrow, but the Eros of mythology is considered to be a beautiful youth, beardless but definitely on the cusp of manhood, probably around the age of seventeen.

Some say the male god of love was the product of Aphrodite and Ares, while other myths place his origin story at the beginning of time. In this narrative, Eros is considered to be one of the original primordial beings, which would make him a sibling of Pontus, Gaia, and Erebus. They say that love makes the world go round, and it seems as if Eros has been present since the dawn of time. Since the gods and goddesses, as well as the Titans, were pursuing each other romantically since day one, it is safe to say that Eros is probably much older than the Olympians.

He is one of the more mischievous gods, as he would make mortals and immortals fall in love by shooting them with his magic love arrows. He did this mainly for sport. In fact, he was one of the more unpredictable and uncontrollable gods. Even mighty Zeus could not control the little love deviant.

For being one of the oldest forces of love in the world, Eros did not take that many lovers himself. The love story of Eros and Psyche is one of the most popularized in the world today. As the story goes, Psyche was a beautiful princess from the mortal world, the daughter of some unnamed Greek king. She was so beautiful that the men of Greece turned away from the temples of the goddess of love to worship the lovely princess. New words needed to be invented to describe the exquisite intricacies of her beauty.

Aphrodite, being Aphrodite and prone to a high degree of jealousy, did not take kindly to this. She sought to fix her Psyche problem by marrying her to the most hideous man in the world. Naturally, to make mortals magically fall in love, one would need the assistance of Eros and his magic love arrows. So, Eros flew off to do his duty for Aphrodite. However, when he came upon the princess, he was smitten by her beauty and was unable to fulfill his task. Instead, he whisked Psyche away to a secret palace, hidden far away from the sight of Aphrodite.

Psyche Revived by Cupid's Kiss by Antonio Canova, 1787–1793. This work is based on a story from The Golden Ass.
Kimberly Vardeman from Lubbock, TX, USA, CC BY 2.0 via Wikimedia Commons; https://commons.wikimedia.org/wiki/File:Psyche_revived_by_cupid%27s_kiss,_Paris_2_October_2011_002.jpg

He visited her there night after night, and they lay together in sweet bliss just before the morning came. He would always leave her before the first light of day could reveal his identity. He kept this secret from her, asking that she never look upon his form and to give him her absolute trust that he was her love. Psyche and Eros were very much in love, and she was his completely, giving herself to him night after night while blindly trusting him.

Their happiness was not to last, though. Psyche's sister was jealous of her sister's contentment. She wanted to see her joy ruined, so she told Psyche that her secret love was a horrid monster, unable to be looked upon by mortal eyes.

At first, Psyche paid no mind to her sister's toxic words, but as time passed, her doubt grew stronger. Eventually, it got to be too much, and one night, she took an oil lamp and gazed at her secret love. Much to her surprise, there laid the most beautiful and desired of all the gods. Just as she was about to retreat, a drop of oil from her lamp fell and landed on his shoulder. Eros woke up in a startled daze and fled from Psyche. The poor girl was distraught. Her lack of trust had caused Eros's love and trust to flee as well. Still, she could not give him up, so she searched all of Greece for a trace of her love.

Unluckily, Psyche came upon the temple palace of Aphrodite, whose hatred and jealousy for Psyche still burned bright within her, perhaps even more so for breaking the heart of her favorite vassal. She forced the poor girl to complete a series of backbreaking and humiliating tasks. Eros, who was still deeply in love with Psyche, hid from her sight and assisted in each task so that she would be victorious and gain the favor of the goddess of love. Over time, Aphrodite came to like the girl and reunited her with Eros, who made her his wife, an immortal. She became the goddess of the soul. He bestowed upon her a pair of butterfly wings so that she would always be with him in the heavens, and they had a child named Hedone together, who was the goddess of sensual pleasure.

Hephaestus

Hephaestus's start in life was not bright or cheerful. When he was pulled from his mother, Hera, the goddess of motherhood and childbirth, she took one look at his sickly form and tossed him from the great height of Mt. Olympus. His upper body was perfectly healthy, but his legs did not seem to develop properly, and there was no room on Olympus for imperfection, at least in Hera's mind.

Hephaestus did not die when he fell to the earth, though. He was rescued by the sea goddess Thetis and her sisters and taken to their underwater grotto, where they raised him in secret, unbeknownst to his hateful mother, who presumed him to be dead. Over the years, Hephaestus's strength grew. While his lower body would always remain disabled, he built up his upper body. This strength made him the finest craftsman and metalworker in the world. He made beautiful necklaces and brooches for Thetis and her sisters, and they loved him dearly.

One day, when Thetis was sunning herself on the beach, Hera looked down from her perch in the sky and saw the beautiful jewelry adorning Thetis. She demanded that the goddess inform her where she had acquired such exquisite pieces. Thetis revealed that it was her very own abandoned son. Hera was instantly filled with regret and begged Hephaestus to return to Mt. Olympus. She offered to build him the most impressive and well-equipped workshop in all the world and give him the beautiful Aphrodite as his wife. Hephaestus accepted and returned to Olympus a prodigy. His work was the pride and beauty of Olympus. He made weapons, armor, and totems for all the gods and their children. He even made two golden women that he used to assist him in walking.

Hephaestus is also credited with being the creator of the first woman, Pandora (yes, that Pandora who unleashed all the evils onto the world), as a punishment for mankind. In the creation of mankind, Zeus was against providing man with the knowledge of fire. Prometheus, the creator of mankind, wanted more for his creations, so he stole away the secret of fire and gave it to humanity. Zeus was furious with Prometheus. He ordered the Titan to be chained to the side of a mountain in the underworld where a vulture would feast on his immortal and thus regenerating liver for all time. Who do you think made the chains that were strong enough to subdue a Titan? If you guessed Hephaestus, you would be right.

For added measure, Zeus evened the score by setting man's development back with the creation of the first woman. Legend has it that Hephaestus molded her from the clay of a riverbank, not unlike most creation myths surrounding humanity, whether those myths originated in North America or Jerusalem. He gave her bewitching features similar to that of the immortal goddesses and bestowed upon her a voice and a mind that sought to undo the spirit of man. In other words, women were the "Achilles' heel" of men.

Dionysus

The story of Greek mythology's resident god of partying and general merriment began with a high degree of death and heartbreak. Dionysus's mother, Semele, was killed while she was still pregnant. Hera saw her husband's love for the princess of Thebes and tricked Zeus into conjuring a lightning bolt that struck Semele in the chest, killing her instantly. Zeus had to act quickly if he was to save his unborn child. So, he removed the still growing fetus from Semele's womb and sewed Dionysus into his own thigh, carrying him to term. This was not the first or the last time Zeus birthed a child from his own body. Dionysus's sister Athena was born from the very skull of their father.

Hera's animosity toward Zeus's many wives and lovers could only be matched by the raw contempt she displayed toward his progeny. She continued to hunt Dionysus, who was successfully hidden for years by the satyr Silenus and his band of nymphs from Mount Nysa. It was during his time with Silenus that Dionysus first discovered the secrets of cultivating grapes for wine and taught mortals how to make the libation.

Eventually, Dionysus came to live with his aunt so he could be better protected from Hera. Semele's sister Ino and her husband Athamas welcomed Dionysus into their home. However, the joys of raising their nephew were not to last. Hera eventually found the child and his adoptive parents, and she drove Athamas to madness, causing him to murder his son and drive Ino and their other child to jump off a cliff to their deaths. (Some versions say Ino was the one to go mad.)

Needless to say, Dionysus was cast to the wind. The experience drove him mad, beginning his long history as the god of not only wine and festivities but also madness. Dionysus would do his fair share of damage to the mind of mortals throughout his tenure as an Olympian.

Before he earned his status in Olympus, he was hunted by not only immortals but also mankind. They did not respect the god of wine, and they tried to attack him and his divinity more than once. One of the main perpetrators to try such a maneuver was the king of Thebes. Dionysus retaliated by driving all of the king's daughters to madness, provoking them to rip apart their father limb from limb.

Eventually, Dionysus was welcomed back to Olympus by his father, having proved himself worthy with his ruthless yet carefree lifestyle. Dionysus adorned himself in skins and wore a wreath of vines around his head. The god of wine was constantly attended by his cult of satyrs and maenads, who were unmatched in their madness and cravings for wine, sex, hunting, and occasionally human flesh.

Dionysus himself had quite the insatiable sexual appetite and got hot for just about anything that moved. He would often get maidens and nymphs drunk and then proceeded to have his way with them. One of these rapes resulted in twins, the first of which was eaten out of sheer rage by the mother. Dionysus eventually settled down and married the princess Ariadne, who had been deserted on an abandoned island by Theseus and was later rescued by the god of wine.

Dionysus also had a few male lovers; in fact, that is where we see the more affectionate side of the god emerge. He was described as a beautiful youth and had many equally beautiful lovers. For instance, there was the young satyr Ampelos, who was killed while trying to mount a wild bull. He was added as a constellation amongst the stars by the mourning god. Ampelos became the constellation Vindemitor, the grape-picker.

Chapter 5: The Goddesses

Hera

Without a doubt, if jealousy, greed, and impulsivity had a human form, it would be the goddess Hera. She was the patron goddess of marriage, the sky, and women. She was the queen of the Olympians and a royal pain in the behind—in particular, a pain in her husband's behind. As you have probably gathered thus far, Hera could not abide the numerous affairs of her brother-husband Zeus.

While Hera was meant to be the protector of women, she had no qualms harming women she despised, usually those who fell victim to Zeus's unfaithful nature. The list of her victims is endless. Oftentimes, Zeus would transform his lovers into wild animals to save them from the wrath of his queen, but Hera was just as wily as her husband and hunted these women in both human and animal forms. In alphabetical order, these were Aegina, Elara, Iynx, Semele, and Othreis.

What's interesting is that despite her immense jealousy, she never had any affairs of her own. Incredibly enough, she stayed loyal to Zeus throughout their entire marriage. In the early years of their courtship, they were truly one of the happiest couples in the world. Their wedding was such a joyous affair that it lasted for two hundred years.

The goddess was very judgmental and often the first of the Olympians to deal out punishments to mortals and immortals alike. When Aphrodite was jumping around in one too many beds, including that of Dionysus, Adonis, and Zeus, Hera cursed her pregnancy (the identity of the father remains unknown since many different versions of the myth exist). She laid her hands on Aphrodite's swollen belly and cursed her child to be born with a bulbous form and an overly large penis. At first, Aphrodite was repulsed by her child, but it all turned out well in the end. The child, Priapus, made his gargantuan appendages work to his advantage, and he became the god of vegetable gardens, with his giant member linked to the fertility and large growth of crops. So, in the end, Hera's actions had a positive outcome, even if the intent was malicious.

She did have a few favorite heroes, with the main being Herakles, who started out as the enemy of the goddess but soon won her friendship and admiration through his heroic deeds. She actively aided in the success of Jason and the Argonauts' quest for the golden fleece. In many ways, Hera's moral compass for justice was right on target. Although this side of Hera wasn't seen as often as her vengeful side, she had a fervor for the pursuit of justice that matched her beauty. This goddess didn't back down for anything or anyone.

The Greek king of the Lapiths, Ixion, once dared to cross the goddess by attempting to rape her. She escaped the grasp of King Ixion and took the matter to her lord and husband, Zeus. Zeus would not convict this man without concrete proof of his crimes, so Zeus sought to entrap Ixion and crafted a cloud from the heavens to take the shape of Hera. Ixion overtook the cloud and bragged that he had his way with the goddess, which, whether he had or had not, was not a great thing to boast about since Zeus would undoubtedly hear. Zeus then apprehended him and tied him to an ever-turning wheel in the sky.

Demeter

Demeter was the goddess of agriculture and, more specifically, grains. She is often depicted as an older woman bearing bundles of wheat with a golden crown laid upon her head. She sustained the earth with her bounty, and for this reason, she wielded a tremendous amount of power and influence amongst the Olympians. When her anger flared, she didn't hesitate to cause a famine. In fact, her main weapon of punishment was to cause mortals to feel immense hunger. This was her sentence for Erysichthon, who dared to incite the anger of Demeter by cutting down the goddess's holy grove.

Like a true mother, Demeter showed a great deal of favor and care to all mankind. She took many demi-gods under her wing whom she found to be worthy of her patronage. One of these heroes was Triptolemos. He was an Eleusinian prince who hosted the goddess Demeter most graciously when her daughter Persephone went missing, during which time she went scouring the earth for nine days, imbibing no nectar or ambrosia. Triptolemos offered Demeter comforting words, which encouraged her to pursue her search for her most beloved child. As a reward for his heart and hospitality, Demeter taught him the ways of cultivating grain and made him a herald unto man so that he could deliver the secrets of the earth to every household. This was an immense honor and responsibility; the Titans and other gods had not even been afforded such trust and confidence. She even gifted a golden-winged chariot to Triptolemos so that he could carry her gifts across the world with great ease.

Demeter had a fair number of lovers in her lifetime but far less than that of her brothers and other goddesses. She took a romantic liking to mortals more for who they were as people rather than their legendary good looks or meager deeds. The only immortal consensual lover she took was her brother Zeus, which resulted in the birth of the goddess and queen of the underworld, Persephone.

Although Hera was Zeus's true wife, he always carried a deep love for his sister Demeter and was known to strike down her lovers with extreme jealousy and prejudice. This is what befell poor Iasion, a prince of the island of Crete. He slept with the goddess in a plowed field and was killed almost instantly by Zeus's thunderbolt. However, Zeus did not get there fast enough, and Iasion impregnated Demeter with twin sons, Plutus and Philomelos.

There indeed was something about Demeter because almost all of her brothers were either interested in sleeping with her or marrying her offspring. Poseidon, true to his nature, even raped his own sister. Legend has it that Poseidon pursued Demeter with relentless "passion" while she was searching for Persephone. This moment was one of the lowest and most vulnerable in the goddess's history. In an attempt to escape Poseidon's grasp, Demeter transformed herself into a mare and started to graze in an open field. Poseidon was not so easily fooled and came up from behind her as a stallion and took her forcefully. From this union, the immortal horse Arion was born. He would become the mount for many prominent heroes, including Oncius and Herakles.

Hestia

Hestia was the firstborn child of Cronos and Rhea; therefore, she was the first to be swallowed and the last to be regurgitated. Without a doubt, Hestia seemed to be the most inherently talented and assured out of all her siblings. The other original Olympians and, for that matter, the later generations as well, could all be insecure, jealous, and dependent on one another and mortals for assurance of their divinity. Hestia never behaved in such a manner, and from the start, she seemed to possess a wisdom and self-awareness uncommon amongst the gods and even the Titans. Her physical appearance is thought to be that of an older woman. She is typically veiled and holds a kettle.

There were several virgin goddesses amongst the Olympians, but the first was Hestia, who was the goddess of the hearth and the home. She provided light during the night in every home across Greece. The warmth that stems from her is not only a physical light but also an emotional light. Hestia's fire was what cooked the meals of the world and thus brought humanity together. Meals and drinking were some of Greece's largest camaraderie activities, so naturally, the goddess of the hearth was very highly venerated among the various cults of Greece.

The link between Hestia and fire is the concept of transformation. Symbols and substances were consumed and then transformed in the fire. This meant that some of the sacrifices dedicated to the gods by fire were dedicated in honor of Hestia. Without her, Greek worship would have been meaningless, regardless of whether the worship was directed toward the other gods and goddesses. "Among mortal men she was the chief of the goddesses."[52]

Although the myths surrounding the goddess are few, Hestia has quite a few hymns dedicated in her honor. She was hailed as one of the most respected and honored of the Olympians, with her vow of chastity protected and enforced by the king of the gods himself. Even Poseidon opted for a more dignified approach in his pursuance of Hestia. Instead of heading right for his rapist tendencies, he asked Zeus for her hand in marriage. He was, of course, denied, and Hestia was given watch over the divine hearth in Olympus.

There was one other incident in the goddess's romantic history where her chastity was almost overtaken. The fair Titan and mother to the Olympians, Rhea, was hosting a banquet for all the illustrious and divine immortals of the world. Gods, nymphs, satyrs, and spirits alike attended her festival, which had no shortage of wine. Fair Hestia laid her head down on the ground for a short spell in order to rest. In her innocence, she never suspected she was being watched by another. Priapus (if you can recall, he was the god of vegetable gardens with the enormous appendage) saw the figure of a female resting on the ground. Whether he knew it was the goddess or some random woodland nymph is still debated. However, he approached her with lust and sought to force himself upon her. Just as he was about to pounce, a donkey that was tied to a tree nearby let out a giant bray, startling the goddess awake. She screamed at the sight of Priapus's huge member, thus alerting the party guests to the situation. Priapus fled before they all arrived, but his name carried great shame from that day forward. This was likely because Hestia was highly revered by gods and mortals alike.

Athena

Athena can be best thought of as the woman prepared for any and all situations. She was the patron goddess of wisdom, arts and crafts, battle strategy, weaving, and pottery, and she was the patron goddess of heroes. Her identification with war is wholly different from that of her brother Ares. Athena saw war as a time for men to

---

[52] Homeric Hymn 5 to Aphrodite 18 ff (trans. Evelyn-White) (Greek epic circa 7th–4th BCE).

show that their wits could win the day, not brawn and muscle. The goddess could hold her own in battle and once engaged in a fight with the god of war, Ares, in which she triumphed. For this reason, the heroes who she took under her wing usually were the brightest, smartest, and most curious among men. Think of Odysseus, who was arguably her favorite man among mortals.

She was also the most credited Olympian when it came to teaching a variety of skills to the human race. She even beat out her uncle Poseidon for the patronage of Athens, the most innovative and progressive Greek *polis*. As the legend goes, the gods entered into a competition of gifts to see who could provide the most well-liked gift to the people of Athens. Poseidon provided the people with a whole sea, where they could fish and ride the waves to find new islands. Athena decided to plant an olive tree for the people. The gods and men judged that Athena was the victor, and ever since then, the tree of life, the olive tree, has grown strong on the Acropolis. Some even say that when the Persians conquered Athens, they laid waste Athena's tree. The next day, the tree grew back, doubling its height in the process.

There are very few moments in Greek mythology in which Athena does not succeed in her endeavors. Ever since her birth, she was ready for action, and it was the very circumstances surrounding her birth that made her one of the most famous and beloved of all the gods and goddesses of Mt. Olympus.

Athena's mother was the immortal Titan Metis, the patron divine being of kingly wisdom and council. She was the first official wife of Zeus, and as such, Zeus found her to be his most trusted confidant and right-hand woman in all matters. She was clever—maybe too clever. Zeus was indeed his father's son and feared that Metis or her offspring might hold more favor with the gods and humanity and, therefore, usurp his throne one day. Heeding the advice of Gaia, Zeus devoured his wife so that her powers of determining between good and evil with ease would seep into his own consciousness.

However, the great Zeus did not know that Metis was with child. At the end of Athena's gestation period, Zeus developed a horrible splitting headache. The pain was far greater than anything the god had ever experienced before. He was in so much pain that he called for Hephaestus and begged him to open his head up with his mighty ax so that whatever was in there might escape and provide him some relief. Hephaestus was reluctant, but he did as Zeus commanded. He swung his ax high and brought the blade crashing down on Zeus's skull. Out sprang Athena, fully armed with a spear, shield, and helmet. There were no first steps or childhood for Athena; she was born grown. She instantly had a deep sense of autonomy, her father's relentless spirit, and her mother's views on right and wrong.

Pottery depicting the birth of Athena from Zeus's forehead, c. 570–560 BCE.
https://commons.wikimedia.org/wiki/File:Exaleiptron_birth_Athena_Louvre_CA616_n2.jpg

Athena was far too busy in her self-improvement and that of humanity to develop any kind of sexual desire for mankind. She viewed them as her students, not her playthings, but she also did not seek the attention of any immortal either. She was, of course, a beautiful, stately goddess, but she found the whole idea of coitus to be revolting. One of the most well-known myths about her repulsion to sex is the transformation of Medusa. Medusa, the

Gorgon from the story of Perseus, was once a beautiful maiden (she is also characterized as a nymph in some versions). She came from the island of Kisthene, which was somewhere in the Red Sea. She was so lovely that she tempted the god Poseidon, and it is no surprise that the god of the roaring seas came to overtake her.

The story goes that Medusa attempted to hide in the shrine of the virgin goddess but was unsuccessful. Poseidon followed her there and took her on the hard marble floor. The goddess tried to cover her eyes with her shield, but she was unable to remove herself from their presence. While some would think the goddess would feel sympathy and heartache for the maiden, her initial reaction was nothing but disgust. Athena knew what to do to fix this issue of Medusa's beauty. She transformed her into a hideously scaled monster, with snakes for hair and a gaze that would turn any living thing of flesh and blood to stone. This snake became one of Athena's primary symbols and can be seen decorating her armor.

Aphrodite

Aphrodite was the goddess of love and beauty, the famed Venus de Milo, an inspiration for a million and one women throughout history, and, without a doubt, one of the most villainous of all the goddesses. The beauty of Aphrodite was inhuman (literally since she was birthed from the sea foam where the testicles of Uranus had been discarded). In most classical Greek art renderings and pottery, she is shown without clothing, making her the ultimate symbol of body positivity in Greek and Roman culture. The Greeks marveled at the beauty of the human form every chance they got, which was one of the main reasons that the ancient Greek Olympics were held entirely in the nude.

Naturally, the goddess of love and beauty was unmatched in charms and her looks, right? Wrong! Although Aphrodite was considered to be the fairest amongst all the goddesses and mortals alike, her personality was not; at times, she was the antithesis of sexuality, self-sufficiency, and confidence. No one likes a jealous partner. And like Hera, Aphrodite had enough jealousy and insecurity to last her several immortal lifespans. She was quick to punish those who questioned her beauty or matchmaking abilities. For this reason, she had a great dislike of the virgin goddesses— Athena, Artemis, and Hestia. She was deeply hurt that these women found her position on Olympus to be a waste of time.

Although Aphrodite was a very vain goddess, she had a soft spot for men and women desperate for love. Everyone deserves companionship, but for some, it is harder to find. One of the more positive myths surrounding Aphrodite was her favor and patronage of the king of Kypros (Cyprus), Pygmalion. The king had taken his throne as a celibate man, and no matter how hard he or his court tried, they could not seem to arrange a marriage. The king was a gentle soul that any woman would be fortunate enough to call her own, but alas, he remained single and in a state of perpetual loneliness. That is until the goddess took pity upon him. She had heard the prayers of Pygmalion and sought to find him a match at the first opportunity.

She could have sent her son Eros to bewitch one of the many ladies of the kingdom to love the king, but she didn't feel the need to resort to such an action. The king would provide his own template for the ideal lover in the form of an ivory statue. This lonely king had quite the artistic nature and had worked for many moons on a statue of incomparable beauty, one filled with curves. He laid with this statue every night, caressing her as if she were a real woman. This may sound a little off and strange, but one shouldn't be so quick to judge, considering all the modern methods humans use to get aroused these days.

Then came the festival of Aphrodite, in which many bulls were sacrificed in honor of the goddess. Her spirit was present at each and every one of these banquets. When the king stepped forward to make his offering, he prayed to the goddess of love and asked her to send him a woman likened to that of his beloved marble lady. Aphrodite heard the king's meaningful and sincere prayers, and she was all too happy to oblige.

Instead of sending a woman born of flesh and blood, the goddess did one better. Pygmalion returned to his bed that night to lay once more with the marble woman. As he was resting his head upon her bare bosom, he noticed that her chest seemed to rise and fall. The king quickly brushed the thought aside, knowing that such things were impossible. Yet the breathing continued, and when he went to take her hand, he felt the warmth and softness of human skin. He raised his head, and his eyes met that of a maiden's, young and bashful. The king lay with his ideal love the whole night, giving thanks to the goddess for finally bringing him his perfect love and ultimate bliss.

Artemis

The last of the virgin goddesses was Artemis. She was seen as forever young, beautiful, and chaste. She was the huntress of the night, the lady of the moon, the twin sister of Apollo, and the patron goddess of young girls. Artemis commanded the entire respect of Olympus and the mortal world. Without a doubt, she was one of her father's favorite daughters; anything Artemis asked for, she received. Upon her request, Zeus gifted two golden bows and arrows to her and her brother so that they might hunt together. He also fulfilled many other divine requests from his young daughter, such as making her goddess of the dawn and the crop-killing frost, as well as making the stormy mountains her hunting domain.

From day one, her precocious nature was evident when shortly after her own birth, she assisted her mother, Leto, in delivering Apollo. This made her the goddess of childbirth. She worked closely with Hera, who was the patron mother goddess of women and child labor. While she was the protector of young children, Artemis was also tasked with bringing sudden death and disease to young female infants. Her twin brother Apollo had the same charge but for all the male babies of Greece.

Unlike the other virgin goddesses, who were usually depicted as mature women, Artemis never seemed to age past what Vladimir Nabokov (the writer of *Lolita*) would have termed a "nymphette." She was seen as a young girl just on the cusp of womanhood but still young enough to be considered a sexual innocent. She is rarely ever seen without her crescent moon crown, and she is typically flanked by a faun or buck. She is also always seen with her bow and quiver. Artemis is the natural world personified. She was both nurturing and cruel, wild yet orderly, and she was always quick to provide for others when she felt that they were deserving.

Artemis, like her sister Athena, had very little fear of confrontation and battle. For instance, she and her brother Apollo slew the giant Python that had been sent by Hera to torment their mother, Leto. In defense of her virginity, she was unparalleled in her ruthlessness. Actaeon, a young prince of Thebes, once came upon the goddess bathing and dared to steal a peek at her naked form. The goddess felt so violated and disrespected that she transformed the young prince into a stag and set his own dogs on him. They ripped him voraciously limb from limb. She exacted similar punishments on any man who dared violate her chastity, even if it was only with their eyes.

Artemis rarely kept company with the other gods and goddesses of Olympus, save for her brother. Most of the time, she preferred to keep to the company of wild animals and a select entourage of maiden attendants she protected with the fervor of a mother bear. She loved them, and they loved her. When one of them fell from grace and succumbed to the temptations of sex, Artemis was quick to exact punishment, although these punishments were far more merciful than other pettier immortals. It has been told that one of her maidens, Callisto, fell prey to the charms of Zeus and became pregnant with his child. When Artemis discovered that her own father had deflowered one of her maidens, she went ballistic. In her rage, she transformed Callisto into a large bear and sent her away into the wilderness to deliver her child. Later, when the goddess took her bow to go hunting, she came upon the bear. She did not recognize that it was Callisto, and she fired her weapon. Callisto was killed instantly. When Artemis discovered the truth, she was filled with unbearable remorse. So, she cast the figure of Callisto in her bear form into the stars to become the constellation of Ursa Major.

Persephone

It was said that Persephone was such a radiant beauty that all the gods of Olympus made Demeter offers for her hand in marriage, including Poseidon, Ares, and Apollo. Her mother would accept none of these offers, for her love for Persephone was too great to ever part with the sweet child. Persephone was also highly favored among her other chaste siblings, in particular Athena. The two half-sisters were raised together on the same island, and they would pick flowers together for hours on end.

The most famous myth surrounding Persephone is her abduction and rape by her husband/uncle Hades. He also fell instantly in love the moment he saw Persephone. The god of the underworld was a perpetually gloomy figure, so when Zeus saw his fondness for the girl, he gifted Persephone to Hades as his bride in order to ease his loneliness. Perhaps he felt guilty for his brother living in exile amongst the dark depths of the earth. However, Zeus knew that Demeter would not separate willingly from her daughter, and so he instructed Hades to abduct Persephone when she and Demeter least expected it.

The Rape of Proserpina by Gian Lorenzo Bernini, 1621–1622.
Gian Lorenzo Bernini, CC BY-SA 4.0 , via Wikimedia Commons;
https://commons.wikimedia.org/wiki/File:Rape_of_Prosepina_September_2015-3a.jpg

One day, when Persephone was gathering flowers in a field near her mother, Hades rode up from a dark crack in the earth. He snatched her up in his chariot and dragged her down to his kingdom. Demeter was furious and scoured the earth for her daughter. For nine days, the goddess wandered the earth, enduring all sorts of mistreatment at the hands of the other gods. She didn't eat or drink any nectar or ambrosia for this entire period either. When she discovered that Persephone had been taken by her brother, she approached Zeus on Mt. Olympus and demanded the release of her daughter. Zeus would not oblige, so Demeter caused a famine and scourge on all the animals, forests, and fields.

Eventually, a bargain was made in order to save humanity so that they would not starve. Zeus commanded Hades to release Persephone back to Demeter, but her daughter could not leave. In the early days of Persephone's captivity, she would not eat or drink anything out of protest. She was eventually tricked into eating a few seeds from a pomegranate, the fruit of the dead. Once a soul had eaten the food of the dead, they could never depart the underworld.

The gods were able to meet halfway on this one. Persephone was permitted to emerge from the underworld for one season to spend with her mother. She would, however, be required to return to the underworld once her time was up. The time of year when Persephone returned to the land of the living was when the first light and vegetation of spring break through the cold of winter and snow. When she was below the surface, the world darkened due to her mother's sadness and grief.

Chapter 6: The Gigantomachy

Let's take a step back now. The Olympians had cast down the reign of their father Cronos and imprisoned his siblings in tormenting punishments that would be carried out until the end of time. Although Gaia had called for the removal of her son from the throne of the world, she was not content with the punishments bestowed on the rest of her children. In fact, she scoffed at the greed of the Olympians. These children were no different or better than her son or her husband before him. These gods were not worthy to rule over the heavens and the earth. Their actions greatly offended Gaia, and she proclaimed in her frustration, "Have they forgotten to revere the earth, their mother?"

From her bitterness, she gave birth to a new race of children from the deepest underbellies of Tartarus, a race of giants, large, brooding, lawless, and lethal. Many sources describe the giants as being clad in shining armor, with beards and hair that brushed the floor. Their lower bodies were covered in scales, and they are sometimes referred to as the scaly sons of Gaia. They stood between nine and twelve cubits high, at least according to the Greek 5th-century epic composed by Nonnus of Panopolis. The height of one cubit is about forty-five centimeters or one and a half feet, making each giant thirteen feet or taller. These giants had grown in the deep womb of their mother, and they had been sired by Uranus himself. When Cronos had castrated his father and tossed his genitals into the sea, there were several other divine specimens that resulted from this action. There was Aphrodite, who grew from the testicles themselves; the Furies, goddesses of vengeance; and the giants (sometimes referred to as Gigantes). This specific generation of giants was known as the Thracian giants, so named for the location of their birth.

Gaia stirred up the giants to war by proclaiming that they needed to avenge her and the Titans by overthrowing Olympus. They needed to cast down Poseidon and put him in chains at the bottom of the sea and rip out Apollo's golden curls. Typhoeus, the great unclean serpent, could take control of Zeus's thunderbolt, and these beastly giants could claim the goddesses for themselves and jest about the rape of Athena, Artemis, and Aphrodite. The giants were crazed and enraged by the poisonous words of their mother, so much so that they already thought themselves the victors. They began to hurl stones and flaming oak trees at the gates of heaven and tormented mankind, attempting to provoke the Olympians to war. Little did they know they would be in for one of the greatest battles of their time.

Zeus sent out one of his most trusted messengers, Iris, and she convened a council of the immortals from every corner of the world in order to aid the gods in their battle. Even Hades and his queen, Persephone, emerged from their dark dwelling place to defend the existence of Olympus. When all the immortals had gathered, Zeus addressed them all with a war speech. The following excerpt is translated from Hesiod's *Theogony*.

"Deathless army, whose dwelling-place is, and must ever be, the sky, ye whom no adverse fortune can ever harm, mark ye how Earth with her new children conspires against our kingdom and undismayed has given birth to another brood? Wherefore, for all the sons she bore, let us give back to their mother as many dead; let her mourning last through the ages as she weeps by as many graves as she now has children."

The war is thought to have taken place on the plains of Phlegra, but some believe that it occurred in Thrace, which was the original birthplace of the giants. There is also a historical and cultural connection to be highlighted with this location. The Thracian tribes that existed north of Greece were considered to be barbaric in comparison to the sophisticated Greek civilization. Thus, these tribes' lawlessness is metaphorically attached to a race of vengeful and jealous abominations.

When the war kicked off, nature was drastically thrown off balance. Each time the gods were provoked, there was an equal and opposite reaction in the natural world. Rivers changed their direction, mountains collapsed, and huge swells flooded the land. In addition to this, the giants also armed themselves with the elements of their mother Gaia in order to defeat the great weapons of the gods. There was very little that could rival the craftsmanship of the gods' Cyclopes-forged weapons, but the giants were still coming for them, strapped for battle. They hurled great mountains and entire islands against the gods. It was nothing for them to grab an island right out of the sea and hurl it toward the heavens. The entirety of the earth was in disarray, but the battle still raged on, with each god and goddess contributing to a great and bloody victory. However, the most referenced Olympians in the Gigantomachy are Zeus, Athena, Ares, and Hera. There is also special attention paid to the mortal allies of the gods in this war, particularly the hero Herakles.

The entire atmosphere of the battlefield was clouded, as it was filled with the dust of ancient mountains and ash. There was so much disarray that it was hard to tell the difference between the two armies. Still, Ares was the first to charge into the fray, his shield and breastplate glistening red, his helmet sitting high on his brow. With a mighty swing of his sword, he cleaved into the giant Pelorus's groin, tearing him from stem to stern. He then proceeded to ride over the dismembered figure of the giant until his wheels slid slick across the earth with blood and ripped flesh.

Athena also showed no hesitation in joining the battle. True to her nature, she was able to defeat her enemies with very little energy and a great deal of finesse. During this battle, Athena wore the Gorgon Medusa's head on her own breastplate. She knew this would be enough to stop anything in her path. She stood steadfast, with her spear and shield calmly reserved at her side as she thrust her breast forward. The giant Pallas was the first to be turned to stone. Fear gripped him, and he exclaimed, "What is this icy feeling that grips my limbs?" He dropped to his knees with a groan, which was soon turned into rock. In frustration over the loss of two of his brothers, one of the giants heaved his brother's stone corpse at Athena. She stepped to the side with the same ease as before, and Pallas exploded on the mountain behind her.

There is another version of Pallas's death that is just as riveting. In a blind rage, he charged the goddess, careful to turn his eyes to the side as he did so to avert his gaze from the petrifying stare of the Gorgon. Athena was not fazed. With a swing of her shield, she deflected the blow of the giant while simultaneously bringing her sword from underneath. With one great swipe, she cleaved off the giant's right arm. With this deathly blow, he let his gaze slip and caught the eyes of Athena's breastplate. This finished the giant for good.

Athena could not be stopped in her defense of Olympus. Her most heroic act came when she managed to bury the giant Enceladus underneath Mt. Etna. To this day, Enceladus remains there, generating the volcanic lava that stirs within.

The remainder of the Olympians disposed of the remaining giants. Artemis, seeking to defend her honor, which had been offended by the blasphemies of the giants, flew into battle armed with her bow and arrow. She slew the giant Aigaion. Her brother and Herakles, one of the greatest heroes among men, slaughtered the giant Ephialtes. Apollo sent an arrow soaring into the giant's left eye while Herakles took the right. Hephaestus bested the giant Mimas by hurling hot molten iron into his face.

Poseidon pursued Polybotes throughout the seas and finally managed to run him down at the island of Nisyros. Poseidon broke a piece of the island and threw it at Polybotes. The chunk of the island came in contact with the giant's torso, crushing his organs and killing him instantly. Hermes, who was armed with Hades's helmet of invisibility, bested the giant Hippolytus in his wily fashion. He swung his mighty sword and, with a few blows, cleaved Hippolytus in half. Dionysus, armed only with his thyrsus (a staff or wand wrapped in vines with a fennel cone mounted on the top, typically used in Hellenistic cult rituals), killed the giant Eurytus.

An image on a cup dated to the late 5th century BCE that shows Poseidon attacking
Polybotes, with Gaia in the background.
Sailko, CC BY 3.0, via Wikimedia Commons;
https://commons.wikimedia.org/wiki/File:Aristophanes,_kylix_attica_con_gigantomachia,
410_ac_ca._02.JPG

Herakles also managed to destroy the only immortal among the
race of giants: Alkyoneus. As long as he remained within the
confines of his ancestral homeland, the plains of Pallene, he could
not be wounded or killed. He was considered to be the king of the
giants, along with his brother Porphyrion. Athena found a loophole
around Alkyoneus's immortality. After Herakles fired countless
arrows into the giant's torso, Athena advised him to drag
Alkyoneus beyond the border of the plains so that he could perish
in agony. Herakles also killed the giant Leon and skinned him in
order to fashion a protective cloak from his rock-hard exterior.
Athena did the same with the skin of her victim Pallas.

The Fates managed to take care of a few of the beastly giants and disposed of Agrios and Thoon, beating them to death with bronze maces. Even the race of immortal horses born of the wind and ocean immortals lent their hand in the battle to destroy the giants. Some, of course, sided with the usurpers. These were Xanthus and Balius, who would become the horses of the tragic hero Achilles.

It was these immortals and those born of mortal women who fought for Zeus in the war of the gods that received the title Olympian if it had not already been bestowed upon them. Of course, Zeus was the most impressive immortal in the Gigantomachy, as he brought an end to the most powerful of the giant race, Porphyrion. When Porphyrion rushed to rape Zeus's wife and queen Hera, the god of the skies hurled thunderbolt after thunderbolt directly at the giant, who was struck dead by these blows.

During the Gigantomachy, there was plenty of treachery against the king of the gods. Zeus had few allies but numerous enemies, even those he considered to be his friends. This included Olympos, a giant of reason who raised Zeus and taught him the order of law and the secrets of the earth. Olympos betrayed Zeus by supporting the giants in their revolt against the gods. This was devastating for Zeus, and in his anger, he struck down Olympos. He was so grieved over the death of his foster-father that he built Olympos a great tomb and named the resting place after himself so that people would think it was the grave of Zeus, causing it to always be visited and revered. The only giant to survive the war was Aristaeus. He was spirited away to the island of Sicily by Gaia and transformed into a dung beetle so that he could be hidden from the gods.

Chapter 7: Typhoeus

Typhoeus was a volcano demon. His weapons of choice were great smoldering volcanic rocks that he hurled at Olympus, and from his mouth poured the endless fires that were stored at the center of the earth. There is much debate around the parentage of the greatest of calamities and the father of all monsters. Some say he was the accursed child of Hera, born from her rage at Zeus for having given birth to Athena.

Hera, true to form, did not take her husband's newest "offense" lying down. She beset the help of Gaia and the great underworld to grant her a child that would not be Zeus's. She asked that Mother Gaia give her child the strength to defeat the king of the gods and be sent as a plague to torment mankind. Gaia was moved by her pleas and fulfilled her request. Queen Hera did not visit the bed of her husband for a full year, not that he seemed to care or notice (he had plenty of other prospects to keep him distracted). At the end of that year, she labored greatly to birth the monster of all monsters, and from then on, fear reigned throughout the world, even at the heights of Olympus.

Some other sources say he was born from the depths of Tartarus and that he was Gaia's last-ditch effort to overthrow the Olympians. Typhoeus took the shape of a collection of some of the most powerful and terrifying animals in nature. His lower half was that of a snake, with multiple long scaly bodies. These led into the torso of a man, but this was where Typhoeus's link to mankind or any kind of humanity ended. From his back sprouted two great wings that easily blew away the clouds and cleared trees from the land with one quick flap. His hair and beard hung heavy in large and stinking smoky mats. His eyes glowed red with the fire of the underworld, and his ears came to sharp points at the top, which were just as serrated and dangerous as his gnashing teeth.

The strength of Typhoeus was unrivaled in the world of Greek mythology. Even Zeus had his fears and doubts about his abilities to defeat Typhoeus. His head passed the great clouds, and his serpent tails gripped and warped the earth. His voice bellowed and growled from deep within him, as would a lion or a bull as they built up to attack. It was said that his war cry was the cry of all these beasts put together, along with a soft chorus of hisses.

Typhoeus is known as the father of all monsters. With the great serpent maiden Echidna, the pair managed to conceive some of the most feared and respected monsters among men and gods. These children feature prominently in other tales, often being cast in the standard role of "Greek hero's opponent" or, better yet, "creature to be slain in order to prove one's worth to a bunch of whiny immortals." Oftentimes, these monsters never instigated the fight. However, the children of Typhoeus and Echidna also birthed some monster babies that caused serious drama. So, villainy was definitely a family affair in Greek mythology.

The first child that Echidna bore was Orthros, the hound of the giant Geryon. Orthros was a two-headed dog with a serpent tail. Orthros was tasked with guarding the red cattle of Geryon on the island of Erytheia. He was ferocious and dedicated to his mission. He was slain by the hero Herakles, who was sent to fetch one of these prized cattle as one of his twelve labors. In the process, Orthros's master was also slain. Not all of Typhoeus's children pursued evil day and night; some were just average monsters committed to the task with which they had been charged.

From Typhoeus's union with Echidna also emerged the most famous employee of Hades and the guardian of the gates of the underworld: Cerberus. This monster ate raw flesh and had three ferocious heads that swiveled and snapped in every direction. He prevented souls from escaping their fate in the dark depths of the earth. However, he could be bested with teamwork. Just like

Orthros, Herakles was also charged with the capture of Cerberus as one of his twelve labors. He was successful only with the help of the queen of the underworld, Persephone, and the bright-eyed Athena. It was an inside job with the logistics of the smartest strategist on Olympus, possibly the world.

Their third child, the Hydra, was born of the great serpent but nourished at the breast of Queen Hera. The milk of the goddess fueled a monstrous and highly formidable beast that stalked the swamps of Lerna. Best described as a "drakonian serpent" by Stephen of Byzantium, the Hydra had a very special regenerative feature to its body, making the monster hard to wound and kill. The beast had nine heads, with eight mortal ones and one immortal, which was the head that rested in the middle. Every time it lost a head, one grew in its place. This was a skill discovered by (you guessed it) none other than Herakles.

Typhoeus was also the father of the Chimera, a fire-breathing monster with three different animal heads. The middle head was a lion, the right one was a dragon or serpent, and the left head was a goat. All these heads were attached to the body of a lion and finished with the classic Greek mythology monster tail, which took the form of a snake. It also had a goat's udder located underneath its rear end. The Chimera would become the mother of other famous monsters, such as the Sphinx and the Nemean lion.

The emergence of Typhoeus from the underbelly of the earth was a clear sign of attack. Zeus and the rest of the gods knew that this new beast would eventually show up at the gates of Olympus. The Olympians fled to Egypt and transformed into animals in order to hide from Typhoeus. He was so ferocious and blood-crazed that the gods feared for their immortal souls. Well, all of them but Zeus, who sought to act first before Typhoeus struck with his fury. Zeus knew that if the monster began developing his raging momentum that he would not be able to stop him.

Zeus called to Hephaestus and ordered the smith of the gods to forge thunderbolts of considerable strength and energy for him. Hephaestus took to this task day and night. Zeus then began his battle with the great Typhoeus, striking him with repeated thunderbolts, weakening his spirit and buying the king of the gods time to decide how to best defeat the beast for good. Zeus then hurled the strongest bolt deep into the sea, splitting open the earth and causing the hot fire from its core to melt away the layers until the gaping mouth of Tartarus was revealed. With a final blow, Zeus managed to back Typhoeus into the pit, and he sealed the crack in the ocean floor, locking the father of monsters away in the dark for all eternity.

According to tradition, Typhoeus still has some influence over the winds of the earth and particularly the seas. From his prison beneath the crusts of the planet, he is able to cause cataclysmic events, such as land swells and rogue waves that send sailors and fishermen to their deaths.

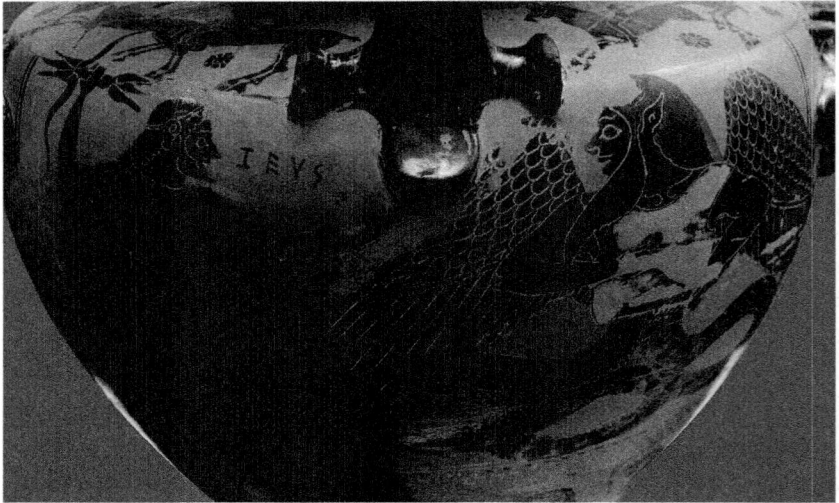

Greek pottery with a depiction of Zeus throwing one of his thunderbolts at Typhoeus, https://commons.wikimedia.org/wiki/File:Zeus_Typhon_Staatliche_Antikensammlungen _596.jpg

Chapter 8: The Creation of Man, the Flood, the New Generation, and Women as the Curse of Mankind

When the time came for the creation of mankind, the task was appointed to the Titan who had fought with the Olympians to defeat Cronos: Prometheus. While there were other Titans that stood with Zeus in the battle for the throne of the world, Prometheus was the most trusted of his generation. Zeus gave him a second-in-command, his brother Epimetheus, to complete the task of making all mortal creatures, human beings and animals alike. Epimetheus was the Titan of afterthought and excuses. He was the son of Iapetus and Clymene and the husband of the first woman ever created. Her storyline is very similar to the biblical Eve. This was none other than Pandora. In both these stories, women were blamed for releasing the negative aspects of creation onto humanity.

Epimetheus and Prometheus were by no means perfect with their own creations. In fact, they upset Zeus a great deal with how they chose to handle the creation of mortals. Both animals and men were fashioned from the same base: a little bit of clay and some water for shaping. This is not dissimilar to other creation myths. It mimics the biblical narrative, as well as a few indigenous legends. When it came to the individualization of men and animals, Epimetheus was not thinking clearly and gave all of the predatory physical qualities to the animals and beasts. He bestowed upon them long claws to defend themselves and to tear into flesh. He also gave them thick fur and scales to protect them from the elements. He made their sense of smell and taste heightened, and he made their eyes glow in the dark. These frightening little lights in the night would plague the dreams of men.

Essentially, men were left shivering and bald in the winds of the world. This simply would not do. Prometheus was willing to go to extreme lengths in order to preserve the dignity and overall happy existence of humanity. So, for men's comfort and pleasure, he stole the knowledge and prowess of the mechanical arts from Hephaestus, along with a piece of the divine flame from his workshop. He also took the knowledge of crafts and intellect from the goddess Athena. Prometheus gifted these to humanity so that they might warm their houses, cook their food, and work their metals. They could now fashion weapons and protect themselves from the beats that Epimetheus had so fervently armored.

When Zeus heard what Prometheus had done, he was enraged. It was not the fact that Prometheus had stolen intellectual and physical properties from not one but two Olympians, but it was what he did with those gifts. Zeus had a very tumultuous relationship with humanity. In fact, before Prometheus's draft of mankind, there were other kinds that came before. These beings were created by the Titans, mainly by the hands of Cronos and his brothers. This was the first generation of mankind known as the gold generation. These beings wanted for nothing and were considered to be perfect.

But they were maybe a little too perfect. The Greek theologian Hesiod considered these beings to be immortal. In fact, he believed that Cronos fashioned their body composition in a way that allowed them to age backward. When they were at the end of their days, these beings did not know pain or strife. They simply reverted to their original spirit form and roamed the earth as demons. When the reign of the Titans and Cronos came crashing down, so, too, came the end of the line of the golden generation because they would not worship the Olympian order. In all honesty, they probably considered themselves to be equal heirs of Cronos since they had been his most prized creations. They likely would have thought themselves better than his actual children. And why not? They were perfect beings, after all.

There were several generations of men before the generation created by Prometheus, Epimetheus. The next generation after the golden beings was aptly named the silver generation of humanity. These beings were the creations of Zeus, and to make sure history would remember his insecure daddy issues, Zeus made sure that this generation was physically and intellectually inferior to the Olympians. These humans were not only ugly and dumb but also bored. The only task that Zeus bestowed upon them was the worship of the gods and the planting of grain. In the end, the silver generation refused to pay the gods the homage they thought they deserved, and Zeus ended up terminating the entire race and sending them to Hades to become blessed spirits of the underworld. How blessed was this, though?

The generation that came after silver was naturally bronze. The third generation, the bronze generation, was even more lackluster than the silver generation. Zeus created these humans out of ash trees. They were warlike, exclusively carnivorous, and very capable smiths, building their houses and weapons solely out of bronze. Their chief characteristic was that they were prone to quick and emotional decision-making. Over time, this began to annoy Zeus. He hated his creation for the very thing he created them for, to be simplistic and subservient beings incapable of evolving. This generation was satisfactory to the gods until they weren't, as they would eventually cause wars and riots, being too stupid to see that they brought the most suffering upon themselves. Zeus thus brought about a great deluge and flooded the world in order to rid the land of these brainless human beings.

The only two survivors of the great flood were the northern Greek king of Thessaly, Deucalion, and his wife, Pyrrha. Deucalion was the son of the Titan Prometheus, and his father managed to warn him of Zeus's plans to flood the world. In the classical and biblical fashion, Deucalion constructed an ark in order to save himself and his wife from the rising waters. They were washed on top of Mount Parnassus. There, they fathered the Hellenic human race by casting stones behind them as they made their way up the mountain, as instructed by the god Hermes.

After that came the final generation of men, the men created by the hands of the Titans instead of the gods. The truth of the matter was that the Olympians (mostly Zeus) did not make good human beings. The best version of humanity that came before the final generation was undoubtedly the gold generation, as they did not pose any significant threat or challenge to the Titans. Only when the Titans were again involved with the creation of mankind did the blueprint finally stick.

In the ancient world, metals were symbolically attached to divine concepts. The "gold standard" is a really appropriate phrase to apply here, although it might be a bit little cliché. The metals used to describe the different generations of humanity become less and less filled with luster, value, and opulence as time marched on. They also became more rooted to the earth (common metals), but they were more capable of adaptation and preservation and could be directed in a variety of innovative ways. The final generation of humankind, made from clay and water, was the most grounded version. These men were different from the gods, thus making them safe from their divine and vengeful insecurities.

Yet, Zeus still hated them with all his heart. Cooperation was not one of his strong suits, and all of Zeus's wisdom seemed to have left his body the day his daughter Athena was born. When he had discovered that Prometheus had dared raise these humans up to the intellectual and creative level of the gods, he forced Hephaestus to create an "Achilles' heel" for the human race. He created a woman who would unleash unto humanity all the ills of the world.

Pandora, the first woman, was endowed with gifts from all the gods. She was beautiful, cunning, wise, and curious. This perfect specimen of femininity was gifted by Zeus to Epimetheus, who, true to form, cluelessly took Pandora for his wife, not bothering to consider Zeus's intentions. Prometheus smelled a whiff of Zeus's deceit, and he instructed his brother not to accept a wedding gift from the king of the gods. On the day of Pandora's wedding, Zeus handed her a large jar and instructed the couple to never try and open the vessel for a great power dwelled within that could escape through even the smallest crack.

Prometheus begged his brother and sister-in-law to return the gift, but they refused, not wanting to offend the great Zeus. Over time, the temptation grew too much, and Pandora could no longer resist not knowing what was in the jar. She lifted the top ever so slightly, and in the same instant, a thousand horrors poured forth, hardships that humanity had never known like toil, sickness, all manner of plagues, jealousy, lust, and greed. This was Zeus's plan all along, for humanity to be brought down a peg.

We will always be our own greatest champions and enemies. While human beings are capable of great love and creativity, we also have a natural predilection for self-sabotage.

Chapter 9: Herakles, the Greatest Hero of Them All

He was known as Hercules to the Romans but Herakles (or Heracles) to the Greeks. He was the most highly venerated and favored demi-god amongst the Olympians and mankind. This honor, however, came at a giant cost, for Herakles, without a doubt, has endured more suffering than any other Greek mortal. Even among the immortals and demi-gods of Greek mythology, his strife takes a higher rank.

The story of his chaotic life began the day he was born. He was thrust into a world of family conflict and jealousy. Herakles was the son of Zeus and Alcmene, who was the wife of Amphitryon and the granddaughter of Perseus. Yes, the same Perseus who defeated the Gorgon Medusa; he was also a demi-god sired by Zeus. So, in actuality, Zeus snuck into the bed of his great-great-grand-daughter disguised as her husband and impregnated her with Herakles. When the boy was born, his mother noticed that he showed an incredible degree of strength and physical stamina. This was the only reason he managed to survive his childhood.

Hera, true to form, was none too pleased with her incestuous cheating husband, and honestly, she had plenty of reasons to seek some sort of revenge. One of the saddest arcs of Hera's story as a wife is that she could never punish her husband for his cheating outside of torturing his many mistresses and their children. She loved her husband and didn't want to hurt him. In response to Herakles's birth, Hera sent two large snakes to strangle the infant in his crib. Herakles's strength saved him for the first time. He seized the serpents by their throats and squeezed until their movements ceased.

If Hera could not steal the infant's life, then she would take away his destiny. Before Herakles's birth, Zeus had prophesied that this son would inherit the Mycenean kingdom and become one of the greatest rulers the kingdom had ever seen. Hera managed to place another child as the king of Mycenae, the feeble and premature Eurystheus, the child of Alcmene and Amphitryon. Hera tricked Zeus out of this oath, and thus, Herakles was stripped of his rightful place on the throne.

After Herakles managed to survive Hera's first assassination attempt, the goddess went mad with frustration and decided, as a last resort, to go with one of her usual punishments. She caused the hero to lose his reason and sense of time; ultimately, she drove him mad. She didn't inflict this punishment until years later, when Herakles had reached manhood and was managing to gather some shred of happiness in his life.

After Herakles defeated the Minyans and saved the city of Thebes from being destroyed, he was given the daughter of King Creon, Megara, as a wife. The two were very much in love and had three children together. Although Herakles had found a place of repose, it was ripped away from him in one swift moment of madness. Although he had been able to cope with these fits for years after Hera had first infected his mind, his mental tenacity wore down. One day, he murdered his wife and children. When Herakles came back to his senses, his grief and heartbreak for the loss of not only his life partner but also his beloved children were indescribably unbearable. After some time, he decided to take action. He tracked down Apollo, the god of truth and healing, and he begged his half-brother to either heal him of his grief or strike him down.

Apollo, who knew what his wicked stepmother Hera had done, decided on a different course of action to aid Herakles in his guilt. He told Herakles that it was not his fault what had come to pass and that if he was up to the challenge, there was a way for Herakles to heal and atone for his actions. At the end of this journey, Herakles would attain immortality and no longer suffer from the loss of his wife and children. These actions would come to be known as the twelve labors of Herakles. They were feats of incredible physical and intellectual strength that would come to define and cement this hero's place in mythological history.

Apollo told Herakles to go to his cousin, Eurystheus, who was both his rival and the current king of Mycenae. He had to ask the king to bestow any tasks he could think of upon the demi-god. Herakles must then complete them to regain his honor. Apollo knew he was asking a lot from Herakles in this endeavor, as he would not only go through hell in order to repent but also suffer at the whim of a king whom Herakles considered to be an inferior man. As anyone who has ever worked under an incompetent leader or manager could tell you, this was indeed a challenge.

This Roman relief, dated to the 3rd century CE, depicts the twelve labors of Herakles. From left to right, you can see the Nemean lion, the Lernaean Hydra, the Erymanthian Boar, the Ceryneian Hind, the Stymphalian birds, the girdle of Hippolyta, the Augean stables, the Cretan Bull, and the mares of Diomedes.
https://commons.wikimedia.org/wiki/File:Twelve_Labours_Altemps_Inv8642.jpg

Eurystheus set Herakles twelve impossible tasks, in addition to nine minor tasks (these are often not included in many myths). These tasks had a high risk of death and no real hope for success. However, when dealing with the demi-god of demi-gods, the odds were pretty even. The first of these tasks was defeating the Nemean lion. Perhaps you remember it from before. It was the son of the great terror Typhoeus. The Nemean lion inhabited a cave in the mountain valley of Nemea in the kingdom of Argolis. The lion's hide was impervious to weapons, so in order to defeat this great animal, Herakles would have to go toe to toe with the lion in a contest of strength and will. In classic Greek fashion, Herakles wrested the lion entirely in the nude. (This mirrors the real-world tradition of ancient Olympic wrestling, which was completed entirely in the nude in the dirt, with each wrestler first rubbed down head to toe in oil. Just let that spectacle sit with you.) He managed to grasp the lion around its throat and strangled it to death. Afterward, Herakles skinned the Nemean lion and wore its hide as an impenetrable cloak. He also requested that the figure of his opponent be placed amongst the stars. So, Zeus honored the great lion by casting him as the constellation Leo. This is one of the hero's trademark symbols, and the skin of the great lion aided him in the remainder of his labors.

Next, Herakles traveled to the faraway swamps of Lerna, which was beside the kingdom of Argos. There dwelled the infamous Lernaean Hydra with her nine heads, the middle of which was immortal. This beast was personally reared by Hera, and as such, it was as if the goddess was using her champion against the hero. Hera was no fan of Herakles, after all. This was, without a doubt, the most dangerous foe Herakles had faced to date, and as such, he required the assistance of his good friend Iolaos to best the beast. For this reason, Eurystheus declared the labor unlawfully completed, which meant it would not be counted as a successful quest. Herakles would have to perform and successfully complete an additional labor.

Herakles managed to defeat the Hydra with the aid of Athena and Iolaos. The Hydra also came with its own reinforcements in the form of a giant crab. The goddess instructed Herakles on how to defeat the Hydra. She told him that every time he cut off a head, he would need to cauterize the wound to ensure that another could not grow in its place. So, Herakles fetched an oak branch off a tree nearby and lit it. With his bow and arrow, he shot the Hydra in the torso to subdue it long enough to cut off one head at a time with enough time to brand the wound. After he had repeated the process with each of the heads, there was only the immortal middle head left to defeat. This he crushed with a giant boulder, bringing the Hydra's reign of terror to an end.

After this grueling labor had been completed and denied authorization by the king of Mycenae, Herakles set out on his next task, one that would take nearly a full year to complete. Eurystheus had charged him with capturing the Ceryneian Hind, which is more commonly known as the Golden Stag of Arcadia. This animal was one of five sacred gilded deer gifted to the goddess Artemis by the nymph Taygete, who was one of the more essential and prominent figures of the natural Greek world. She was the daughter of Atlas and Pleione, and she inhabited the mountainous area of Laconia. With Zeus, she would give birth to the ancestors of the king of Sparta. The animals she gifted the goddess were of great importance to Artemis, and all five of them pulled her chariot.

Herakles finally managed to capture the animal by wounding it with an arrow in its flank. At one point, the stag tried to escape its captor, and in the ensuing struggle, Herakles accidentally tore off one of its golden antlers. This was tucked away for safekeeping, and Herakles attempted to haul the animal back to Mycenae on his shoulders. On route to the kingdom, the hero was stopped by Artemis and her brother Apollo. Artemis was furious that her sacred animal had been treated in such a manner, and she sought revenge on Herakles. After hours of arguing back and forth, Herakles managed to calm the goddess's anger, explaining the goal of his twelve labors. The goddess allowed him to haul the animal back to Mycenae just as long as he planned to release the stag after it had been presented to the king. The hard task for this specific labor was not only capturing the animal but also surviving the wrath of a goddess who didn't typically allow such infractions. She would have likely preferred to transform Herakles into a wild animal, one that would be ripped apart by her hunting hounds.

After he had regained his strength, Herakles set out on his next impossible task. This time, he traveled to the snowy mountain region of Erymanthia, where the Erymanthian Boar was known to reside. Occasionally, the great beast would come down from the mountains to hunt and terrorize the villages of mortal men in the farmlands of Psophis. So, Herakles traveled all the way up the snowy mountain to a cave where the boar was resting. The boar caught the scent of our hero and charged him as he was standing at the entrance of the cave. Herakles jumped swiftly out of the way, and the chase was on. He ran after the boar for a good couple of hours, finally netting the great beast. He managed to take the boar alive all the way to the chamber of Eurystheus.

Upon seeing the terror that was the great Erymanthian Boar, Eurystheus, true to his cowardly nature, dove headfirst into a giant pithos jar that was buried underneath the earth. Herakles took the opportunity to tease his cousin and acted like he would shove the live boar into the jar with the king, which caused Eurystheus to cower even further inside the vessel. This gained a chuckle from the rest of the people in the throne room. When the king finally emerged from his hiding place, he gave Herakles his next labor and made sure this one would pay the hero back for his torturous behavior.

Herakles was charged with cleaning the stables of King Augeas, who ruled over the Epeians of Elis in the western region of the Peloponnese. This was not the noblest of tasks, and the job needed to be completed in one day, which was practically impossible, considering that there was about a week's worth of oxen feces caked to the floor of the barn. True to form, Herakles gave the same dedication to the labor as the other ones for the right price. Some say he was to be paid in gold, while some sources indicate that Herakles had been promised a quarter of the oxen. The king was sure he would never have to reward Herakles because there was no earthly way that he could perform the task in one day. The king promised to pay the hero a fair wage for his assistance, and the two men shook on their deal.

With his great strength, Herakles managed to push giant boulders into the River Alpheus, diverting the stream onto the plain and into the barn. The strength of the water washed away the manure from all twenty oxen and swept away the dirt and impurities from the stalls. King Augeas couldn't believe the ease with which the hero completed the task and refused to pay Herakles what he was due. The hero was so angered that he swore destruction on the entire kingdom of Elis. When his labors were completed, he would come back and exact his terrible vengeance on the land and its people. His campaign was delayed for quite some time after the completion of this labor due to a lack of resources and an army, as well as a sudden illness that befell the hero. However, when Herakles regained his strength, he overtook Elis just as he had promised and crushed the skull of the king with his bare hands.

Before all that transpired, though, Herakles needed to continue with his labors for the good of his soul. The sixth labor was to rid the world of the Stymphalian birds that lived on Lake Stymphalia in Arcadia. These man-eating birds were initially discovered by Jason and the Argonauts, who found out the hard way their proclivity for the flesh of anything and everything. After that, these birds developed a taste for man meat and became the terror of Arcadia. In addition to their hardy appetite, the birds could also shoot razor-sharp feathers from their wings that sliced through the air like arrows. The parentage of the birds is hotly debated, but one thing the ancient scholars all agreed upon is that these birds were raised for some period of time by the god of war, Ares. As such, the god probably used the giant raptors in one or all of his many battles, although they are never named directly.

Herakles was not fazed one bit by what were surely some terrifying birds. He drew them out from their hiding places in the thick bushes and vines that ran along the eastern side of the lake by creating loud noises by casting large stones against one another. As each bird flew to attack him, he shot them out of the sky with his arrows. Now you may ask yourself, how come no one ever succeeded in killing the birds this way before? The propulsion of Herakles's arrows and the swing of his sword were mightier than most men. When he shot an arrow from his bow, the strength was almost akin to the shot from Zeus's lightning bolt. Herakles's strength made him closer to the gods than humans.

The seventh labor of Herakles features perhaps one of the most famous mythical animals in Greek legends: the Cretan Bull. This bull fathered the Minotaur with the queen of Crete, who had seen the beauty of the animal and couldn't help but be overcome by unimaginable lust. Bestiality was not common in ancient Greece, so this act would have been very disturbing to the average Greek.

The Cretan Bull was said to be born of the sea as a gift to mankind by the god Poseidon, and it was to be sacrificed in his honor. However, when the king of Crete saw the beauty of the animal, he could not offer it in sacrifice. Instead, he turned the bull out to pasture and gave another in homage to the god of the sea. Naturally, this was not a good idea, and Poseidon cursed the king, saying that the bull would be the ruin of him. He drove the creature mad to the point where it pursued the queen (who herself had been driven mad with longing for the bull, most likely by Poseidon as an act of revenge) and continuously terrorized the people.

Herakles now needed to capture the animal and take it all the way back to Mycenae to present to the king. He succeeded in his task and afterward set the creature free to return to its home island. Why he freed the bull and the boar after killing many of the other animals and creatures involved in his labors cannot be said. However, it would seem that the Cretan Bull was a god in its own right; it was certainly on the same divine level as Herakles since it was a child of one of the big three gods—the brothers Zeus, Poseidon, and Hades. Perhaps Herakles respected the bull far too much to put an end to his life. It was not until the hero Theseus that the days of the Cretan Bull came to an end, and his likeness was placed among the constellations as the astrological symbol Taurus.

Herakles's eighth labor was the most devastating to his soul. After he had released the Cretan Bull, Eurystheus issued a more dangerous task for Herakles to complete, something that would test his constitution as a demi-god. Herakles had faced off against many evil creatures during his labors, even creatures that hungered for human flesh, but such was their way as natural predators. In his eighth labor, Herakles would encounter something far more sinister: a human being who fed the flesh of other human beings to his animals.

The king of Thrace, the terrible son of Ares and Cyrene, was Diomedes. He fed his horse a diet of human flesh, which turned the poor animals away from their natural gentle inclinations, turning them into beasts unrecognizable as horses with unnatural aggression. In the dead of night, Herakles, with a few very brave volunteers, set off to kill the guards to the king's stables, after which he captured the horses and placed them on a ship that was waiting at the coast. With the animals successfully captured, Herakles dismissed the volunteers to sail back home, leaving the horses under the charge of his squire and long-time friend Abderus, a son of Hermes.

While Herakles was in pursuit of Diomedes, Abderus was attacked and eaten by the mares. Diomedes had done his work well; the horses were uncontrollable, even for a demi-god and experienced warrior like Abderus. After Diomedes had been captured, Herakles returned to the ship, where he discovered the remains that were once his best friend. In anger, he found the king and fed him alive to his horses. This seemed to quell the horses' insatiable appetite for man flesh. Herakles hauled the steeds back to Mycenae and presented them to the king, who once again scoffed at Herakles's efforts. Our hero was too devastated over the loss of Abderus to respond.

At this point, Herakles was tired of fighting. For the ninth labor, he sought every sort of road possible to peacefully achieve his quest. Eurystheus next asked him to bring him the belt of Hippolyta. She was the queen of the Amazons and one of the greatest warriors in Greece. She certainly had the most feared cavalry. Amazon warriors were known for charging into battle on horses and mowing their opponents down. These were no ordinary warriors Herakles was up against, and if possible, he wanted to avoid a fight.

When he arrived on the shores of the Amazons' island with his company of warriors (just in case), Hippolyta came down to the beach with her entourage of fighters. She inquired why one of the most legendary heroes in all of Greece had rowed all the way to her shores. Herakles informed her of his request. He knew the weight of what he was asking of Queen Hippolyta. The belt had been gifted to her by Ares, and as such, it was irreplaceable.

Surprisingly, Hippolyta was more than willing to hand over the belt in order for Herakles to complete his tasks. It is unknown why the queen showed such selfless generosity, but perhaps she had heard tell of the hero's labors and pitied him for having to suffer such an ordeal. Hera, however, suspected ill of Herakles and his company and decided to start a fight, just to be safe. She proceeded to go from Amazon to Amazon, whispering to their inner conscience that Herakles was there to kidnap the queen. The Amazons, having all had this same collective thought, suited up for battle, mounted their horses, and charged down to the beach. Seeing the entire army coming his way, Herakles ordered his men to slay the queen's warriors. He shoved his sword into the queen's chest and ripped the belt from her body. He made a quick getaway before the army reached the shore, making off with a belt that he had sought to acquire peacefully but did so in blood due to another goddess's insecurities. He took the blood-stained belt back to Eurystheus and laid it before the king's feet. Eurystheus then gave Herakles his next task.

On the island of Erytheia in the westernmost known reaches of the earth, somewhere near Iberia, lived a giant who went by the name of Geryon. He was a peaceful enough giant, despite his very intimidating presence. He was known for his three torsos and four sets of wings. He was the son of two great forces of nature, Callirhoe and Chrysaor. His mother, Callirhoe, was a rain nymph from his native Erytheia, and his father, Chrysaor, was a giant, the son of Medusa and the twin brother of Pegasus. Geryon was definitely one of the strongest contenders that our hero had come up against thus far.

The task was to bring King Eurystheus the peaceful giant's prized herd of cattle, the red calves of Geryon. The light of the magnificent sunset that fell over the western waters had stained the entire herd red. It is no coincidence that the "red calf" trope appears in one of Greek mythology's most well-known stories, as it is seen in many ancient sources. The Greeks indeed got around and were more than willing to share their stories with other societies and vice versa. Some of the most influential literature in history has come out of the Mediterranean region.

So off Herakles went on his task, borrowing his mode of transportation from Helios. The sun was kind enough to lend Herakles his solid gold drinking vessel, which was large enough to row across the sea to the island of Erytheia. Of course, the physics of this transportation is iffy at best, but one has to imagine there was a great deal of rowing on Herakles's part. Regardless, he sailed the seas in a giant cup.

In order to acquire the cattle, Herakles would need to fight his way past the two levels of security that Geryon had set up to look after his beloved herd. Herakles's first task would be to get past the shepherd, the fearsome giant Eurytion, then somehow best the fearsome two-headed canine Orthros. And then after that, if he was still in one piece, he would need to go toe to toe with the three-bodied Geryon himself. One has to think that Herakles would have rather gone after one hundred Nemean lions rather than attempt to steal any cattle from Geryon. But penance is penance, and Herakles had to endure this punishment to relieve his suffering from murdering his family. Of course, one has to wonder at what point had Herakles suffered enough.

Herakles managed to slay the cattle herder and then the brave Orthros. Finally, he found himself facing the terrible Geryon, who stood stoic, ready to protect what was his. In terms of the law, Herakles had come to kill and steal, although he is meant to be seen as the protagonist of this tale. However, if one looks at it from the other angle, he is also the antagonist. In the end, Herakles drove his sword into the back of Geryon and then herded the cattle on board his ship and set sail back to the Peloponnese.

Thus far, Herakles had successfully completed ten of the twelve tasks assigned to him. There were two more. Eurystheus tasked Herakles with retrieving the golden apples from Hera's tree and bringing them back to Mycenae so that a tree might be planted in the king's garden. The tree and its fruit were guarded by the Hesperides, the daughters of Nyx. They were the goddesses of the golden light of dusk. They were named Aegle, Erytheia, Hesperidia, and Arethusa.

These goddesses guarded the precious treasures of not only Queen Hera but also all the immortals. When Perseus set out on his quest to slay the Gorgon Medusa, he also stopped to visit the Hesperides in order to obtain weapons powerful enough to slay a Gorgon. Despite the Hesperides being charged with the protection of these items, they were not always the perfect security detail. One assumes that their parentage afforded them such a position of power.

Together, these four women stood guard over Hera's tree. It was a precious gift given to her by Gaia on the day of her wedding to Zeus. The Hesperides were also assisted in their watch by a hundred-headed serpent who went by the name of Ladon. Herakles had already bested more fearsome monsters than a hundred-headed dragon, and as such, this task was probably a walk in the park for our hero. He easily delayed the dragon and then proceeded to take the apples by force, once again ferrying them all the way back to Mycenae to be left in the hands of an ungrateful king.

Atlas, the Titan condemned to hold up the sky, plays an interesting role in the more popular version of this myth. On his way to gather the apples, Herakles found Atlas. Since it was his daughters who oversaw the apples, he thought Atlas would have an easier time. Someone had to hold the world up, though, and Herakles took the burden upon his shoulders so his task could be fulfilled. Atlas retrieved the apples as requested and was then kind enough to offer to deliver them to the king himself.

But Herakles was not moved by the Titan's compassion. He suspected that if Atlas left with the apples, he would never return. Instead of playing his hand, Herakles agreed but asked if Atlas could take the world for a moment so he could make himself more comfortable. Atlas sat the apples down and shouldered his burden once more. Herakles did not hesitate; he grabbed the apples and ran.

In a variation of the myth, Athena righted this wrong before the precious fruit could be carved open and their seeds extracted. She stole the apples from the king's personal chambers and returned them to the Hesperides. Most versions end with Herakles successfully delivering the apples, though.

The final task that King Eurystheus set for our hero was to retrieve the three-headed guard dog of the underworld and the pride of the great Hades: Cerberus. This task was probably one of the most treacherous in terms of location, given the fact that many heroes had succeeded in entering the underworld, but few were victorious in actually leaving in one piece or at all. Herakles managed to capture the hound with the help of Hermes, Athena, and Persephone. Given the sheer number of immortals needed to execute this plan successfully indicates the mess Herakles would have been in if he had attempted the task on his own. Hermes lent Herakles his winged shoes in order for him to gain more speed. Athena revealed the best ways to tackle the beast by using the dog's weight against him. Finally, Persephone would aid Herakles in getting back to the surface with his prize.

After this, Herakles's labors had been completed, and his guilt had been absolved for the crime of murdering his wife and three children. At the end of the labors, the gods were impressed with Herakles's physical and mental tenacity and awarded him a seat on Olympus, along with immortality.

Chapter 10: Jason and the Argonauts

Greek myths involving the most famous heroes, be they demi-gods or full human beings, always start with some sort of dramatic backstory, a tale to build up the coming drama of the hero's journey. Just like in the real world, our stories do not start with us; they start with stories that come before us, building into a collective narrative of interconnected lives. The legendary myth of Jason and the Argonauts has been reflected and drawn from in various adaptations. People are still retelling the morals of this amazing tale and basing new stories on names and concepts used in the original myth thousands of years after the story was first told.

The story of Jason and the Argonauts begins with a golden fleece that belonged to a winged ram. No one knows the origin of this particular ram. All that is known is the unfortunate fate of the animal and the destiny it provided one Greek hero. The ram was captured by King Aeetes of Colchis and sacrificed to the gods. However, the ram's golden fleece was preserved from the sacrificial flames and locked away from the daylight and the eyes of other mortal kings who would seek to possess the fleece's inherent wealth and magical power. The king hid the fleece in a far-off cave on the island of Colchis and employed the services of a fire-breathing dragon to guard the fleece day and night. If you have ever read Tolkien, you now know where the dragon-like characteristic of guardians and hoarding treasure originates, for this theme was employed in the myth of Jason and the Argonauts.

Centuries later, on the island of Iolkos (Iolcus) in Thessaly, the good King Aeson gave birth to his son and heir, Jason. Like all good family dramas in the ancient world, sibling bonds counted for very little. King Aeson's half-brother Pelias sought to take control of his brother's throne. He accomplished this easily enough by poisoning the reigning king. Jason's mother, Queen Alcimede, was not so easily fooled as the rest of her husband's court. It is also possible they themselves had been privy to the heinous murder of her beloved husband. To keep her son safe from the clutches of her brother-in-law, Alcimede sent Jason away to be raised by the centaur Cheiron (also spelled as Chiron). Shortly after she turned her son over to Cheiron, Alcimede died, succumbing to heartbreak over the death of her husband and the separation from her only son, whom she was sure she would never see again.

Jason's new guardian, Cheiron, was the wisest and the oldest of his kind. The centaurs were a breed and tribal confederation of half-horse men that inhabited Thessaly. Cheiron was, in fact, the half-brother of Zeus, and as such, he was a very respected figure in the Greek world for his prowess as a capable leader. He was also known for his intellect and kindness. Cheiron nurtured the young Jason, teaching him invaluable life skills, such as reading and writing in several languages, self-defense, and offensive fighting tactics. Cheiron was the living embodiment of strength through grace, and his name is seen in many different Greek myths. He is heralded as potentially the most famous centaur in Greek mythology. If anyone reading this has ever read any Percy Jackson books, the figure of Cheiron appears there; he is the trainer of all the demi-gods in the modern world.

When Jason grew into a man, he asked Cheiron to let him go before the king and demand his rightful inheritance to the throne. Cheiron was very fond of his protégé and ward. He did not want to see the boy he had raised go before a mad and dishonest king. But Cheiron knew that this was Jason's destiny, and as such, he told him to go before the king but keep his wits about him. Jason knew that he would never be able to slay his uncle in the throne room with so many swords pointed at his back. He would come in a diplomatic fashion and demand the return of his throne.

Years before, Jason's uncle, King Pelias, still fearing for the security of his throne, visited the Oracle of Delphi and consulted her as to what his fate might be if Jason should return. Pelias had no guarantee that his nephew was indeed dead, for he had no knowledge of what Alcimede did. He certainly would never have guessed that Jason would be left under the charge of one of the most feared and respected creatures of the ancient world. The Oracle informed Pelias to be wary of a man that came before him without one of his sandals.

Hera, who had overheard everything Pelias confessed that day, sought to end the evil king and his lordship over Iolkos. Years prior, Pelias had murdered his stepmother in cold blood at the entrance to Hera's temple. For fear that someone would discover what he had done, especially the goddess, he banned all his subjects from worshiping at the temple of Hera. Hera was one of the more insecure goddesses who needed lots of attention, and if she didn't get it, she could be ruthless. She was definitely the wrong divine being to mess with because if anyone mortal or immortal knew how to hang onto a grudge, it was Hera. She was always seeking out chances for revenge, and this time, she would make sure that Pelias suffered for his crimes against her and her worshipers.

On Jason's way back to the palace, he saw an old woman trying to cross a treacherous river. He assisted her, but he lost one of his sandals in the current. Pelias would have liked to chop Jason's head off right then and there when he saw the young man enter his throne room with one sandal, but he knew that this would tarnish his reputation as king and potentially shine a light on his brother's untimely and somewhat suspicious death. All rulers find it exceptionally hard to rule a kingdom that despises their very existence. At some level, kings and queens do need to care about how their people consider them as rulers.

However, Pelias was very cunning. He, too, sought to deal with the issue in a diplomatic fashion. He informed Jason that he would return the throne to him if he retrieved the coveted golden fleece from the dragon-guarded cave on the island of Colchis. He believed that his nephew would never be able to beat the beast and that he would more than likely die on the quest.

However, Jason would not be going alone. He commissioned one of the best shipwrights in all of Greece, Argos, to build him the largest and sturdiest ship the Greek world had ever seen. Under the guidance of the patron goddess of craft Athena, Argos built the *Argo*, a twenty-two-meter-long vessel with fifty oars and a low drought that allowed the ship to take on a considerable amount of water without foundering. The oars, anchor, and mast were all removable, which allowed the vessel to be rolled onto the shore of any landmass. This would prevent the ship from being destroyed in their absence or stolen.

Crafted from the oak and pine trees of Iolkos, the *Argo* was a blessed vessel, and the men aboard her sturdy deck were nothing but the finest soldiers in all of Greek mythology. These men were known as the Argonauts. The word Argonauts is translated from ancient Greek as "Argo sailors," with "nauts" meaning sailor or voyager. Some of the most famous heroes of Greece came to aid Jason in his quest, including the demi-god Herakles. The Argonauts numbered around fifty men and demi-gods, who were all willing to fight or die trying for the glory of the rightful king of Iolkos. Although they knew they were taking part in a noble deed and serving the rightful king, the men also wanted their names to be remembered. Being involved in such a dangerous quest would surely get their names written down in the book of Greek history, whether or not they survived the experience.

Jason and his crew first docked on the island of Lemnos in order to find fresh water and possibly resupply their food stores. When they landed on the shores of Lemnos, they noticed a distinct foul odor in the air. The island reeked of dead fish. They scoured up and down the shores, looking for whatever marine life carcass was causing such a horrific smell. Little did they know that the smell was coming from the inhabitants of Lemnos. Years prior to the arrival of Jason and his soldiers, the island of Lemnos was once a place of peace and prosperity. That is up until the moment its inhabitants neglected to regularly worship the goddess Aphrodite. It is a symbolic irony that even gods and goddesses, in all their seeming perfection, were often the most insecure. This is something that is true of most humans as well.

Despite her legendary beauty and seemingly confident persona, Aphrodite was rife with insecurities. She often wondered if she deserved her place on Olympus, and despite being the patron goddess of one of the most sought-after human experiences in the world (love and sex), she was less loved by the people of Greece. No one seemed to worship or respect her on the same level as some of the other goddesses, like Athena. Women and men alike respected, admired, and prayed often to that goddess. One of the most famous cities in the ancient world and by far the most famous in all of Greece, Athens, was named after Athena.

So, when the lovely ladies of Lemnos dropped the ball on offering regular prayers and sacrifices to Aphrodite, that did not go over well. Perhaps the women of Lemnos were too busy with their daily lives to make it to every temple and shrine, or maybe they did this as a deliberate insult to the goddess. Either way, it did not end well for the women or their husbands. Aphrodite cursed all the women of the island to reek of a foul fish odor, and she made sure there was no cure. And the smell was foul. It greatly affected the lives of the Lemnos women but none more so than their sex lives. Husbands turned away from their wives, and the young ladies yearning to get married were not attracting any suitors. The men of Lemnos were probably 10 percent faster on foot than every other man of Greece because they were constantly running away from the women of their island.

Eventually, all of the husbands took to bedding their Thracian slave girls, who were not affected by the curse. Angry and heartbroken, the women of Lemnos proceeded to murder every man on the island, even the younger boys. They could no longer deal with the rejection and humiliation that came with their affliction. This was the true intention of Aphrodite's curse: first loneliness and then utter extinction. However, the Lemnos ladies moved on and functioned as any Greek society might. They elected a queen to rule over them, Queen Hypsipyle.

After a while, the women accepted the fact that they would never know romantic love or affection again—well, heterosexually anyway. Still, they did have a serious population problem. And although the women suffered, they wanted to continue the culture and polity of their island. But to do that, they needed children. They were out of luck there. All the men were buried or gone, and they couldn't just steal men from the other cities and islands of Greece. That was an easy way to start a war they could not possibly win.

Their luck changed when Jason and the Argonauts arrived on the shores of Lemnos. These sailors were more than ready to fall into the arms of any woman who crossed their path. Now, you may ask yourself, how in the world did the Argonauts and Jason stand the fish smell wafting off these women? Well, when Aphrodite saw that her curse had been fulfilled, she gave the women a break and changed the conditions so that the women would reek of dead fish only on certain days of the year. Over time, the women also learned how to manage the condition with native root plants that grew on the island so that they were not as rancid when those days of the year finally came around.

This seemed to have worked well enough because after six years, the island was back to its original population size. Queen Hypsipyle took Jason as her personal companion, and she was his first lover. Together, they conceived twin boys, Thous and Euneus. After those six years, Jason worried that his men were becoming too comfortable in the beds of these women and that in another year, they would not want to leave their new families. So, he ordered his men to prepare for their journey, and in the morning, while their lovers and wives slept, they set sail once more into the horizon.

They traveled on the sea from Lemnos to the Hellespont and the Propontis (Sea of Marmara), now located in modern-day Turkey. Lemnos was a Greek island located in the northern Aegean, so while the trip was not that lengthy, the men still needed to freshen up their water supply on this particular leg of the voyage. The land of the Propontis was ruled over by King Cyzicus. The king's generosity toward his people was legendary, and he was extremely welcoming of strangers, treating them as honored guests under his own roof.

King Cyzicus greeted Jason and his men with open arms and decided to host a fine and expensive banquet for the Argonauts and toast to the good fortune of their journey. What a time they must have had because the king's men and the Argonauts passed out right in the banquet hall. The next morning, the Argonauts woke up before the king, who was sleeping off a fairly nasty hangover. They went out into the wild to collect supplies for the remainder of their journey. In all of the merriment and drinking, the king kept forgetting to warn Jason of the terrible creatures that plagued his otherwise perfect kingdom.

The Argonauts sailed to another portion of the Hellespont and left Herakles in charge of the ship while they searched for game and water. As Herakles was lying on the sand with the sun in his face, he heard a rumble from deep within the earth. As it grew, the ground started to vibrate with intensity. Herakles jumped to his feet and ran back for the ship as the huge Gegenees burst through the layers of the earth. The Gegenees were giants with six arms. Herakles feared that without his men, he would be beaten by the Gegenees.

They were going to try and attack the ship so that the Argonauts could not escape. Brave Herakles managed to hold them off for an impressive amount of time, all the while yelling and screaming for reinforcements. Jason was the first to hear the cry of his comrade and commanded the Argonauts to return to the ship, their swords drawn. They got down to the beach and stood aghast at the site of the Gegenees. After many relentless hours of fighting the giants, the Argonauts were victorious and hopped back onto the *Argo* before any more misfortune could come their way. However, they had no way of knowing that the greatest tragedy of the journey was yet to come.

By the time Jason and his men were able to set sail, it was well past sundown, and sailing on the seas at night was difficult, given the fact that any light was swallowed by the dark abyss around the ship. The Argonauts meant to sail away from the Propontis, but in the confusion of the night, they sailed right back toward the land of the Doliones, the inhabitants of the Hellespont. Good King Cyzicus saw a ship approaching his coast from his balcony in the throne room, but he could not make out the ship's inhabitants. All he saw was the light of their few torches. Since the king was not expecting any more visitors, he thought that Jason and his men were pirates who had come to lay waste to his shores. The king ordered his men down to the docks and told them to be armed and prepared for battle. The Argonauts were unaware that the king and his army were going to lead an attack against them. All they heard were the war horns of someone, and thinking they were far away from the land of Propontis, they did not deduce that it was, in fact, their friend and ally sending the charge to attack them.

Amidst all the confusion, King Cyzicus was slain by a rogue arrow, and he died right there on the deck of his ship. When light broke the horizon, both the Argonauts and Cyzicus's men were horrified. They despaired over the death of one of the finest rulers the kingdoms had ever seen. They held a grand funeral for the legendary Cyzicus, and every person in the kingdom, from the city to the countryside, came to honor his memory. The crowd was sobbing for a life that had been so needlessly lost, but none more so than our hero Jason, for he felt responsible for the death of his friend and ally. Although everyone assured Jason that Cyzicus's death was an accident, one that was provoked by the king himself, Jason carried that sunken feeling of absolute guilt for the remainder of his days.

As if the death of Cyzicus was not enough, the Argonauts had not seen the end of death, misery, and loss. Off the coast of Mysia, the *Argo* nearly crashed onto a body of rock formations. In order to divert the ship in time, Herakles dug his oar into the waves and managed to steer the ship out of danger. However, just as the ship cleared the rocks, Herakles's oar snapped right in two. He told Jason that he intended to go ashore with Hylas, his beloved squire, in order to find another large oak tree, from which he would fashion a new oar. Jason agreed, and off the two men went into the forest.

While Herakles went on his search for the perfect oak tree, Hylas, ever the loyal and loving ward, went to fetch fresh water for his master so that he would have something to quench his thirst while he worked on the oar. Hylas found a cool mountain lake, clear as crystal, with waters that seemed to glimmer, gleam, and even flirt with the young man as he approached. Little did Hylas know that the waters were indeed flirting with him. This was the work of a water nymph. She emerged onto the smooth rock shore of the lake and lured Hylas into the water with sweet words and kisses that lapped at his feet. Eventually, Hylas followed her so far into the water that his head went under the smooth waves. Since he was bewitched by the immortal nymph's spell of love, Hylas was unaware that he had begun to drown.

After some time, Herakles noticed that his friend had failed to return. Hylas never left his master's side for this amount of time. Herakles called out for him and searched far and wide, but his squire failed to answer. Herakles began to become hysterical, and he ran down to the *Argo* to request a search party. Most of the Argonauts did not see the need for such a fuss over one squire, but Herakles refused to leave without Hylas. This began to break down the relations on the *Argo*, with half the men refusing to leave without Herakles and the other unwilling to postpone the progression of the journey. Soon, Jason faced the threat of a mutiny.

However, Hera (remember, she had a lot staked on the success of Jason and his men) sent word to the sea god Glaucus, the patron god of fishermen. He was the ideal being to pacify and mediate the situation, given the fact that Glaucus had once been human; he had gained immortality by eating a very rare sea herb that had been sewn into creation by Cronos himself. Glaucus knew very well the tensions that could be aboard a vessel and reassured the Argonauts that it was the will of the gods that Herakles stay on land to search for his friend.

Before they set sail once more into the breach, Glaucus advised Jason to leave Herakles a second-in-command, so Jason ordered Polyphemus to stay behind with Greece's greatest hero and make sure he came to no harm. If Herakles perished, it would be Polyphemus's responsibility to make his way back in order to report the death.

Now missing two of their most skilled warriors, the Argonauts set sail with a pit in their stomachs. Even though Glaucus had reassured them that this was fated, they still felt less than confident about surviving the remainder of their journey, especially since they were sailing toward their next destination to restock their stores. In northwestern Anatolia was the land of King Amycus (or Amykos), lord of the Bebryces, a hoard of stocky bare-knuckle fighters that were feared throughout mainland Greece, Asia Minor, and Mycenae.

Amycus was actually a demi-god himself. He was the son of Melia, the naiad daughter of the Titan Oceanus, and Poseidon. Given his parentage, Amycus had inherited both his mother's and father's turbulent nature and sought to fight any stranger who dared step foot on his lands. Seeing Jason and the Argonauts roll onto his shores greatly angered and intrigued the king, as word had already spread throughout Asia Minor of Jason and the Argonauts and their quest for the golden fleece.

King Amycus approached the Argonauts and challenged Jason to a fistfight right there on the spot. One of Jason's better qualities as a man and a leader was recognizing where his strengths lay, and he knew that he was no match for a demi-god son of Poseidon. In the most gracious manner, he beseeched Amycus that he might be able to select one of his men to fight in his stead, for who would be responsible for the well-being and command of the Argonauts if he should fall. Jason made it seem like his chosen tribute would have no chance of winning the fight against Amycus, and so, the king of the Bebryces accepted Jason's offer. Little did Amycus know that in Jason's company was the legendary boxer Polydeuces, who was also a son of Zeus.

The fight was well-matched, demi-god against demi-god, and what a fight it was. There were plenty of nail-biting moments where it seemed that either boxer could be the victor. Right hooks landed firmly on jawlines, and the spectators witnessed fast dodges and swings that would have taken the head off of most mortals. However, in the end, Polydeuces had bested Amycus. He managed to kill the king with an uppercut right to Amycus's lower jaw. The sheer amount of force broke the king's jaw and shoved his nose bone into the fore of his brain. The scene was grotesque, to say the least, and Amycus died a horrible death.

The Bebryces were outraged over the inhumane death of their king and sought to avenge his death by doing away with Jason and the Argonauts. They were no match for Jason's cunning wit and intellect, though. Jason had undoubtedly realized that Polydeuces was the superior fighter when he set the challenge, and he had already prepared for the outcome of what would happen if Amycus fell. As the fight between the two men was drawing to its close, Jason had his men slowly move into their main fighting formation so that when the Bebryces attacked, they would be ready. The Argonauts managed to push back the attack and drove their enemies into the hills.

After reboarding the *Argo*, the men sailed past the Bosporus (or Bosphorus, a strait in northwestern Turkey) and finally made port in the land of Thrace. After trudging for some time on foot, searching for more supplies, they came upon a man who was just sitting down to enjoy his midday meal. Jason went to approach the man to ask him where they might find game to hunt when all of a sudden, two winged and beastly creatures appeared from seemingly nowhere and began to torment the man. At first, Jason ordered his men not to engage these creatures, but when he saw that the man was blind and that the beasts were desecrating his food, he and the Argonauts engaged them and drove them away. They helped the man reset his camp, light his fire, and get him a fresh pot of food back on the flame. The man was so grateful to the Argonauts that he invited them to join him for the meal and revealed himself to be Phineas, a legendary seer who had been gifted with visions of the future. Phineas could predict all potential variables for changes in the destiny of men and all potential outcomes of the future.

His greatest gift also became his curse. Phineas lost his eyesight because of his predictions concerning the many offspring of Zeus. The lord of the skies did not need his already crazed and jealous queen knowing the whereabouts of his potential wives and children. Phineas was able to expose Zeus to any common stranger. Phineas would discuss the fate of men very casually, and he knew the information could circulate its way back to Hera through her network of prayers and spies. Also, she was a goddess and very tuned in to the world of women.

Zeus cursed Phineas, causing him to go blind all of a sudden. He could have easily killed the seer, but in the end, Phineas was a useful and rare source of information, only secondary to the Oracle of Delphi. Zeus's curse was a warning shot, alerting Phineas that he was to keep his mouth shut from now on. However, Zeus had plenty of petty nature in his godly form and wanted to make sure Phineas wouldn't suddenly have a wave of courage and go back to his old ways. So, Zeus sent the Harpies to visit Phineas every once in a while. They tormented and intimidated the old man, reminding him who was in charge. This torture was too much to bear, and it traumatized Phineas to the point where he no longer attempted to see the future. He was too afraid to even use his gift.

So, the Argonauts and Phineas talked through the night, with the young sailors, heroes, and demi-gods all enthralled by the stories and knowledge of the old seer. This was the most Phineas had spoken to other people in years, and he spoke freely. He then heard the story of the Argonauts' journey, the lands they had visited, their tragedies, and their triumphs. Phineas was so moved and compelled by their journey that he offered them his services; he would look into their future and predict their best outcome for survival. However, in return for his visionary guidance, he requested that the Argonauts help him dispense of his tormentors, the vicious Harpies. Jason and his men were already quite fond of Phineas, and they agreed to help.

Luckily for the Argonauts, this was not a big favor to ask, as they were well equipped to deal with the situation. Two in Jason's crew, Zetes and Calais, were the children of Boreas, the Titan of the north wind. They were very capable flyers. The Harpies didn't stand much of a chance in the grand scheme of things since they were far less agile flyers. If it had not been for their sister Iris, who intervened at the last second, the Harpies would have been slaughtered. (Yes, the same Iris who was the goddess of the rainbow and the messenger of the gods.) Iris made the Argonauts a promise that the Harpies would leave the old man be. She also said that Zeus would not be made aware of their absence so long as Phineas thought twice about whose future he looked into.

After Iris and the Harpies departed, Phineas looked into the future of the Argonauts' journey and saw the Symplegades or Clashing Rocks. These were two giant boulders that had once been a whole island. This island was split from the seafloor by Poseidon. The boulders had a tendency to shift apart and then crash back together again, but for a few perilous minutes, the passageway would be open. This was the fastest way to the other side. It was the route that the Argonauts would have to brave if they wanted to stay the course and not add a lot of additional time to their journey. Time was always on Jason's mind; the crew had lost so much time at the beginning of their journey that they could not afford to waste more. Phineas told them they could time their sail through the Symplegades by sending a white dove through first. If she made the journey and returned, they would know it was safe enough to sail through.

When the Argonauts approached the massive rocks, they were unlike anything one could imagine. And the passageway between them was even more narrow than Phineas had originally described. The worst part, of course, was the small amount of time the rocks seemed to stay apart from one another. It seemed to truly be a matter of minutes before the two boulders crashed together again. If the ship attempted to sail between them, it was obvious the men and the *Argo* would be wiped clean from the face of the earth forever, with not even their bones remaining intact.

Jason was willing to take the risk. He believed that it was worth it, and this gave his men courage. They sailed as close as they could without being pulled into the current of the rocks, and then they sent out the dove. She was gone for a little while but returned to the ship safe and seemingly unharmed. The Argonauts took this as a blessing and decided to attempt the pass. They prayed to the gods for strength and speed and set their oars.

Onward they rowed, entering the passageway with fear in their hearts but strength in their conviction. They could hear the sounds of the rocks creaking and moaning in the seas, sounds coming from the lowest depths of the earth, the sound of rushing anxious water sloshing back and forth against every inch of the ship. It was not smooth sailing by any means. What's worse was the disappearing light. Jason began to notice that the sun's rays were growing weaker and weaker, a sign that the tops of the boulders would crash together at any minute. Jason ordered his men to row for their lives as he steered the ship through the perilous pathway. The light was dying, the tunnel was becoming increasingly dark as they rowed on, and Jason feared they would not make it through after all.

Just then, it was as if the boulders ceased to be moving toward one another. They miraculously had just stopped moving altogether. Jason could not see Athena, but she was at the top, holding the two boulders apart, which gave the Argonauts just enough time to make it through. As soon as they were clear, she let the two cliffs meet once more.

The remainder of the Argonauts' journey to Colchis was relatively uneventful other than a surprise attack by the remainder of the Stymphalian birds, those birds that managed to survive

Herakles a few years prior. Herakles's defeat of the birds had echoed throughout Greece, and pretty much every person had a basic concept of how to drive the beasts away with loud noises. Jason and his men went to work throwing objects at the birds and beating their swords and spears against their shields, fending the birds off as they did so. They managed to succeed but lost one of their crew, Oileus, in the ensuing frenzy. He was struck in the chest by one of the razor-sharp feathers and was dead before he hit the deck of the *Argo*.

Finally, Jason and his men had completed their voyage and arrived on the island of Colchis. Hera had been in their company for the entire journey and had planned from the outset to aid Jason in his ultimate quest of obtaining the golden fleece from the clutches of a dragon, if not purely for her own gain. No matter how brave Jason was, he was only a man. He was not impervious to flame and fire, and he was completely devoid of any physically superior gifts like those that had been bestowed on Herakles. As they approached Colchis, Jason wished more than ever that he had convinced Herakles to remain aboard the *Argo*.

However, he was unaware of the plan that the goddess Hera had concocted in order for him to survive. King Aeetes happened to have a daughter, Medea, the high priestess of Hecate, who was the goddess of magic. And it just so happened that Medea was more than skilled in the magical arts. She would be a powerful ally for the Argonauts, but her heart was cold and withdrawn. Hera knew that only by a spell of love would Medea be willing to aid Jason and his men. Before the *Argo* ever touched the shores of Colchis, Hera had called upon Eros to stand by and remain close to the princess. When the opportune moment arrived, he would shoot Medea with an arrow of love, and from then on, she would be infatuated and deeply in love with the young prince.

When the Argonauts approached the city of Aia, they were given a royal escort to the court of King Aeetes, who welcomed the men as his most honored guests—well, that is until the king discovered the real reason the Argonauts had come to Colchis. Aeetes had half a mind to strike down the young prince right on the spot, but such acts were frowned upon in the democratic world of the ancient Greeks. Such actions often provoked generational blood feuds between kingdoms, and King Aeetes, for all his greed and faults, still cared for the peace and prosperity of his subjects.

That doesn't mean that the king was willing to give up his prized possession. Instead, he informed Jason that he was more than welcome to try his luck with defeating the dragon that guarded the cave, as well as the two fire-breathing bulls that Aeetes had added as extra security measures. Jason would need to tame both of the bulls. He would then need to use the animals to plow a giant field in which he would plant the teeth of a dragon. Those teeth would become soldiers, giant and merciless, and Jason would also need to slay them in order to claim his prize. And after all that, he needed to deal with the dragon guarding the fleece.

Jason could not refuse the king. He knew that if he did not take this challenge, he would be declared a thief, and King Aeetes would be well within his rights to cut down the hero where he stood and assign the Argonauts the same fate. Jason could forfeit his own life, but he would not make that choice for his men.

As Jason and Aeetes were discussing the terms of Jason's attempt to possess the golden fleece, Medea walked in. Eros was at the ready with an arrow already notched into his bow, and as soon as the main doors of the hall swung open for Medea to make her entrance, Eros shot her in the hip. Mortals did not feel the sting of Eros's arrows, so the princess continued forward without so much a stumble in her steps. When she lifted her eyes, the very first gaze she met was that of our hero Jason. Aeetes introduced his daughter, who was fairly lovely, with jet black hair and glowing dark eyes. In fact, Medea was hailed as being one of the most "bewitching" women of Greece. Her other distinguishing characteristic was her unyielding and ruthless nature, which was matched equally with her beauty. In psychological terms, the princess was borderline sociopathic. She was beautiful but crazy, and even with Eros's arrow of love still dug into her hip, no one could say for sure if her newfound love for Jason would match the love she had for herself. Eros wasn't going to leave anything to chance, so he also shot Jason for good measure.

Medea went to claim her seat next to her father's throne, and she held Jason's gaze for almost the entire time. As for Jason, he was having plenty of trouble focusing on the king and not his daughter. One final stipulation was that Jason would attempt to acquire the fleece on his own. He could not enlist the aid of his men. Jason was more than happy to accept those terms. He would need all of the Argonauts alive and well in order to row the ship back to Iolkos if he was to succeed in obtaining the fleece.

That night before Jason was to make his attempt, Medea visited him in his chambers. As Jason was lying in his bed, the princess seemed to evaporate through the walls. He never heard the door to his chambers open and close. She drifted to his side. No words were shared between the two lovers; they simply fell into one another's arms. Whilst lying in the afterglow of their love-making, Medea informed Jason that she was the only person who could ensure the success of his venture. Jason sat up and listened to his lover's proposal intently. Medea said that she would concoct an ointment that would protect him from the flames of the bulls. It would allow him to get close enough to tame and harness the animals, after which she would also help him soothe the dragon and tell him how to defeat the soldiers that would rise from its teeth.

However, Medea had some conditions of her own. She would not be willing to perform any of these tasks or divulge any information if Jason did not take her back to Iolkos and make her his queen. She assured Jason that without her help, he would surely die, leaving the hero very little choice. He also seemingly loved the princess, a side effect of Eros's arrow of love. How much he believed in her love, however, is not known. Nevertheless, he agreed to Medea's terms, and true to her word, she told Jason everything he needed to know in order to survive his perilous quest.

The next day, Jason bid his men farewell and ordered them to watch him from the cliffs above, all except the legendary and well-known musician Orpheus and Medea. She provided Jason with the ointment as promised. He slathered this all over his body before redressing and heading down to where the bulls lay in their field. Jason was able to approach the bulls, despite being consumed in a raging tunnel of hellfire. He made his way toward each animal, and after soft words and sweet nothings, he had both the bulls curled up at his feet like purring cats.

Jason Taming the Bulls of Aeëtes by Jean-François de Troy, 1679–1752.
https://commons.wikimedia.org/wiki/File:Jean-Fran%C3%A7ois_de_Troy_-_Jason_Taming_the_Bulls_of_Ae%C3%ABtes,_1742.jpg

The next portion of the quest was to sow the dragon teeth. The teeth had already been harvested by Aeetes. With the teeth in hand, Jason went about plowing the field with the bulls and planting the teeth in orderly rows. Around a dozen soldiers clawed their way out of the earth. The night before, in Jason's chamber, Medea had assured her hero that what the soldiers possessed in brawn, they sorely lacked in brainpower. After all, these were not normal humans but things closer aligned with the laws of nature. These soldiers were provoked very easily since attack was their only mode of interaction. Thus, Jason threw rocks at the soldiers. Unaware that these stones were being hurled from far away, the soldiers engaged whomever they determined to be a threat, even those among their own brigade. In a matter of minutes, the soldiers had completely decimated one another. The only task left was for Jason to claim the fleece.

The dragon was all that was left. And this dragon never slept. As with most myths, there are different versions. For instance, some say that Medea had given Jason a concoction of herbs that put the dragon to sleep. However, a more exciting version exists. Orpheus, who was among the Argonauts, played a soothing lullaby with his harp. Medea even helped, using her sorcery to ensure the dragon fell asleep. Soon, the great and fearsome dragon was sleeping like a baby in no time. Music sometimes is really the only way to soothe a savage beast.

Once the beast was asleep, the three of them crept closer. Jason tiptoed around the slumbering dragon and found the fleece nailed to a tall but leafless tree bathed in a single ray of sunlight, which had broken through the top of the cave. Jason had never laid eyes on any material that was like the golden fleece. The very fibers seemed to beckon and seduce, which shows how King Aeetes lost his sanity and humanity in order to keep the fleece from the hands of other men. The three victors wasted no time in returning to the *Argo*, where the Argonauts were waiting, ready and prepared to set sail.

News of Jason's victory and hasty exit had made its way back to King Aeetes, who had never expected the young prince to succeed. He was instantly suspicious that someone in his family had aided Jason, but he surprisingly never considered Medea to be the culprit. She was his perfect little girl, and he didn't consider her capable of such treachery, although it was more than plausible to all who were aware of her true nature.

Aeetes called upon his firstborn son Apsyrtus to aid him in the hunt for the Argonauts. Aeetes no longer cared about public opinion or blood feuds; his anger clouded his judgment. The two of them set sail with their personal battalions and were just about to close in on their target. Meanwhile, Medea was below the deck of the *Argo*, performing blood magic in order to stop her father in his tracks. Medea cast a spell that caused a hemorrhage in her brother's brain. Apsyrtus fell onto his hands and knees, nauseous, his head throbbing. One of the soldiers called out to King Aeetes that his son was suffering, and the king immediately dashed to his son's side. But there was nothing that could be done.

The king's son collapsed, but this was not the worst to come. Medea's spell was twofold. While her brother suffered and was unable to comprehend time and space, he started to slowly disintegrate, similar to the appearance and infliction of leprosy. He was covered in boils and soars, but her spell sped up the disease. Before the king could do anything, his son had disintegrated completely, with all the blood from his body washing over the deck and pieces of flesh falling into the ocean. The grotesque and graphic sight halted the king's pursuit. He dared not follow the Argonauts any farther, for he feared that this torment had been delivered by a god. Medea was that powerful and that terrifying.

After a bout with the Sirens, the melodious flesh-eaters who lured men to their death with song, the Argonauts finally found refuge on the island of Drepane, where Jason and Medea were finally married. After a long rest on the island, Jason and the Argonauts made their way back to Iolkos, where the prince sought to finally claim his throne and rule as king. The entire company stormed into the throne room of the king, and Jason thrust the golden fleece at the feet of his uncle Pelias. However, Pelias would not relinquish his throne. With the golden fleece in hand, he could rule for decades and acquire new and very prominent lands. Why would he suddenly give up the throne to Jason now that he had both wealth and power?

Jason would not take this betrayal lying down. And he was even more willing to dispose of his uncle once he learned the truth from Medea that Pelias had murdered his father and caused his mother's heart to break to the point of death. Jason instructed Medea to exact revenge any way she could think, and Medea did not disappoint. One night in court, she gathered Pelias's daughters around her and told them that now their father had the fleece, he would become immortal. The daughters would now live under his sadistic and cruel rule for the rest of their lives. It was a little-known secret that Pelias was unwilling to let his daughters marry or relinquish control over their lives in any way. The girls were practically royal hostages. They could not bear the thought of their father outliving them, controlling their destinies until they were dead and gone. The three girls murdered Pelias and gave the throne willingly to Jason.

However, Jason had a huge problem on his hands. Once he had taken the throne and installed Medea as his queen, there were revolts throughout the kingdom. She was a well-known sorceress throughout the entirety of the Peloponnese, and she was greatly feared by those who knew the extent of her power and ruthless nature. The people of Iolkos would not have a foreign sorceress as their queen. Jason, fearing for the safety of his beloved wife and protector, took her away into exile on the island of Corinth, where he planned to live out the rest of their days in joy and happiness together.

They were happy enough for some time. Medea even gave birth to three of Jason's children. However, soon after they were born,

Jason fell from grace. One night, he approached Medea and asked her permission to propose marriage to the princess of Corinth. All things considered, it was actually unwise for Jason to make this request. Medea was just as possessive of Jason as she was protective, and his request to be with another woman was the ultimate betrayal in her eyes. Jason loved her, but she could be cold and unforgiving, and yet, he believed that she would never bring him to harm. As cliché as it is, hell hath no fury like a woman scorned, and Medea had no interest in sharing her husband with another princess. For Jason to even make this request was a great offense, and the only thing she could think of was revenge.

She killed the princess of Corinth, causing her to go mad and fling herself from the highest cliff on the island. If this wasn't enough, to further punish Jason, she massacred their three young children and laid each one in their marital bed for her husband to find. Once her revenge was complete, she made her way to Athens to seek the throne of another king.

Jason returned home later that evening to find the last joys of his life, his beloved children, slaughtered to the point that they were almost unrecognizable. The loss of a child is the deepest despair. The greatest of all mortal heroes, who had traveled the seas, bested the most fearsome creatures of the ancient world, and won back his crown only to relinquish it for love, was undone by the same ruthless woman he took to be his bride. Jason lived out the rest of his days alone. He had even lost the favor of Hera for breaking his vow to Medea. He died when one of the beams of the *Argo* fell and hit him in the head. Jason died instantly, buried in the ruins of one of the greatest ships to ever sail the seas and as one of the greatest heroes that ever lived.

Chapter 11: Theseus: The Minotaur Slayer

So, you remember how the queen of Crete had been impregnated by the most beautiful bull of all time, the Cretan Bull? From their bestial union came the Minotaur, who would become the terror of Crete. King Minos placed his wife's terrible offspring in a giant labyrinth underneath his palace and began to feed this beast with prisoners and his enemies. Although it was an effective method of implementing fear into his people and disposing of traitors, it didn't exactly leave the right message with the remaining kings of Greece or the king's own subjects. The cannibalistic nature of the Minotaur was disturbing enough, let alone a king who actively sated such a beast. Minos was the same sort of detestable enemy that Herakles went up against in his twelve labors, Diomedes (the king who was feeding human parts to his mares).

These sacrifices soothed King Minos's great shame that his wife had cheated on him with a divine bull. Soon enough, the Minotaur would have more than the enemies of the king to consume. However, the mythology of the Minotaur begins with a king who yearned for a son and a princess who managed to sleep with not only a king but a god and all in a single evening.

Years before the sexual encounter of Queen Pasiphae and the Cretan Bull, the king of Athens, Aegeus, was about to reach his early thirties and still had not managed to have a son. On a diplomatic mission to the kingdom of Troezen, he told the king of his concerns to produce an heir. The good king offered his daughter Aethra for Aegeus to bed for the evening, thinking that perhaps from their union, a son would be produced. The two young lovers (if we can even call them that) spent the night together. Later, slumbering in the afterglow of some decent love-making, the princess had a strange dream—a very strange dream. The goddess Athena appeared to Aethra and told her that the child who would grow in her belly from this night would be an exceptionally blessed child, one destined to perform great and heroic deeds. Athena told the princess to go down to the sea, stand near the water's edge, and wait. Aethra rose from her place in bed and followed the goddess's instructions.

She waited by the edge of the sea, the small waves gently kissing her toes. Although the sources are somewhat hazy, it is possible that the princess was not entirely conscious during her visit to the water; it was as if she was in a state of hypnosis. Right on cue, the god of the seas, Poseidon, emerged from the dark water and proceeded to have sex with the princess. When it comes to producing ideal heroes, the gods and goddesses of Olympus really don't pay attention to things like consent, but most of the mythology surrounding this particular tale makes it evident that the princess indeed enjoyed herself both back in the palace with Aegeus and on the beach that same night with Poseidon.

Oftentimes in Greek mythology, it was not uncommon for one child to have two fathers or two mothers or to be conceived in the stomach of a woman but then placed in the thigh of a man for the rest of the gestation period. The rules of science don't apply when we are talking about divine sperm. So, as mythology would have it, from this double union was born the hero Theseus. His claim as the son of Aegeus gave him lands, a title, and power. His godly patrilineage also gave him abilities that were not common to the world of mortal men. Since his birth was also blessed and orchestrated in some sense by the goddess Athena, Theseus would also have a logical mind, one unclouded by fear and able to rationally calculate the best course of action for success. All these qualities and more would serve him well when he reached manhood and had to fulfill a task that etched his name in the stone of Greek legends.

The next morning after Aegeus spent the night with the daughter of the king (he was unaware of her little late-night visit to the beach), he made preparations to return to Athens. However, before he departed, he left something behind for his future son. Near the same spot where Aethra had lain with Poseidon, Aegeus placed his sword and sandals under a large smooth stone. When his son came of age, Aegeus hoped that he would find the objects and return to Athens with these tools to take his rightful place as prince.

So, Theseus grew up in Troezen with his mother, and when he turned seventeen, she took him down to the water's edge and told him the story of his conception. When the princess had finished speaking, she took her son to the stone where his father's possessions had been stored for nearly two decades. Theseus, a strong youth at this point, rolled away the stone with great ease. His quest to reach Athens and claim his birthright had begun, as did the legend of Theseus and the Minotaur.

Before Theseus set out on his journey, his mother Aethra begged him to go by way of the sea and not to travel on the road. In the ancient world, when you traveled on the open road, it was a dangerous undertaking, one that included thieves who wouldn't think twice about slicing your throat and making off with your possessions. Or even worse, some sort of otherworldly creature could rip your eyeballs from their sockets or flay you alive. Of course, there were threats on the open waters, but Theseus, determined to prove himself worthy of his parentage, decided to travel by road. Armed with the king's sword, Theseus set out, and along the way, he encountered his fair share of trials and victories. He killed every foe he met on the road. These were not innocent travelers but evil men and monsters, defilers of human life. They were feared by many and challenged by none until the young prince arrived.

The first evildoer he encountered was a man who went by the name of Periphetes. This brute was known for bashing in the skulls of travelers with his iron club. What's worse is he didn't steal anything from his victims; the killings were purely for sport. Theseus managed to kill Periphetes, and he took his weapon as a trophy. Also, it wasn't every day that one came across such a fine weapon. The next man Theseus came up against was a far more sick and twisted individual than Periphetes; he was known as the stretcher or Procrustes. This disturbed individual would tie his victims to an iron bed and proceed to stretch their limbs so that they reached the edges of the bed. The unfortunate souls, who were too tall for the bed, would have their limbs chopped off one by one, a hand there, a foot here, until Procrustes was satisfied with the physical dimensions of the torture. Theseus came up against the stretcher and cleaved him in half with his sword.

By this point in his journey, word had begun to reach certain cities in Greece of Theseus's heroic accomplishments. When he arrived in Athens to finally stand before his father, the hero encountered more danger. A few years after his night with the princess of Troezen, King Aegeus had remarried, taking the sorceress and ex-wife of Jason, Medea, as his bride. This was a woman who liked to be in control of her fate and those around her at all times. She knew that her husband awaited the return of his son, and she feared that her claim to rule and influence Aegeus would wane.

When Theseus arrived in the throne room of the king, Medea, being wily in her ways and more than willing to kill for her station, convinced Aegeus that their new visitor could not be trusted. She whispered in his ear to give the young man a cup of poison to drink. It was better safe than sorry. Aegeus offered the drink to his son, unbeknownst of his true identity until the moment Theseus stepped forward to accept the drink. As he took a step toward the king, his sword swung into view. King Aegeus recognized the weapon immediately. This was his son and long-awaited heir. Medea couldn't run out of that throne room fast enough, and she fled to an unknown location.

The reunion between the king and his son was one overflowing with joy. Not long after that, however, their joy was stifled by the unfortunate political situation between Athens and Crete. Before Theseus had arrived, Aegeus had hosted a series of games with all of the neighboring Greek *poleis*. In one of the events, the son of King Minos, Androgeus, was crushed by a runaway chariot. King Minos was so outraged by the unexpected death of his young son that he demanded tribute from Athens. In order to avoid a war with the irrational king of Crete, Aegeus consented to King Minos's idea of reparations. Every year, the city of Athens sent fourteen of the most beautiful and virtuous young men and women to be given in sacrifice to the great terror of Crete, the Minotaur. The ship that ferried the tributes to the island always sailed under a black flag so that passing ships would know that sacrifices were aboard.

When Theseus discovered that his father had essentially been politically forced into such barbary, he decided to put an end to the Minotaur. His plan was to offer himself as a tribute and go into the maze and slay the beast. When he informed his father of his plan, the king would not hear of it. His only son would be sailing toward his potential death. Aegeus had only just welcomed his much-awaited heir back into his life. However, after much debating and convincing, the king finally consented to his son's quest but made him swear that when he was sailing back to Athens, he would raise white sails on his ship, replacing the black sails of death. This way, the king would know his son had survived and was returning home.

So, the day of tribute came, and true to his word, Theseus offered himself up. This was a most special tribute indeed, for the long-lost prince was the prized jewel of Athens. He was the most lovely, the most strong, and the most intelligent youth that Aegeus could offer. Minos was very pleased when he received word that one of Greece's most powerful kings was consenting to let his only son be devoured by an unholy monster. When Theseus stepped off the ship in Crete, he and the other tributes were led up to the palace of the king to be inspected.

King Minos greeted his royal guest, shaking his hand. He then presented him to his young daughter Ariadne, who was immediately struck by Theseus's beauty and charm. The young prince also noted Ariadne's striking beauty. Later that night, the princess visited Theseus in the tribute's quarters, and the two shared a passionate night together. Theseus confided in the princess and told her of his plan to slay the Minotaur. Although he seemed confident in his abilities to succeed in his quest, Ariadne knew that even if he managed to kill the beast, he would most certainly get lost in the maze. Many tributes had died not by a direct attack from the Minotaur but from succumbing to starvation or dehydration. Their corpses lined the walls of the maze and acted as snacks for the beast to devour later.

Early the next morning, Ariadne awoke before anyone else in the palace. She went down to the docks, where she collected a spool of thread from one of the vendors and returned to the bed of Theseus. She woke her love and instructed him to take the spool with him into the maze. Before he entered, he needed to tie the end of the thread to one of the columns just outside the entrance when he was alone. The guards who manned the maze never followed the tributes all the way inside. They were terrified of the Minotaur and for a good reason. The beast did not distinguish between friend or foe, prey or master. If King Minos walked into the maze, he would be treated no differently than the tributes. This spool would act as Theseus's bread crumbs, leading him back to safety once he had slain the Minotaur. Ariadne also managed to obtain a sword for her love and hid it near the entrance. For all Ariadne had done to help, Theseus promised to take her back with him to Athens.

And so, Theseus and the other Athenian tributes were pushed into the dark passageways of the maze. The stench was worse than anything Theseus could have imagined. The decaying corpses and bones of the Minotaur's previous meals were strewn about, shreds of ripped skin clinging to the walls, which were splattered brown with the dried blood of hundreds of victims. The twists and turns of the passageways were sporadic, and the walls seemed to move and change direction at will. The darkness in the labyrinth was all-consuming. The naked human eye couldn't make out more than two to three feet in front of them, but thankfully, not all of the tributes in the maze were all human. As a demi-god, Theseus possessed heightened senses, natural reflexes, and intuitions that allowed him to be on par with the Minotaur in terms of strength and speed.

He couldn't see in the dark, but the air in the labyrinth was thick and cold. Theseus could feel the changes in tension, and he proceeded into the blackness slowly, Ariadne's string tied to his hip. He wasn't the hunted; he was the hunter. For nearly two hours, Theseus listened and walked the maze while trying to make out the faintest sounds and changes in the environment. The rest of the tributes had stayed near the early portions of the maze, hoping they wouldn't encounter the beast.

A mosaic of Theseus and the Minotaur.
https://commons.wikimedia.org/wiki/File:Theseus_Minotaur_Mosaic.jpg

Theseus eventually stopped searching and decided to make the Minotaur come to him. He began to bang his sword on the wall every so often so that the beast could get a sense of where he was but not pinpoint his exact location. Then Theseus heard it: the distinct clip-clop of a bovine hoof. The stench intensified. The strength of the Minotaur's breath seemed to change the air temperature around Theseus as well, even though he could tell the beast was at least several feet away from him. Theseus stood fast, his hand on the hilt of his sword, ready for the moment the beast charged him with its great horns.

The Minotaur stamped its foot on the ground once, twice. It ran right at the young prince, who unsheathed his weapon at the last minute. With one graceful strike, he buried his blade in the Minotaur's neck. The beast, still in shock over the deadly assault, was still trying to run forward, further impaling himself on Theseus's blade until the point broke through the back of his skull. The great terror of King Minos and the island of Crete had been defeated. Theseus chopped off the Minotaur's head for good measure, taking it as a trophy for his father, and proceeded to follow his safety line all the way out of the labyrinth with the other

Athenian tributes, who were all alive and well.

Ariadne couldn't control her happiness when she saw that the man of her dreams was alive. Although Theseus was the main actor in this tale, it was Ariadne who had ensured his survival. Without her brilliant idea, Theseus would have been walking toward his death, and he knew it. He, Ariadne, and the tributes stole away on the ship with black sails and set out for Athens. However, all was not right in paradise, as they say. The ship stopped at the island of Naxos to resupply, and the next morning when Ariadne awoke, she found herself sleeping alone on the beach. Dumbstruck by her situation, she scoured the length of the beach for her love, then looked inland to see if she could see the Athenians up high on the terrain. "Perhaps they were searching for more food or water?" she told herself, but she knew it was a lie. The young princess slowly turned toward the sea and saw the black sails on the horizon. There was Theseus on board his ship, sailing away from the island, the tributes in tow.

Why would he abandon the princess? The myths are a bit hazy with this one. It is thought that jealous Hera had appeared to the Athenian prince in a dream and convinced him to leave the young woman behind. Some say Dionysus wanted Ariadne for himself right then and convinced Theseus to leave her. However, it is also possible that Theseus realized he did not care for Ariadne as much as he thought. Perhaps he was just using her, or perhaps he did not want to spend the rest of his life with her as his queen. Despite being revered as heroes, many demi-gods made a great deal of questionable moral decisions. This was usually done to comment on their human side and their tendency toward imperfection. Demi-god or not, Theseus was still a man. Poor Ariadne was not devastated for long because shortly after her abandonment, she was seduced by Dionysus, who carried her off to become his wife and the mother to two of his children.

On his way back to Athens, Theseus began to regret abandoning the princess. He realized that perhaps he did love Ariadne. He was so distraught over losing a woman he deliberately left on an island that he forgot to change the sails on his ship from black to white, which would indicate to his father that he had survived the terrible ordeal and was returning home. King Aegeus had lookouts posted on the cliffs day and night for the last fortnight so that he would be notified the moment Theseus's ship was spotted. One of the lookouts noticed a black spot coming toward the cliffs, but he couldn't make out if it was the prince or an enemy ship. Eventually, he was able to identify the black sails. The lookout ran all the way to the palace and burst through the doors into the throne room. He threw himself before the feet of the king and wept that black sails had been spotted on the water.

The king, in disbelief, rushed to the cliffs and indeed saw that the watcher had spoken truthfully. There is little despair in this world that is equivalent to the death of a child. Aegeus had lost his son and, therefore, his heart and will to live. The king couldn't bear the pain. Without hesitation, he stepped off the edge of the cliff into the open air below. Theseus saw his father as he impaled himself on the rocks below and was heartbroken for the second time. He was now the king of Athens, but it was a throne he took filled with grief and sorrow. As a demi-god, Theseus was strong and brave, but he lost his love and his father all in one day because of his weakness as a man.

Chapter 12: Perseus and Medusa

The story of the demi-god Perseus begins with the love affair of his parents. Although Zeus had many wives and even more lovers, the man was a very emotional creature. He was a person who fell in love with everything and everyone. It has been said that out of all those women, he loved Danae the best. She was the daughter of King Acrisius and Queen Eurydice, and she was beloved by her people but feared by her father. For years, the king and queen had failed to produce a son to inherit the throne. When their daughter was finally born, their joy was unparalleled, but a dark and disturbing thought had dwelled in the king's mind for years over this very event.

Before Danae was conceived, Acrisius had sought the counsel and divination of the Pythian oracle to determine whether he would ever have a son. Perhaps he had angered or offended the gods in some manner but did not realize it? The oracle informed the desperate king that his line would indeed produce a male heir, but it would not be his. The child would one day grow to dispose of Acrisius and bring ruin to all he loved and held dear. Shortly after Danae was born, Acrisius realized it would be her womb that produced his downfall. When Danae bled for the first time, her father wasted no time in shutting her in a subterranean room entirely made of stone and earth. There was little to no light that reached the princess, save for a skylight above with metal bars over the gap.

Danae stayed there for two winters. Another person would have given up all hope that they would ever leave; maybe, they would succumb to the loneliness and desperation they felt. But not Danae. She somehow never lost her hope in that dark and secluded cell. Zeus had been listening to the girl's prayers. She was strong and stoic, and Zeus fell in love with her gentle yet relentless spirit. One night, he visited her in that prison, coming down through the spaces between the skylight bars as golden rain. In this form, he made love to Danae.

The experience for Zeus was also something different, and when his wife Hera inquired about the reason behind his infidelity, "Zeus who gathers the clouds answered her [Hera]: 'Never before has love for any goddess or woman so melted about the heart inside me, broken it to submission, as now: not that time...when I loved Akrisios' [Acrisius's] daughter sweet-stepping Danaë.'"[53] This would have been hurtful for Hera to hear, but one can assume that Zeus was telling the truth. Zeus had some despicable tendencies, but this sounds like unbridled honesty.

That night brought about the birth of Perseus. Danae gave birth in her cell alone. After her labor was complete, her father wasted no time in disposing of her and her newborn child. After the king's physician had certified Danae's son, Acrisius commissioned his masons to build a sarcophagus. He placed his young daughter and grandson in it and cast the two out to sea.

Zeus had been keeping watch over Danae since she fell pregnant, and as soon as she was tossed into the waves, Poseidon was at the ready. He carried the sarcophagus safely to the ship of a fisherman by the name of Dictys. He ferried her safely to the island of Seriphos, a small and secluded kingdom. Still, word gets around. For the first few days after her arrival, Dictys nursed the young mother back to health. She mostly slept, waking only to nurse her child; Dictys handled everything else. The fisherman had lost his own wife and child years prior, so seeing Danae in this condition

---

[53] Homer, *Iliad* 14. 319 ff, trans. Lattimore. [Greek epic, c. 8th BCE]

broke his heart. He did not want the woman and her young son to be without support, something which he could not provide in his meager surroundings. This child needed a father or at the very least some direct guidance, and his mother, being a single mother and a vulnerable woman, needed the protection of someone in power, someone like his brother, King Polydectes.

Although Dictys had good intentions, his brother did not possess the same kind and generous spirit. He yearned for Danae, and after the king made several advances, all of which Danae turned down, he decided the solution was to kidnap her and lock her away while still trying to court the poor woman. One captivity in a lifetime was more than enough, but Danae was destined to suffer. As for her young son, Polydectes was merciful, to a degree, and sent Perseus off to be raised in the temple of Athena.

In actuality, this was one of the most generous things he could have done for the young hero, for it was the beginning of Perseus's patronage and favor with the goddess Athena. She would later become an indispensable part of his story. Years later, when Perseus had reached manhood, he returned to the house of his former foster father, Dictys, and lamented over the captivity of his mother. Dictys informed the young hero to go before the king and demand the release of his mother. Dictys knew that the king would not let her go willingly and would set before Perseus an impossible task in exchange for his mother's release. Dictys, however, was not entirely unaware of Perseus's lineage. Danae had confided in Dictys like a father, having been so estranged from what should have been the natural love of her own biological dad. She had informed him of that night in her cell when she was impregnated with Perseus. Whatever challenge Polydectes set before the demi-god, Perseus would surely succeed.

When Perseus stepped into the throne room of the king, he saw his mother sitting at Polydectes's feet, chained to the floor. She had changed, as the weariness and turmoil of her circumstances had dulled her spirit, but she was still beautiful. Perseus had to stop himself from rushing to embrace her. It angered and hurt him to see his beautiful and brave mother in such a fashion. Whatever the obstacle, Perseus would complete his task one way or another or find a way to kill the king.

He demanded the release of his mother, and Polydectes agreed to comply if and only if Perseus would go on a quest for the head of the legendary and fearsome Gorgon Medusa. Remember her? She had been raped by Poseidon and then maliciously cursed by Athena, the goddess of wisdom and rationality. Medusa had to live the rest of her days with snakes for hair and a gaze that turned any living creature into stone. Perseus consented to kill the Gorgon or die trying, and he turned to leave the throne room. He looked back only once to catch the glance of his mother's eyes, rimmed with tears yet stoic and bluer than the Aegean Sea.

Zeus, who had been following the escapades of his son and former lover since the day Perseus was conceived, beseeched the gods and goddesses of Olympus to aid Perseus in his quest and to bestow upon him gifts that would help him to slay the Gorgon. Hades selflessly gave Perseus his very own helmet of invisibility. The mighty Hephaestus forged a steel sword with a golden handle for the young hero. Athena presented him with a reflective bronze shield, and Hermes gifted him a pair of winged sandals. All of these gifts would be necessary for Perseus to best Medusa, who was well equipped with the best defense mechanism of any man or animal. On top of this, she was also a gifted archer. Not to mention she had years of pent-up aggression and rage toward the world of men and gods for her current predicament.

After collecting his gifts from the gods and bidding farewell to Dictys, Perseus set out on his quest for Medusa's head. For starters, getting to the dwelling of Medusa would be a trip and a half. Her cave was located deep beneath Mt. Olympus in caverns that were as old as the original Titans. Medusa would not be the only foul creature lurking in those dark passageways and halls made of stone. Eventually, Perseus found his way to the entrance of her cave. Mastering all of his courage, he entered the darkness. The coils and hisses of serpents were his guides for finding Medusa, and lucky for him, when he did find her, she was fast asleep. The hero finding his hunted target in a deep slumber was not unusual in Greek mythology. Certain versions of Theseus and the Minotaur recount how Theseus found the beast asleep and was able to kill it with great ease. Even asleep and with her eyes closed, though, Medusa was dangerous. Perseus did not want to chance anything, as a non-direct gaze could have the same full blast radius of a wide-awake Gorgon.

He turned his back to face the monster and held up his shield to use as a mirror in order to locate Medusa. Carefully stepping backward, he lifted his sword high in the air and brought it crashing down at the base of Medusa's neck. The decapitated monster wiggled and wretched as her head went rolling away from her body. From her severed neck sprouted her twins, Pegasus and Chrysaor. The former would become Perseus's personal mount, and he would be crucial for the success of his remaining quest.

Perseus did not move a muscle, and he wouldn't open his eyes until he heard complete silence. Once Medusa's body had stopped involuntarily convulsing, Perseus used his shield again to find her severed head and laid his cloak over it for good measure. He then wrapped it up, chucked it in his satchel, mounted the winged steed Pegasus, and began to fly back to the island of Seriphos to free his mother from her captor.

Perseus with the Head of Medusa *by Benvenuto Cellini, 1554.*
Xosema, CC BY-SA 4.0 via Wikimedia Commons;
https://commons.wikimedia.org/wiki/File:Florencia_-_Firenze_-
_Perseo_con_la_cabeza_de_Medusa_-_Benvenuto_Cellini_-_01.jpg

On the way back, our hero encountered another damsel in distress, Andromeda, the daughter of King Cepheus and Queen Cassiopeia, who were lords of Joppa in the Levant. Some say that the king and queen were the rulers of Ethiopia, but their origins were not from mainland Greece or the surrounding Greek islands. At a party one evening, the queen had boasted arrogantly that her daughter was the most beautiful creature in the world. Her boasting got worse and worse until she crossed a line mere mortals dare not cross. She exclaimed that her beloved child was even more lovely than the Nereids, the nymph daughters of Poseidon. Various versions of the story interchange the object of her offense, for sometimes it is Aphrodite or Thetis, but the bottom line is that she greatly offended the immortals.

As punishment, the god Poseidon threatened to destroy the city of Joppa by unleashing the monstrous Cetus, a sea creature and the doomed spawn of Poseidon himself. Poseidon, who was perhaps the least merciful of the gods, provided the king and queen with one method of saving their beloved kingdom and all the innocent souls under their dominion. He instructed them to sacrifice their one and only child to Cetus by chaining her onto a rock in the Mediterranean Sea. Only her blood would sate Cetus and save the city.

Now, any sort of political choice is not made lightly and always presents a few cons and pros, either of which can tip the scales toward a certain decision. The decision that King Cepheus and Queen Cassiopeia reached was that the life of their city was worth more than that of their daughter. They were young, and the queen's womb was still functioning, but replacing a city and their people would be nearly impossible after a divine and very aggressive sea monster virtually wiped them clean from the face of the earth. Andromeda also cared about the life and safety of her people, so she willingly allowed herself to be led down to the shore and strapped to the boulder to await her fate as the martyr of Joppa.

Perseus was flying by at the time and saw the fair maiden upon the rock. At first, he took no great notice of her predicament, but as he flew closer, he saw the fair beauty of the maiden and then the rolling waves that seemed to grow larger and larger as they approached the princess. Finally, Cetus's head broke the surface of the water, and out he sprang from the sea, a gigantic serpent. His slimy form crawled its way onto the shore, ready to devour the tender princess. Perseus immediately recognized the danger, and he knew what he must do to stop the monster and save the princess. No creature made of flesh and blood was a match for the stone-cold gaze of a Gorgon's severed head, most of all, the severed head of the deadliest Gorgon in all the ancient world.

Perseus dive-bombed his winged steed, and as he descended, he whipped out the terrifying head, readying himself to face it toward Cetus. When the sea dragon made eye contact with Medusa's head, it immediately began to recoil and retract, unable to comprehend the ice-cold feeling seeping its way into its veins and muscular tissues. Fear gripped the serpent and shone from the hollow yellow in its bright eyes, which were the last body parts to be rendered motionless and dead for all time. Legend has it that Cetus can still be found in his stone form in the ancient Levant somewhere near the Red Sea, while others say it is at the edge of the Mediterranean.

Perseus cut Andromeda down from her boulder, loaded her up onto Pegasus, and flew to the castle to demand her hand in marriage from her parents. The king and queen would have immediately obliged, given the fact that the rescuer was the answer to their prayers for having saved not only their beloved daughter but also their fair city. However, their daughter's hand was already promised to another. This did not seem to faze Perseus, and he asked the king and queen to bring forth the inconsequential prince. Perseus saw that the prince was a weak and cruel man who resented Perseus for having been the one to rescue his betrothed.

Perseus wasted no time and pulled forth Medusa's head from his bloody satchel. The prince didn't even have time to scream before he, too, was turned to stone. The king and queen were more or less elated, if not slightly terrified, of their soon-to-be son-in-law. Perseus and Andromeda headed back to Seriphos to finally rescue Perseus's mother from her own non-consensual marriage, one bonded not in love but with chains.

Perseus had to be cunning. He knew that his mother would be sitting at her designated place of imprisonment, at the feet of King Polydectes. He first went to see his adoptive father, Dictys, both to say hello and to help him concoct a plan to set his mother free. Upon seeing that Perseus was not only alive and well but also victorious in his quest and married to the lovely Andromeda, Dictys wept with happiness. Dictys said that he would request Danae come visit him at his home to help mend some old fishing nets. Danae usually came by herself when she visited Dictys, so he knew his brother would be alone in the throne room.

On the day of Danae's visit, unbeknownst to her, Perseus walked into the throne room to present Medusa's head to the king as he requested. Polydectes was floored. He did not expect Perseus to survive his quest, and he was thankful that his mother was not there to see that her son had succeeded. Polydectes was already thinking of ways to have Perseus killed before his mother could ever discover that he had returned. Before he could even get out a greeting to his stepson, Perseus revealed the severed head of the Gorgon and turned the king to stone right there on his throne. For good measure, Perseus came up behind the stone king and pushed him off the throne, causing the statue to shatter into a million pieces. This was the end of the malignant Polydectes. Few would mourn the evil king.

When Danae returned to the throne room, she saw her own son sitting on the throne with his new queen beside him. Few mothers in the history of the ancient world felt such unparalleled joy and relief at seeing their son. Danae must have gasped in happiness, for her son was not only alive but had also inherited the keys to the kingdom. It is typical of ancient tales, whether they are considered to be mythological, biblical, or otherwise, to end with the death of a most beloved son or the parent. The story of Perseus and Medusa is one of the rare exceptions where the hero and parent are reunited in a happy ending.

Chapter 13: The Trojan War

The *Iliad* and the *Aeneid*, which recount the story of the Trojan War, are some of the most circulated stories in the modern world. Thousands of years after its inception, the tale of the Trojan War still captivates readers with its lessons of human flaws, strengths, desires, and hopes. The characters' names and personas have been elevated in the pages of history and mythology for their unique sense of telling the story of many. For instance, who of us hasn't felt the sting of unrequited love? Plus, some people are just really unlucky. The sense of triumph and travesty that is accessible to every human being can be found in the pages of the *Iliad* and the *Aeneid*.

As we expressed earlier in this book, the main subject of a Greek myth never begins with the story itself but with a few others instead. Context and background were very important to the Greeks. Who one was depended on where one came from, and their circumstances eventually trickled down into a single destiny. The rest of the story was dictated by one's choices.

The story of the Trojan War begins with the wedding of Peleus and Thetis, the parents of the hero and legendary fighter Achilles (you know you're a major influence on the world when a whole portion of the ankle is named after you and your story, but more on that later). Thetis was the daughter of the second-generation Titan Nereus and his nymph-goddess wife, Doris. Together, the two had fifty daughters, the eldest of which was Thetis. She looked after her sisters and, like her parents, could shapeshift into any marine creature. The family inhabited a series of sea caves buried deep within the underbelly of the Aegean, and there they remained, peaceful and relatively undisturbed.

That was until the day that Peleus struck a bargain with Zeus for the hand of Thetis, the loveliest and adored of her sisters. The Oracle of Delphi had prophesized that Thetis's son would be twice as great as his sire. Zeus could not allow himself to succumb to Thetis's charms, nor could he allow any of the other immortals the chance to have her as their wife or lover. The child that would come from her womb could be powerful enough to kill them all and disrupt the world order. Thus, Zeus plotted to have her betrothed to a mortal man. This was when Peleus, the king of Phthia, stepped onto the scene. He was powerful enough to be respectable but would not produce a son greater than the gods.

His child, however, would still be considered a demi-god, given his mother's impressive divine lineage, and would make a name for himself as one of the greatest fighters the world had ever seen. Although demi-gods typically are not immortal beings and are by no means 100 percent invincible, they can succumb to death and injury given the right circumstances. To ensure her son retained some of her invincibility as an immortal, Thetis took him to the River Styx when he was a small child. She held her baby by one of his heels and dipped his entire body into the waters of the dead. However, the spot where she had held Achilles did not enter the water. His heel was his only weak spot. How Achilles was able to survive being submerged in the river is largely debated. Usually, those with any mortal heritage who fell into the river would not survive, hence the need for a boatman to ferry the souls of the dead into the underworld.

The wedding of Peleus and Thetis was a very joyous affair, and all of the immortals were invited to the wedding except for Eris, the goddess of discord. Despite not receiving an invitation for obvious reasons, the goddess still took the decision to heart. All things considered, it was unwise for the happy couple to disrespect her in such a manner and not expect some kind of retaliation in return. Eris devised a plan to ruin the wedding festivities. She sent a golden apple to the feast as a wedding present, and she addressed it to "the most beautiful of all the goddesses."

Naturally, Hera, Athena, and Aphrodite all thought they had a claim to the apple. Zeus sent the apple, along with the three goddesses, to the city of Troy, where the goddesses would be judged by the young Prince Paris. "Let the hands of men be soiled with this unpopular decision," thought Zeus. Paris was damned if he didn't judge and damned if he did. He had no way of knowing just how much his decision would affect the rest of his kingdom and change the face of the Greek world for all time.

The goddesses approached Paris when he was out one morning hunting with his guards. He came to a large clearing with one tall olive tree right in the middle. The area was completely silent, and Paris climbed down from his horse to collect a few of the beautiful olives. Suddenly, he heard another party make their way into the clearing. Hand on his sword, ready for any friend or foe, he turned quickly and was shocked to see three goddesses standing before him. Paris fell to his knees. Each goddess offered him a gift if he declared her the most beautiful. All the goddesses offered generous gifts, but Paris was persuaded by Aphrodite's enticing offer. At the end of the day, she was the best judge amongst the three goddesses as to what the prince's heart truly desired. She offered him the hand of the most beautiful woman in the world: Helen, the reigning queen of Sparta. This was obviously an issue, but the fact that Helen belonged to another man did not dissuade the young prince from claiming his prize.

Paris made the journey to Sparta under the false pretense of a political mission to discuss the terms of imports and exports with the Spartan king, Menelaus, a great warrior who came from a prominent royal family. His brother, Agamemnon, was the king of Mycenae, and he was on a political quest to unite and rule over all the *poleis* of Greece. Although each Greek city-state had its own particular ruler or king, it was Agamemnon who declared that all of these men would answer to him and be at his beck and call for any sort of need. It was a position that required a great deal of strength and strategy. Paris was playing with fire by seeking to abduct the beautiful wife of Agamemnon's favorite brother.

When Paris walked into the throne room, Menelaus greeted the young prince with open arms and orchestrated a whole banquet in his honor, not knowing that he had just invited a snake to dinner. As for Helen, she was immediately smitten with the young prince's handsome features and fine manners. (Some accounts say she did not care for Paris in the same way he did or that Aphrodite intervened to make sure they loved each other; we chose to go with the romantic version.) Her current husband, Menelaus, could be a cold and brutish warrior without the finer subtleties and touch of a man that a woman of Helen's status preferred. Although Menelaus loved Helen and vice versa, there was a certain spark of passion missing. According to some accounts, Helen was just a prize to Menelaus, a beautiful jewel to make other men more envious of his stature and position. It only took a few encounters for Helen and Paris to be absolutely enthralled with one another. After about a month of their affair, it was time for Paris to sail back to Troy.

Little did Menelaus know that below the deck of the Trojan ship was his prized bride. When he discovered that Helen was missing from her chambers, he went ballistic. He had no idea where she could have gone until a fisherman came to the court of the king and revealed that he had seen her board the ship and share a kiss with the young prince the night before the Trojans were to set sail.

Upon their arrival in Troy, King Priam, Paris's father, and Prince Hector, Paris's older brother, were outraged at what the young prince had done. However, it was too late to undo the wrong that had been done. Even if Helen was returned, it was not in Menelaus's nature to forgive, and Paris would have met an unfortunate death regardless. Who knows what ills and abuse would have been done to Helen? Priam was a soft-hearted king who ruled and commanded respect and power through his wisdom and kindness. He loved his sons dearly and would never wish them to come to any harm despite their mistakes or failings.

While Helen was being greeted by the entirety of the Trojan court and nobles, Menelaus was sailing to Mycenae to request the help of his brother in a campaign against Troy. They would sail to the city, reclaim Menelaus's wife, and lay waste to the entire city. Agamemnon willingly agreed. Men with all the power in the world usually only care about one thing: gaining more power. Agamemnon cared very little for his brother's pretty little wife, but he cared very much for the stature and power provided in decimating perhaps the greatest city in Anatolia, which is now present-day Turkey. This was already shaping up to be one of the most legendary wars in Greek history, and Agamemnon sought the allegiance of some of the greatest kings and warriors of all time. His list included Odysseus, king of Ithaca; Ajax the Great, a descendant of Zeus and the cousin of Achilles; and, as one might have guessed, the brave and fearsome Achilles himself.

Over one thousand ships set sail for the coast of Turkey. Achilles commanded his own ship and a force of specialized soldiers, the Myrmidons, which were widely acknowledged as the most fearsome men in Greece. These soldiers would do anything their general asked without delay. Also sailing with Achilles was his best friend and most trusted advisor Patroclus.

For the first few years of the war, all of the battles were evenly matched, with plenty of casualties on both sides. Hector, being the eldest prince of Troy, always led his army onto the battlefield. He was also one of the most skilled warriors Troy had ever seen, and he even held his own against Ajax the Great. Hector was guarded by Apollo during this battle, and Athena chose Ajax as her champion. Even the gods took sides in the war. Apollo was the patron god of Troy. He would always look out for members of the royal family, as the city of Troy had maintained his patronage for hundreds of years, currying his favor with gifts and sacrifices of immense worth. When their dance of death was over, both men greatly respected the other. Hector presented his sword to Ajax to honor the hero's great skill and speed; Ajax would later use this sword to kill himself.

One battle ended in great tragedy for Achilles. At one point during the war, Achilles is upset with Agamemnon. The great king had taken his slave, Briseis, for his own, even though Achilles was the one to enslave her. He refused to fight as a result, which was devastating for the Greeks since he was one of their strongest fighters. But unless his prize was returned to him, he would not go on the battlefield.

Although the Greeks entreat him to fight, showering him with promises of wealth and the return of his slave, Achilles refuses. He was going to sail home, and he told the other Greeks to follow his example. Patroclus found this reaction to be in poor taste. He could not stand the thought of his fellow Greeks being slaughtered while the Myrmidons stood down.

The Trojans had advanced their attack by this time, as they wished to drive the rest of the Greek army into the sea. Little did they know that Zeus had already prophesied that the Greek army would be the victor in the war, but the king of the gods was not above humbling or punishing the hero that had stepped out of line on the battlefield.

Patroclus went to Achilles and begged him to allow him to fight in the battle. In addition to this request, he also asked permission for the honor of wearing Achilles's armor into battle. Achilles could not deny his most beloved friend's request, but he told Patroclus to only fight long enough to drive the Trojans back from the ships.

Patroclus, filled with courage, ran into the battle, fully outfitted in Achilles's distinct armor. He managed to rally the Greek forces and pushed back the Trojans. He even ended the life of one of Zeus's favorite mortal sons, Sarpedon. Hector had to pull his men back to the safety of the city.

However, Patroclus was driven drunk with blood lust. He knew a potential victory was on the horizon. Some variations say that Apollo robbed him of his senses, which led to Patroclus following the Trojans all the way to the city gates. This was exactly what Achilles had told him not to do. As Patroclus advanced, he took as many Trojan lives as he could.

Eventually, he came face to face with Hector and was slaughtered. With one clean jab of his spear, Hector skewered Patroclus. It wasn't until the end of the battle, when the bodies were being removed from the field to be cremated, that news of Patroclus's death reached Achilles. Every soldier of Greece knew who the man was, and one soldier ran to tell Achilles. He couldn't believe it, but when he saw the body, he dropped to his knees and began to wail. Once his wailing had ceased, Achilles felt nothing but rage and anger toward Hector.

Without authorizing his next move with Agamemnon, Achilles immediately mounted a chariot and drove it all the way to the city gates of Troy. The archers were ready to dispose of the warrior, but Hector ordered them to stand down. He was sure that his skills on the battlefield were akin to, if not better than, Achilles. Hector was also a man of honor and would not simply dispose of Achilles when the warrior had come to his gates seeking one-on-one combat. He would have disgraced his family's name and honor if he did not accept the challenge.

The fight that ensued between the two warriors was a dance of death, as the two men were agile and cunning. Hector eventually began to tire, but Achilles's anger fueled his strength. With one thrust of a spear, it was all over. Hector laid there in the dust as Achilles went over and tied his feet together. He fashioned Hector to the back of his chariot and rode all the way back to camp with the crown prince of Troy dragging behind. The sight was too much for King Priam to behold, and he fainted at the sight of his firstborn and heir being disrespected in such a manner. This also greatly angered the gods, as it displayed a severe lack of honor and self-control, especially since Hector had asked for his body to be treated respectfully. Hector had not singled out Patroclus for a kill; in fact, he had thought he was battling Achilles since Patroclus was wearing his armor. What Achilles did to Hector's body was not necessary in the eyes of many, and the warrior would pay for his offense.

A fresco of Achilles dragging Hector's corpse.
https://commons.wikimedia.org/wiki/File:Triumph_of_Achilles_in_Corfu_Achilleion.jpg

Achilles was brought down by Paris, who was fairly gifted with a bow and commanded the archers high up on the walls of Troy. During another campaign to overtake the city, Paris saw Achilles below in the swarm of blood and bodies. He took aim and let loose his arrow, aiming right for Achilles's exposed leg. The legs were one of the only regions of the body to not be covered by any form of armor. The wound, he thought, would give another soldier enough of a fighting chance to kill Achilles. Little did he know that the gods were on his side. At the last moment, Apollo pushed Achilles a little further so that the arrow went right through the tendon in his heel (hence the name for this body part being the Achilles' heel). This was his only weak point, and it caused the remainder of his organs to shut down. The greatest warrior in all of Greece was defeated and lay in the dust for all to see.

After the death of Achilles, the morale of the Greek army was at its lowest point. The Trojan War lasted ten long years, and it seemed as if the fighting would never cease. The city of Troy had built its walls strong and high, and it was nearly impossible for all the armies of Greece to overtake the city without serious casualties. And now they had lost one of their best warriors. The Myrmidons refused to go onto the battlefield for any other master besides Achilles, not even when Agamemnon threatened them with execution. The kings of Greece were desperately trying to persuade Agamemnon to abandon the campaign and sail home. He feared what would happen to his kingdom if he lost this war, though. If the Trojans could beat him so easily, it might give other empires ideas about invading territories he had worked so hard to acquire.

Then salvation came in the form of an idea, an ingenious and deceitful idea from the mind of Odysseus. He was by far the most cunning and intellectually gifted out of all the Greek kings. He knew that the Trojans were very devout subjects of the gods and that they would never refuse a sacrificial offering.

Odysseus told Agamemnon to have his men break down one of the ships. They would use the planks and the nails to construct an offering that King Priam would not be able to refuse. This offering was the Trojan horse. Inside, the horse would be filled with Greek soldiers. Once they were inside the city walls, the men would open the gate for the remainder of the Greek army. Odysseus told Agamemnon to have all the other ships sail around to the far side of the coast and to leave a lookout so that they could confirm the gift had been received.

Depiction of the Trojan horse on a Corinthian pot, circa 560 BCE.
https://commons.wikimedia.org/wiki/File:Trojan_horse_on_corintian_aryballos.JPG

The lookout in the tower of Troy called out that there were no more Greek ships spotted on the coast. An envoy was sent down to the shores and reported back that the Greeks had, in fact, departed but that they left a gift on their way out. They thought perhaps it was an offering to the god Poseidon for a safe journey home. Some sources say it was an offering to Athena and that by taking the horse into the city gates, Troy would be impregnable.

Cassandra, Priam's eldest daughter, cautioned her father to dispose of the offering by burning it right then and there on the beach. Priam was a man devoted to the gods and would not hear of anyone burning an official offering of such stature, especially to one of the more temperamental gods. The good king decided that the horse would be brought into the city and placed inside the temple of Poseidon (or Athena, depending on which version you read). It would serve as a reminder and honor of the victory won against all the armies of Greece.

However, Cassandra had been cursed by the god Apollo to know the future. This sounds pretty nice, except he made it so that no one believed her. And Priam's decision turned out to be a fatal mistake. When night fell, and the whole city lay in their beds fast asleep and oblivious to the impending danger, the Greek soldiers crawled out from the horse and opened the gates to the city. In a matter of hours, the entirety of Troy was engulfed in flames. We will spare the gory details of what happens when a city is overtaken, but you can use your imagination.

Like Achilles, some Greeks would end up paying for their lack of honor. Even though they had won the war, they did so with trickery and deceit, which was far different from beating your enemies on the open battlefield. Many of the Greeks who sailed for home did not survive the journey, or their trip was delayed by trials and hardships. In fact, when some reached home, they found their wives married to others, having believed that after so many years, their husbands were never coming back. One of the fortunate ones to make it home was Odysseus.

However, before he reunited with his queen Penelope, he would spend several years sailing the ancient world, being tested with a few legendary trials of his own. His story would become one of the most famous myths of all time and one of the first to be put down in writing. We are referring to none other than the *Odyssey*.

Chapter 14: The *Odyssey* and the Return of Heroes

Many years before Odysseus had been called to fight in Troy, he married his wife Penelope, and the two had a son named Telemachus. It was a joyous day when the prince was born. The entire kingdom rejoiced, but none more so than Anticlea, Odysseus's mother. She saw that her son's happiness was now complete, and if her son was happy, the kingdom would be as well. Odysseus was beloved by the entire kingdom, and his son and heir would grow up amongst the people, learning how a king ruled.

However, Odysseus never got to see his son grow, as he was away for ten long years in the campaign for Troy. And for ten years after the war ended, Odysseus strived to return home to the bed of his wife, Penelope. However, the anger the gods felt toward the Greeks was doubly true for Odysseus. The Trojan horse was his brainchild, and after his plan succeeded, he forgot to pay homage to the god Poseidon, lord of all horses and the master of the seas (the very sea on which Odysseus was to set sail). Odysseus's thoughtlessness created his worst enemy. Poseidon was one of the least forgiving of the gods, and as such, he swore that Odysseus would never again see the shores of his beloved Ithaca. Instead, he would suffer on the high seas and be steered into any potential danger.

During the years Odysseus was trying to get home, a brigade of suitors eventually made their way to the palace. They were led by the vilest amongst their company, Antinous. These suitors made a mess of the king's great hall, but neither Penelope nor Telemachus (now a young man) had the authority or the strength to make the suitors leave. They all believed that the true king was dead and that there would be no consequences for their actions. Meanwhile, Odysseus had already set sail from Troy and vowed that despite Poseidon's vow of destruction, he would return home a victor.

For his first interference, Poseidon set a thick fog over the Aegean, separating Odysseus from the rest of the Greek fleet. The ship sailed aimlessly, as the lookout could see nothing but fog. There seemed to be no end to the sea and no land in sight. Just then, land seemed to appear out of nowhere. The men were hopeful that the island was inhabited by mankind, for they could seek shelter, rest, and perhaps find a new and correct course for Ithaca.

The instant that Odysseus set foot on the island, he knew that it was no place of men. All he could make out in the distance was the faint sound of sheep and goats. Herds would not be without their shepherd, but who and what exactly was the shepherd was the real question to be answered. Odysseus sent two of his scouts to see what the island held. The men found no signs of civilization or manmade structures of any kind. The only thing they found on the whole island was a vast cave that seemed to disappear down into the depths of the earth. In this cave was nothing save for a great deal of goat cheese. But who made the cheese, and where was the master of the herds?

While the men were overjoyed to find this cave of plenty, Odysseus was still hesitant, and the knot in his stomach would not go away. The king was famed for his mind and instincts, which could smell danger a mile away. He found it suspect that the cave contained no tools or weapons of any kind. How did these men fend for themselves, shear their sheep, or create the heavy stone door to the cave?

Outside the cave, Odysseus's men were busy collecting firewood to prepare their evening supper, and they found a large footprint, one that was ten times larger than any print made by a human or animal. Why the men didn't think it necessary to report the print to their leader is unknown. They must have thought that the being who left the print was long dead; things like giants were rarities in the world of the Greeks now. And what were the chances they had stumbled across one? So, Odysseus's men made camp inside the cave and proceeded to get roaringly drunk. The ship had run out of fresh water a while ago, and the Greeks would mix their wine with water; otherwise, it was too strong. The inebriated men continued to laugh and joke, making an excessive amount of noise. This was not the brightest thing to do, considering these men had no idea where they were or whose company they were going to find.

Just then, they felt the earth shake. They could hear the bleating of the sheep not too far off, as well as the deep breath of something very large making its way back to the cave. It was not a shepherd after all but a cyclops by the name of Polyphemus, a son of Poseidon. Polyphemus was astounded to find Odysseus and his men in the cave. He quickly shut the large stone door to his cave and inquired who were these men to be so bold as to eat his food.

Odysseus, ever the politician, decided to try and reason with the cyclops, explaining that they had eaten from his stores but only because they were so hungry. In fact, they wanted to trade goods for the things they had eaten. Polyphemus was not interested in what the men had brought to trade, declaring that he did not eat the food of men but only meat. He then seized one of Odysseus's soldiers, tore the man in two, and ate the upper half of his body. The remaining soldiers leaped to their feet, ready to defend their lives, but Odysseus knew how dangerous it would be to try and fight a cyclops. He told his men to stay calm.

The king was very clever; he told the cyclops that he would be his next meal, willingly and freely. However, if the cyclops ate him, he would never possess the magic inside of Odysseus. It was not uncommon for the world of men and magic to collide, and quite a few mortals had magical gifts similar to that of Phineas the seer or Medea the sorceress. This caught Polyphemus's attention, and he asked for Odysseus's name. Odysseus told him that his name was Nobody (yes, literally nobody) and then offered him some wine to drink. Polyphemus had never heard of or tasted wine, and the cunning king of Ithaca told him that it was the drink of the gods.

Cyclopes were looked down upon by most of the immortals; they occupied a lesser status, despite their immense skill and strength. Polyphemus quickly drank the "wine of the gods" while one of Odysseus's soldiers played him a soft lullaby. Polyphemus then fell into a deep sleep. However, the men still had a fairly large issue on their hands. The stone door was immovable. Only the giant cyclops could move the stone and set the men free. However, clever Odysseus had a plan.

He had his soldiers collect all of the sheepskins that Polyphemus used for his bed. He then set about to fashion a giant lance. This he used to blind the cyclops's eye, who ran to the stone door, opened it, and called out to his brothers that Nobody had blinded him. It was a very clever move indeed. The soldiers were then able to sneak past the blinded Polyphemus by wearing the skins of his sheep. Odysseus suffered the loss of a few of his men against the cyclops, but all in all, the company had a fairly impressive survival rate, despite the horrific manner of death their comrades faced.

Laconian pottery showing the blinding of Polyphemus, circa 565–560 BCE.
https://commons.wikimedia.org/wiki/File:Odysseus_Polyphemos_Cdm_Paris_190.jpg

The rest of the company returned to the ship and sailed away as fast as they could. From the deck of his ship, Odysseus called out to Polyphemus that his fate to be blinded had been sealed by his own father, Poseidon. If the god had not made the ship veer off course and land on Polyphemus's island, the cyclops would still have his sight. While Odysseus was one of the cleverest kings in the history of Greek mythology, he was known for his immense pride and somewhat boastful nature. The man who thinks he is the smartest in the room is oftentimes the hardest to get along with. These men rarely learn from their mistakes as well. So, it is no surprise that Odysseus was quick to add insult to injury by provoking Poseidon yet again.

The men sailed for months, and their extreme thirst nearly killed them all until they finally saw land. It was yet another strange island with more potential surprises. Odysseus went off on his own to look for water for his men. When he finally found a freshwater source, the stream somehow evaded his pitcher. Every time he lowered the vessel to obtain some of the water, it moved out of his way. Odysseus was sure this was some sort of madness or illusion brought on by extreme thirst or hunger, but it was none other than Poseidon who was refusing the hero and his men the right to a drink of water.

Odysseus then heard the voice of someone. It was the king of the island greeting Odysseus. "I am Aeolus, the keeper of the winds, and this is my island." Aeolus told Odysseus that he meant him and his men no harm and that he actually wanted to help the hero in his quest to return home. Aeolus thought Poseidon was being unfair. In some versions, he actually despises Poseidon, thinking him arrogant and selfish since Poseidon never gave the wind its due credit for its influence over the high seas.

Odysseus and his men got along with Aeolus, and Aeolus was very fond of Odysseus for his clever mind and inquisitive nature. Despite his hubris, Odysseus knew that there was something to be learned from his failures. Aeolus gifted a bag of the winds (minus the east wind) to Odysseus, telling him to use it in his most dire time of need to push his ship all the way home. Soon after, Odysseus and his men returned to the ship and set sail. All Odysseus could think of was returning to his beloved wife, and for the first time in months, he was absolutely sure that he would return to her and their son soon.

However, Odysseus's men were all too curious about what their master had retrieved from the island. What kind of treasure was Odysseus hiding? Most believed it to be gold, and after such a treacherous journey, they expected their fair share. Just then, the lookout called from the top of the crow's nest. The shores of Ithaca were in sight! But the men would not allow the ship to dock until they had opened the sack and retrieved a portion of the gold. They could never have known that the winds were stored inside.

They released the winds, which caused a great storm. The ship was pushed far from Ithaca to the other side of the world. The ship's supplies had gone overboard as well. Just when home was within grasp, it was all taken away. The men despaired, while Odysseus lost his trust and confidence in his crew.

However, there was no time for harsh grudges when survival was on the line. Odysseus sent his men off to find whatever game there was on the island. Then out of nowhere, a pig ran down onto the beach where the remainder of the men were resting. They immediately set about trying to catch and kill the pig to cook it for their evening meal. One of Odysseus's soldiers who was sent on the hunt burst through the bushes; he seemed to have been chasing after the pig as well. He ran toward Odysseus and begged him to stop the men from killing the pig, for it was Polites, one of Odysseus's own soldiers.

All the men laughed in his face until he told them the cause of Polites's affliction. It was a witch, Circe, a great and powerful sorceress. They had landed on her island, and she had turned every last man in the hunting party into animals, all except the one soldier who escaped. Odysseus believed the soldier's tale. He told his men to stay with the ship. If he did not return by sundown, they were to sail away from the island and never look back. Odysseus went ahead alone. He would not risk putting any more of his men in danger.

Just as the soldier had said, Odysseus followed the same path up into the hills, but he came across a giant black bear. In order to avoid the beast, he began to climb the side of the mountain. When he was about to reach the top, Hermes appeared to Odysseus. He had been sent by Athena; she had been watching over the hero since he left his home nearly fifteen years ago. She, too, despised Poseidon and wished for the king of Ithaca to succeed in his quest. Hermes offered Odysseus an herb from the face of the cliff. He told him to eat this plant for it would protect him from the witch's curse. Hermes told Odysseus that when the witch saw her curse did not affect the king, she would try to conquer him another way—in the bedroom.

Odysseus came across the giant stone palace, which was surrounded by animals of all types: lions, tigers, bears, and a few monkeys—the whole cast of the Wizard of Oz. Then he saw the witch standing in the doorway surrounded by all her animals; he recognized a few of his men amongst the droves of creatures. Each one seemed to be crying out for help. She offered Odysseus wine with honey, a drink the king knew was meant to transform him into an animal. Circe sat back on her throne and waited for her potion to work. Odysseus drank and drank, but he remained a man.

This confused, angered, and aroused the witch. Odysseus pulled out his sword, meaning to end her life, but Circe conveniently reminded him of the fact that his men would remain animals without her magic to change them back. She then made him an offer. She would release Odysseus's men from their captive forms if he took her to bed. As he was having sex with Circe, one by one, his men regained their human forms. She told Odysseus to bring the rest of his men to her palace, and they would eat and drink their fill until they were rested and ready to continue their journey.

Circe Offering the Cup to Ulysses by John William Waterhouse, 1891.
https://commons.wikimedia.org/wiki/File:Circe_Offering_the_Cup_to_Odysseus.jpg

All the while Odysseus was lying in Circe's bed, he still dreamed of his wife, of meeting her again, feeling her embrace, and basking in her smile. Circe noticed this of her hero and inquired how he could lay in her bed every night but still think of his wife? Fair question. Odysseus was by no means a hostage of Circe. He could have left with his men after a few days of rest, but he still found himself returning to her bed of his own volition. Odysseus's men had even asked when they would be leaving, but the great hero had no response. He was happy for the first time in years, and it was hard for him to leave that all behind. He had children with Circe, and they deeply loved each other. He wanted to linger in Circe's bed, whisper sweet nothings to each other, and enjoy each other intimately. Heroes in Greek mythology are sometimes defined more by their faults than by their deeds, and one of Odysseus's biggest faults was his affinity for beautiful goddesses.

Eventually, Odysseus's men were able to convince him that it was time to continue the journey. Circe offered Odysseus advice for finding his way home to Ithaca. She said one man and one man alone would be able to point Odysseus in the right direction. This was Tiresias, the prophet, who had long been dead and was currently living in the underworld. Circe told her lover that he must cross the River Styx and sacrifice a lamb, then enter the flames in order to find the prophet.

The entire time Odysseus sailed for the underworld, he thought of his son, who had now been many years without a father, and his wife, who surely suffered more than anyone. Meanwhile, Penelope's suitors had grown bolder and continued to linger in the king's palace, demanding an answer from her in regard to who was to be her new husband. It was customary that guests could not be turned away, and the men were abusing this custom to the extreme. However, Penelope was just as clever as her husband and managed to avoid their pestering questions by keeping them in either a state of drunkenness or sleep. She told them that she would choose a suitor once she had completed a shroud for her husband. It was incredibly large, and she unraveled the shroud little by little at the end of the day in order to buy more time. Her suitors remained so inebriated that they didn't even notice.

In the meantime, Odysseus and his company had reached the entrance to the land of the dead. There lay a river of fire ahead that Odysseus had to cross, and he had to cross it alone. Odysseus bid his men a tearful goodbye, as they were sure their master would perish in the flames. Odysseus took his lamb and went forth in search of Tiresias. He found the blind prophet in the depths of the underworld, sitting at the edge of the river of fire, his feet dangling into the waters like he was on vacation in hell. Odysseus made his request and tossed the lamb into the flaming waters. Tiresias then told him that in order to find his way home, he needed to use the constellation Orion and sail toward its brightest star until he reached the straits of Scylla, an insatiable monster of the deep. On one side of the strait would be Scylla, while on the other would be Charybdis, the swirling maelstrom of death.

Before Odysseus returned to his men, his mother Anticlea appeared before him. Odysseus felt a great wave of grief pass over him, for he knew his mother had perished while he had been away.

Little did he know she took her own life in her grief, as she had been waiting for a son that never returned. Anticlea told her son to make haste and return to Ithaca as soon as possible, for the nobles of his kingdom sought to make his wife their own, and Penelope was running out of strength and reasons to resist marrying one of the suitors. It was customary, after all, for a queen to remarry if her husband had been declared dead. Good thing for her that Odysseus's death was still speculation, but that could not last forever. The thing that weighed most heavily on the queen's heart was her son's despair that his father had either perished at Troy or on the seas. Of course, there was the lingering doubt that he had decided simply not to return to his wife and child.

Before Odysseus and his men approached the straits of Scylla, they would have to make their way past the Sirens. The Sirens chanted a beautiful song that caused mortals to drive their ships onto the rocks. It is hotly debated whether the Sirens feasted on the sailors or simply trapped them there, causing sailors to starve since they were unable to leave the beauty of the Sirens' song. Odysseus had received a warning from Circe about the Sirens before he departed her island. She told the king not to listen to the words of the Sirens and that he and his men should plug their ears with beeswax.

Odysseus was an incredibly curious man; he liked to know things that other men did not. One of the things he desired to know was the song of the Sirens. He ordered his men to tie him to the mast of the ship and plug their ears with beeswax. No matter how much he pleaded and cried, they were not to let him loose from his restraints. If he managed to wriggle free, they could not under any circumstances let him enter the water. His men did as they were told, and no matter how their king pleaded and struggled, the men kept sailing as Odysseus listened to the enchanting song of the Sirens.

Odysseus and his men eventually approached the straits of Scylla. Although Odysseus and his men had braved the horrors of the ancient world, they could never have imagined what awaited them in the dark corridor that lay ahead. As they slowly inched their way into the straits, all the light disappeared. It was blacker than any darkness of the night. The air was thick and hot, but the worst part of the whole experience was the quiet. There was absolutely nothing to be heard; even the waves ceased to make noise against the ship. Then, from the darkness, a giant set of jaws lunged forward and snatched one of Odysseus's men from the deck.

It was a horrific sight. The teeth of Scylla were razor-sharp, and the force of her jaws cut the soldier clean in two. His upper body seemingly disappeared into her jaws, and his legs remained upright on the deck of the ship. The men were horrified as the poor soldier's legs began to twitch, his nerve endings unaware that they had been severed from the brain. Scylla then emerged from her dark hiding place. Her form was a grotesque machine of murder, with six long necks, each topped by a single head with razor-sharp teeth. Her claws kept her mounted among the caverns of the narrow corridor. Petrified, Odysseus's men pulled forward. They knew they were unable to best this beast through strength; their only hope was to keep rowing forward and to stay as far from the sides of the cavern as possible.

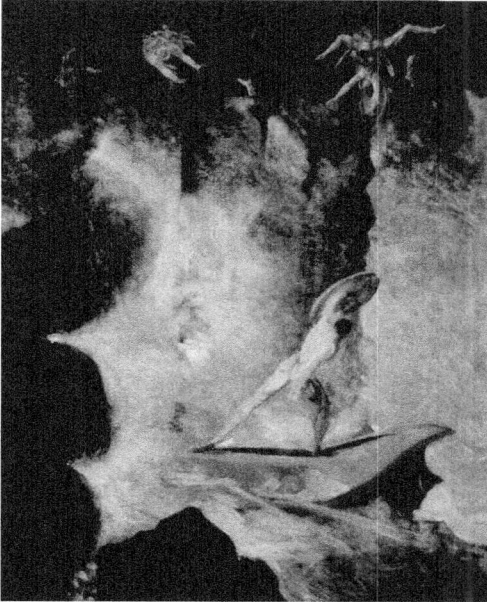

Odysseus in front of Scylla and Charybdis *by Henry Fuseli, 1794–1796.*
https://commons.wikimedia.org/wiki/File:Johann_Heinrich_F%C3%BCssli_054.jpg

They could see the light at the end of the tunnel and rowed furiously toward what they believed to be their salvation, but it was not what they suspected. Soon enough, Odysseus realized that at the end of the strait was a drop, one that led right into the jaws of Charybdis, a creature even more terrifying than Scylla. Her jaws were not filled with teeth but rather rushing water; she was a massive whirlpool. And the ship was headed straight for the drop, and there was nothing that any of the men could do to stop it. Odysseus told his men to jump and try to catch the vines that hung from the ceiling of the opening. Some of the men made the jump, but most did not, falling into the terrifying maelstrom. Odysseus instructed the remainder of his men to let go of the vines, and they all fell into the sea. When Odysseus surfaced, he called out for his men, but none answered. He was utterly alone, floating in an endless sea. Perhaps Odysseus had finally been bested by Poseidon.

Just then, from out of nowhere, appeared an island of white limestone. Odysseus used the last of his strength to swim toward the island and pulled his body onto the soft sand. He had never been happier to see land. From the tall cliffs, he could make out several figures and heard the soft melody of women's voices in the wind. This was Ogygia, the island of the nymph Calypso, a daughter of the Titan Atlas. It was only her and her maidens who occupied the island, and Odysseus was the first man they had seen in a long time. The beauty of the goddess was legendary; she could be compared to the legendary Helen of Troy or even the goddess Aphrodite herself.

Calypso brought Odysseus water and food until he fell into a deep sleep. Odysseus stirred and tossed with nightmares of his journey, the evil things he had seen, the blood he had seen shed, and the terrible loss of his men who had braved the perils of the world for their king. They were all now dead. Calypso came to his side to rouse him. When he woke, he began to weep uncontrollably and fell into her arms. It did not take very long for the goddess's charms and magic to seep their way into Odysseus's blood, making his heart race. The two fell into one another's embrace, and for the second time on his journey, Odysseus was unfaithful to his wife. Only this time, there was no ulterior incentive to save the lives of his men. This mistake was born from the deepest sadness and loneliness a man could feel.

The two became intense lovers, and he confided in Calypso about the terror of the last thirteen years. He requested a ship from

Calypso so that he might return to Ithaca. However, the goddess informed her newest love that there was none to be had on the island. No one came to her island, and no one was permitted to leave. Odysseus tried to escape once or twice by trying to flag down ships he saw on the horizon, but they were all too far away, and the island was nearly invisible to all, the white limestone hiding it in the glare of the sun. Calypso told Odysseus that he would never leave, as she would never let him go.

Meanwhile, in Ithaca, Telemachus was preparing a ship to set sail in search of Odysseus. He was going to leave without one word to his mother. While he was still pondering the implications of his decision to leave, the gray-eyed Athena appeared to the prince on the beach. She told him to sail to Pylos and Sparta to the court of Menelaus for reasons unknown to Telemachus.

For seven years, Calypso kept Odysseus on her island, his memories of Penelope fading more and more with each passing day. He was wrapped in the arms of the goddess every night. (Some say it wasn't consensual on the part of Odysseus, though. In that version, he was more than ready to sail home.) Odysseus felt that the gods had all but abandoned him to be the hostage of a very deranged and clingy woman. However, Athena had not turned his back on the hero. Over time, she made the king of the gods take notice of Odysseus, of his strength, wit, and cunning mind. These two gods would not see Odysseus end his days as a captive. So, Zeus sent Hermes to Calypso, demanding that she release the hero. Calypso cursed the gods, accusing them of being jealous that she was finally happy with a companion. Hermes advised her not to deny Zeus's command.

According to some accounts, Calypso had been blessed with two children by Odysseus. She was happy keeping Odysseus under her enchantment and raising her children. But what could a nymph do against the will of the gods? She told Odysseus he had to go, that he had to leave her island and her sight. There was driftwood on a nearby island, which Odysseus would use to build his ship. Calypso tried everything in her power to make Odysseus stay; she used sweet words, kisses, tears, and even the promise of immortality, but it made no difference. Odysseus thanked the goddess for saving his life and the supplies she gave him and then pushed his driftwood dingy into the sea.

Back in Ithaca, things had begun to take a turn for the worst for Penelope. After seducing one of her maids, Antinous learned why Penelope's shroud was not yet completed after weeks of work. (Some sources say that he even slept with Penelope, while others say that a slave found out and disclosed the information.) He confronted Penelope and gave the shroud to the other suitors to destroy, desecrate, and burn. Penelope was now alone. She had been outed, she was without hope, and her son was far away in Sparta. Telemachus had made the journey to the house of Menelaus and propositioned the king to aid him in the search for Odysseus. Menelaus informed the prince that his father was still alive. He gained this knowledge from Proteus, the prophet and sea god. The king told Telemachus to remain strong; Odysseus would do whatever it took to return to Ithaca.

On the high seas, Poseidon sought another chance to take his revenge against Odysseus for blinding his son Polyphemus. He battered Odysseus with wind, waves, and rain. Odysseus likely thought that surely this would be the end of his days. How would he survive wandering the high seas if his ship was destroyed? Eventually, Odysseus washed up onto the shores of Scheria, which was home to the Phaeacians. He was found in a weakened state by Princess Nausicaa and carried to the palace of the king. There, he received a warm welcome from the king and queen, who were only too aware of who Odysseus was and what his name meant amongst the warriors of Greece. They begged Odysseus to share his tale and how he had come to survive the wrath of the gods. In return, the king would provide Odysseus a ship and the finest mariners in all his land to man it.

Odysseus recounted all of his treacherous misfortunes to the king and his entire court from the time he left Troy until his departure from Ogygia. No one had ever heard such a story of bravery and terror. The king kept his word, and in the morning, Odysseus set sail, finally for his home country. Every night he slept aboard the ship, he dreamed of Penelope. He could not wait to share their bed together once more and finally meet his son, who had been born just before he left for the Trojan War.

When Odysseus arrived on the shores of Ithaca, he wept from joy. He knew the scent of sweet sea air mixed with pine, and he embraced the feel of the sun cascading from between the branches of the forest as he made his way up to the hut of his faithful swine herder, Eumaeus. When the two men locked eyes, Eumaeus dropped to his knees, buried his face in his hands, and joined Odysseus in weeping. From the port below, Eumaeus could make out the ship of Telemachus returning home from Sparta. Eumaeus rushed to the docks, pulled the prince aside, and told him to follow him back up to his hut; he would not tell the prince why, but when they approached, Odysseus revealed himself. Telemachus was suspicious of this man, but having prior knowledge of his father's whereabouts and the word of Eumaeus to boot, he quickly came to believe that this was his father, Odysseus. The last twenty years of Odysseus's suffering seemed to melt away the moment he embraced his son for the second time in his life. Father and son then sat down to concoct a plan to massacre the suitors and restore Odysseus to his throne. He told Telemachus to join the suitors at their usual feast of barbary later that night and to tell no one that Odysseus had returned to Ithaca.

Up at the palace, Penelope had developed a plan all her own to rid herself of the suitors once and for all. She told them that she would marry the man that was able to string Odysseus's bow and fire it through the eyes of twelve rows of axes (that would be through the end of the hilt where there was typically a metal circle). This was an extraordinary task that had only ever been completed by the king himself.

With the help of Athena, Odysseus was disguised as a beggar (many versions say he was disguised when Telemachus came to see him). He entered the palace and found the contest for Penelope's hand in full swing. He saw the untold mess and filth of the guests that had been plaguing his home for all those years. His rage was great, but he held his tongue, knowing that at any moment, his chance for revenge would come. And at that time, Athena would be with him. That night, Odysseus's nurse from infancy, Eurycleia, came to tend to what she thought was an old beggar. However, from one deep look in his eyes, she knew the man's true identity. It was Odysseus, her Odysseus, the boy she had pulled from the womb of Anticlea herself. She wept tears of joy. Eurycleia wanted to run and tell her mistress Penelope, but Odysseus made her swear not to speak a word of his return, or all hope would be lost.

None of the suitors were able to accomplish the impossible task that Penelope had set for them. None of them could even string the bow. When it seemed as if no one would be able to finish it, the suitors began to grumble. She had to pick someone. A beggar stepped forward and asked to try his hand. The other men scoffed, believing there was absolutely no chance that a man of such lowly stature could wield a bow as fine as this. But they eventually agreed to let him try.

Odysseus walked up and took up the bow. Everyone in the hall watched in amazement as the decrepit old man strung the bow with astonishing ease. He placed one of the arrows on the string and fired it through the hoops of all twelve axes. As he completed the feat, Athena's spell was broken, and Odysseus was revealed. While the contest had been in full swing, Odysseus's loyal servants, Eumaeus and Eurycleia, had been collecting all the suitors' weapons and armor. They then locked the doors of the great hall. And once the contest was over, Odysseus and Telemachus, along with a few of Odysseus's loyal servants, began to massacre the suitors without mercy, one by one.

Odysseus and Telemachus Massacre the Suitors of Penelope *by Thomas Degeorge, 1812.*

Later that night, Odysseus was waiting for Penelope in their chambers. Words have not been invented yet for the love these two shared for one another. For twenty years, Odysseus had strived to return to his home, to his wife, to his son, and at long last, that dream was now a reality. He had faced monsters, gods, sexually "enslaving" goddesses, and many other enemies. No mortal man had ever earned such favor from the gods. His mind and iron will were his greatest strengths, but all men need something to live for.

As he and his wife lay in each other's arms for the first time in two decades, he whispered to Penelope that she would never be without him again; she was his world. The story of Odysseus does not end there. It goes on, and today, it inspires people with its many lessons of love, loss, bravery, pride, and friendship. Most of all, the story teaches us that no matter how small we are in the grand scheme of things, we are still able to make all the difference in our own worlds if we are guided equally by our minds and our hearts.

Conclusion

Greek mythology is, for the most part, still entirely relevant in our day and age. Well, no man has ever tried to seduce a woman while in the form of a bird, but we still fall in love, get jealous, act rashly, involve ourselves in good and bad affairs, and strive to find a place of meaning and understanding within the world.

The world began with absolutely nothing, the end of nothing, in fact. And from the darkness emerged a single spark of hope. The Greeks' tales of the cosmic beginning of the world were not so different from the way other ancient cultures viewed the beginning of time, as they have elements of both femininity and masculinity. Gaia was a necessity, just like her husband, Uranus. In fact, Gaia's horrid treatment at the hands of her husband and progeny can be a lesson for the ills mankind inflict on the earth today.

Still, the two halves of femininity and masculinity made one whole perfect world, and it was then subdivided into gods and goddesses, the various representations of what is masculinity and what is femininity. This split dichotomy can be seen in everything that inhabits Greek mythology. The Minotaur was a man, while the monster Scylla was a female. It is no accident that rage, fury, and destruction were embodied by Poseidon, the male god of the seas, just as it was no accident that true wisdom resided in the domain of women, which was embodied by the goddess Athena. Both male and female deities were needed for the ancient Greeks to be able to navigate their world and understand its building blocks, which could be found in everything they could see and touch. Human beings learned how to be human beings from the world surrounding them.

As we have learned by reviewing the myths of heroes, mankind did not always follow the lessons it was provided by the gods and the natural world. Even the best among mortal men and demi-gods made mistakes, and sometimes they learned from it, and other times they didn't. For all his wisdom and wit, Odysseus nearly perished several times due to his prideful nature. Herakles, for all his strength, could not bring his loved ones back from the dead and so had to work through that sadness with the twelve labors, confronting and dealing with his sins while doing so. For all he had achieved, Jason felt the greatest loss of any hero at the end of his days, which just goes to show that success does not bring a person happiness. From Theseus, we can learn to be grateful for the things we have and the help that others are willing to give us, lest karma comes to exact terrible vengeance.

The sheer fact that the gods and goddesses of Greek mythology were subject to and the originators of certain emotions and actions that were also felt and expressed by mankind speaks to the divinity of everyday human life. The final lesson we can glean from Greek mythology is that to be human does not mean to be "other." We are not set apart from everyone and everything else in the world. To be human is to be a part of and subject to a divine world order.

Here's another book by Enthralling History that you might like

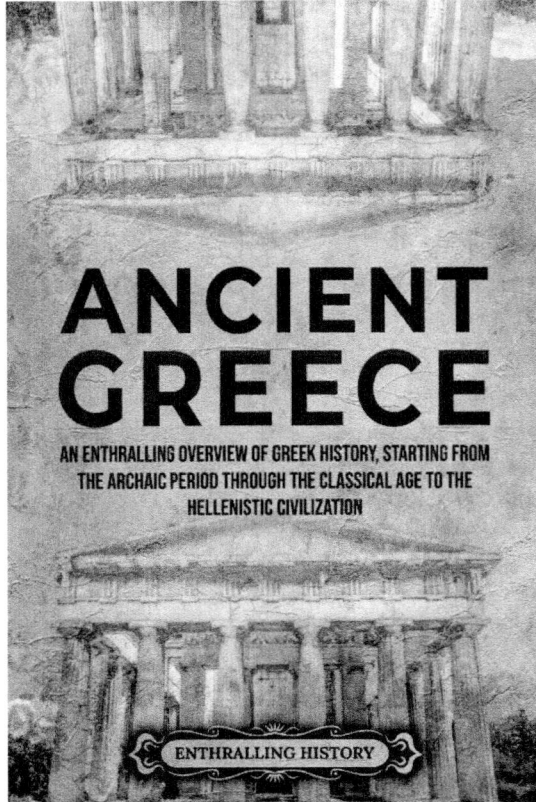

ANCIENT GREECE

AN ENTHRALLING OVERVIEW OF GREEK HISTORY, STARTING FROM THE ARCHAIC PERIOD THROUGH THE CLASSICAL AGE TO THE HELLENISTIC CIVILIZATION

ENTHRALLING HISTORY

Free limited time bonus

Stop for a moment. We have a free bonus set up for you. The problem is this: we forget 90% of everything that we read after 7 days. Crazy fact, right? Here's the solution: we've created a printable, 1-page pdf summary for this book that you're reading now. All you have to do to get your free pdf summary is to go to the following website:

https://livetolearn.lpages.co/enthrallinghistory/

Once you do, it will be intuitive. Enjoy, and thank you!

We forget 90% of everything that we've read in 7 days...

Get the free printable pdf summary of the book you've read AND much, much more... shhhh...

Enter Your Most Frequently Used Email to Get Started

DOWNLOAD FREE PDF SUMMARY

© Enthralling History

Bibliography

Arrian. *Alexander the Great: The Anabasis and the Indica.* Translated by Martin Hammond. Oxford: Oxford University Press, 2013.

Austin, M. M. "Greek Tyrants and the Persians, 546-479 B. C." *The Classical Quarterly* 40, no. 2 (1990): 289-306. http://www.jstor.org/stable/639090

Barron, John P. "The Sixth-Century Tyranny at Samos." *The Classical Quarterly* 14, no. 2 (1964): 210-29. http://www.jstor.org/stable/637725.

Beck, Julien, Despina Koutsoumbab, Dimitris Sakellariouc, Morgane Surdez, Flavio Anselmettie, Nikos Papadopoulos, Ionnis Morfis, et al. "Searching for Neolithic Sites in the Bay of Kiladha, Greece." *Quaternary International* 584 (May 20, 2021):129-40. https://www.sciencedirect.com/science/article/pii/S1040618220308466#

Bennett, Bob, and Mike Roberts. *The Wars of Alexander's Successors, 323-281 BC. Volume I: Commanders and Campaigns.* South Yorkshire: Pen & Sword Military, 2019.

Bennett, Bob, and Mike Roberts. *The Wars of Alexander's Successors 323 - 281 BC. Volume 2: Battles and Tactics.* South Yorkshire: Pen & Sword Military, 2019.

Bicknell, P.J. "Anaximenes' Astronomy." *Acta Classica* 12 (1969): 53-85. http://www.jstor.org/stable/24591168.

Cartledge, Paul. *The Spartans: The World of the Warrior-Heroes of Ancient Greece.* New York: The Overlook Press, 2003.

Castleden, Rodney. *The Knossos Labyrinth: A New View of the 'Palace of Minos' at Knossos.* London: Routledge, 2012.

Chioti, Lamprini. "The Herulian Invasion in Athens (267 CE). The Archaeological Evidence." *Destructions, Survival, and Recovery in Ancient Greece.* American School of Classical Studies at Athens: May 16, 2019. https://www.academia.edu/39196609/The_Herulian_invasion_in_Athens_267_CE_The_Archaeological_Evidence

Clogg, Richard. *A Concise History of Greece.* Cambridge: Cambridge University Press, 2021.

Clogg, Richard. *A Short History of Modern Greece.* Cambridge: Cambridge University Press, 1979.

Coleman, John E. "The Chronology and Interconnections of the Cycladic Islands in the Neolithic Period and the Early Bronze Age." *American Journal of Archaeology* 78, no. 4 (1974): 333–44. https://doi.org/10.2307/502747.

Daskalov, Roumen, and Tchavdar Marinov. *Entangled Histories of the Balkans - Volume One: National Ideologies and Language Policies.* Leiden: Brill, 2013.

Davies, Siriol, and Jack L. Davis. "Greeks, Venice, and the Ottoman Empire." *Hesperia Supplements* 40 (2007): 25–31. http://www.jstor.org/stable/20066763.

Dillon, John and Lloyd P. Gerson. *Neoplatonic Philosophy: Introductory Readings.* Cambridge, MA: Hackett Publishing Company, 2004.

"Downfall of King Constantine." *Current History* (1916-1940) 6, no. 1 (1917): 83–85. http://www.jstor.org/stable/45328408.

Figueira, Thomas J. "Population Patterns in Late Archaic and Classical Sparta." *Transactions of the American Philological Association* 116 (1986): 165–213. https://doi.org/10.2307/283916.

Gellius, A. Cornelius. *Noctes Atticae (Attic Nights).* Volume I, Book III. Loeb Classical Library. http://penelope.uchicago.edu/Thayer/E/Roman/Texts/Gellius/3*.html#8

Guthrie, W. K. C. *A History of Greek Philosophy.* Cambridge: Cambridge University Press, 1979.

Guthrie, W. K. C. *The Sophists.* Cambridge: Cambridge University Press, 1977.

Hack, Harold M. "Thebes and the Spartan Hegemony, 386-382 B.C." *The American Journal of Philology* 99, no. 2 (1978): 210–27. https://doi.org/10.2307/293647.

Heidel, William Arthur. "Anaximander's Book, the Earliest Known Geographical Treatise." *Proceedings of the American Academy of Arts and Sciences* 56, no. 7 (1921): 239-88. doi:10.2307/20025852.

Henderson, W.J. "The Nature and Function of Solon's Poetry: Fr. Diehl, 4 West." *Acta Classica* 25 (1982): 21-33. http://www.jstor.org/stable/24591787.

Herodotus, *The Histories.* Translated by George Rawlinson. New York: Dutton & Co, 1862. http://classics.mit.edu/Herodotus/history.html

Hofmanová, Zuzana, Susanne Kreutzer, Garrett Hellenthal, Christian Sell, Yoan Diekmann, David Díez-del-Molino, Lucy van Dorp, et al. "Early Farmers from across Europe Directly Descended from Neolithic Aegeans." *PNAS.* 113 (25) (June 6, 2016): 6886–6891. doi:10.1073/pnas.1523951113. ISSN 0027-8424. PMC 4922144. PMID 27274049.

Homer. *The Iliad.* Translated by Samuel Butler. Internet Classics Archive. http://classics.mit.edu/Homer/iliad.html

Homer. *The Odyssey.* Translated by Samuel Butler. Internet Classics Archive. http://classics.mit.edu/Homer/odyssey.html

Hooten, E.R. *Prelude to the First World War: The Balkan Wars 1912-1913.* Gloucestershire: Fonthill Media, 2014.

Isocrates. *Letters.* Perseus Digital Library. Tufts University. http://www.perseus.tufts.edu/hopper/text?doc=Perseus:text:1999.01.0246:letter=3.

Jenkins, Romilly J. H. "The Hellenistic Origins of Byzantine Literature." Dumbarton Oaks Papers 17 (1963): 37–52. https://doi.org/10.2307/1291189.

Jones, Adam. *Genocide: A Comprehensive Introduction.* London: Routledge, 2006.

Jones, A. H. M. "The Greeks under the Roman Empire." *Dumbarton Oaks Papers* 17 (1963): 1–19. https://doi.org/10.2307/1291187.

Josephus, Flavius. *Antiquities of the Jews.* Translated by William Whiston. Project Gutenberg. https://www.gutenberg.org/files/2848/2848-h/2848-h.htm

Kaldellis, Anthony. *Hellenism in Byzantium: The Transformations of Greek Identity and the Reception of the Classical Tradition.* Cambridge: Cambridge University Press, 2007.

Kelder, Jorrit M. (2010). *The Kingdom of Mycenae: A Great Kingdom in the Late Bronze Age Aegean.* Bethesda: CDL Press, 2010

King, RJ, S. S. Ozcan, T. Carter, E. Kalfoğlu, S. Atasoy, C. Triantaphyllidis, A. Couva's, et al. "Differential Y-chromosome Anatolian Influences on the Greek and Cretan Neolithic." *Annals of Human Genetics.* 72 (March 2008): 205-14. do: 10.1111/j.1469-1809.2007.00414.x. PMID: 18269686.

Krausmüller, Dirk. "Emperors, Patriarchs, Metropolitans, Deacons and Monks: Individuals and Groups in the Byzantine Church (6th–11th Centuries)." *Scrinium* 17, 1 (2021): 199-238, doi: https://doi.org/10.1163/18177565-bja10048

Lazaridis, I, A. Mittnik, N. Patterson, S. Mallick, N. Rohland, S. Pfrengle, A. Furtwängler, et al. "Genetic Origins of the Minoans and Mycenaeans." *Nature* 548 (August 10, 2017): 214-18. doi: 10.1038/nature23310. Epub 2017 Aug 2. PMID: 28783727; PMCID: PMC5565772.

Lupack, Susan. "Mycenaean Religion." In *The Oxford Handbook of the Bronze Age Aegean,* edited by Eric H. Cline, 2012. 10.1093/oxfordhb/9780199873609.013.0020.

Mansfield, D. F. "Plimpton 322: A Study of Rectangles." *Foundations of Science* 26 (2021): 977–1005. https://doi.org/10.1007/s10699-021-09806-0

Martin, Thomas R. *Ancient Greece: From Prehistoric to Hellenistic Times.* New Haven: Yale University Press, 1996.

Matyszak, Philip. *Greece Against Rome: The Fall of the Hellenistic Kingdoms 250–31 BC.* South Yorkshire: Pen & Sword Military, 2020.

Matyszak, Philip. *The Rise of the Hellenistic Kingdoms, 336–250 BC.* South Yorkshire: Pen & Sword Military, 2019.

Mazower, Mark. *The Greek Revolution: 1821 and the Making of Modern Europe.* New York: Penguin Press, 2021.

Mittal, Rakesh. *Hellenism and the Shaping of the Byzantine Empire.* Marquette University, 2010. https://epublications.marquette.edu/cgi/viewcontent.cgi?article=1001&context=jablonowski_award

"Not War Against Islam – Statement by Greek Prime Minister." *The Scotsman.* June 29, 1920.

Ostrogorsky, George. "Byzantine Cities in the Early Middle Ages." *Dumbarton Oaks Papers* 13 (1959): 45–66. https://doi.org/10.2307/1291128.

Oost, Stewart Irvin. "Cypselus the Bacchiad." *Classical Philology* 67, no. 1 (1972): 10-30. http://www.jstor.org/stable/269012.

Peoples, R. Scott. *Crusade of Kings*. Rockville, MD: Wildside Press LLC, 2013, 13. ISBN 978-0-8095-7221-2

Plato. *The Republic*. Translated by Benjamin Jowett. Internet Classics Archive. http://classics.mit.edu/Plato/republic.9.viii.html

Plutarch. *Cimon*. Translated by John Dryden. Internet Classics Archive. http://classics.mit.edu/Plutarch/cimon.html

Polybius. *Histories*. Book 16. http://www.perseus.tufts.edu/hopper/text?doc=Perseus%3Atext%3A1999.01.0234%3Abook%3D16%3Achapter%3D34

Pomeroy, Sarah B., Stanley M. Burstein, Walter Donlan, Jennifer Tolbert Roberts, David W. Tandy, and Georgia Tsouvala. *Ancient Greece: Politics, Society, and Culture*. New York: Oxford University Press, 2020.

Rhodes, P. J. *Athenian Democracy* (Edinburgh Readings on the Ancient World). Oxford: Oxford University Press, 2004.

Runciman, Steven. *The Byzantine Theocracy: The Weil Lectures, Cincinnati* (Cambridge: Cambridge University Press, 2004), ISBN 978-0-521-54591-4.

Runnels, Curtis. "Review of Aegean Prehistory IV: The Stone Age of Greece from the Paleolithic to the Advent of the Neolithic." *American Journal of Archaeology* 99, no. 4 (1995): 699–728. https://doi.org/10.2307/506190.

Svolopoulos, Constantinos. "The Ecumenical Patriarchate in the Ottoman Empire (1453-1923): Adaptation and Change." *Journal of Modern Hellenism*. 17-18 (2000-2001); 107-123.

Syme, Ronald. "The Greeks under Roman Rule." *Proceedings of the Massachusetts Historical Society* 72 (1957): 3–20. http://www.jstor.org/stable/25080512.

Theophrastus. *Characters*. Translated by R.C. Jebb. https://www.eudaemonist.com/biblion/characters/

The William Davidson Talmud (Koren - Steinsaltz). https://www.sefaria.org/Yoma.69a.14?lang=bi&with=all&lang2=en

Thucydides. *History of the Peloponnesian War*. Translated by Rex Warner. New York: Penguin Classics, 1972.

Treadgold, Warren. "The Persistence of Byzantium." *The Wilson Quarterly* (1976-) 22, no. 4 (1998): 66–91. http://www.jstor.org/stable/40260386.

Warren, Peter. "Knossos: New Excavations and Discoveries," *Archaeology* 37, no. 4 (1984): 48–55. http://www.jstor.org/stable/41731580.

Worthington, Ian. *By the Spear: Philip II, Alexander the Great, and the Rise and Fall of the Macedonian Empire* (Ancient Warfare and Civilization). Oxford: Oxford University Press, 2016.

Xenophon. *The Landmark Xenophon's Hellenika.* Translated by John Marincola. New York: Anchor, 2010.

Young, David C. *The Modern Olympics: A Struggle for Revival.* Baltimore: Johns Hopkins University Press, 1996.

https://www.greekmythology.com/Myths/The_Myths/The_Creation/the_creation.html

https://www.theoi.com/articles/what-is-the-greek-creation-myth

https://classicalwisdom.com/mythology/gods/in-the-beginning-part-1

https://www.theoi.com/Titan/TitanKoios.html

Hesiod, *Theogony* 133 & 207 (trans. Evelyn-White) (Greek epic C8th or C7th B.C.)

Beall, E. F. "Hesiod's Prometheus and Development in Myth." Journal of the History of Ideas 52, no. 3 (1991): 355–71.

https://doi.org/10.2307/2710042

https://grbs.library.duke.edu/article/viewFile/6661/5061

https://www.thoughtco.com/the-five-ages-of-man-111776

https://www.britannica.com/topic/Deucalion

https://www.thoughtco.com/people-around-hercules-Herakles-herakles-118960

https://www.history.com/topics/ancient-history/hercules

http://www.perseus.tufts.edu/Herakles/amazon.html

https://classicalwisdom.com/mythology/spotlight-on-mythology-theseus-and-theminotaur

https://www.theoi.com/articles/the-myth-of-perseus-and-medusa-explained

https://www.britannica.com/topic/Andromeda-Greek-mythology

https://www.theoi.com/articles/jason-and-the-argonauts-myth

https://www.britannica.com/topic/Jason-Greek-mythology

https://www.theoi.com/Georgikos/KentaurosKheiron.html

https://www.greeka.com/thessaly/pelion/myths/jason-argonauts

http://www.argonauts-book.com/hypsipyle.html

https://www.theoi.com/Pontios/Glaukos.html

https://www.theoi.com/Nymphe/NympheMelia4.html

https://www.theoi.com/Pontios/NereisThetis.html

https://www.theoi.com/Pontios/Nereus.html

https://www.theoi.com/Olympios/JudgementParis.html

https://www.theoi.com/articles/short-trojan-war-summary

https://www.theoi.com/articles/was-achilles-a-warrior

https://www.sparknotes.com/lit/odyssey/summary

https://www.theoi.com/Pontios/Skylla.html

https://www.theoi.com/Nymphe/NympheKalypso.html

Printed in Great Britain
by Amazon